Active Server Pages 3
Weekend Crash Course™

Active Server Pages 3
Weekend Crash Course™

Eric A. Smith

IDG Books Worldwide, Inc.
An International Data Group Company
Foster City, CA • Chicago, IL • Indianapolis, IN • New York, NY

Active Server Pages 3 Weekend Crash Course™
Published by
IDG Books Worldwide, Inc.
An International Data Group Company
919 E. Hillsdale Blvd., Suite 400
Foster City, CA 94404
www.idgbooks.com (IDG Books Worldwide Web site)
Copyright © 2001 IDG Books Worldwide, Inc. All
rights reserved. No part of this book, including
interior design, cover design, and icons, may be
reproduced or transmitted in any form, by any
means (electronic, photocopying, recording, or
otherwise) without the prior written permission
of the publisher.
ISBN: 0-7645-4756-9
Printed in the United States of America
10 9 8 7 6 5 4 3 2 1
1B/RX/QR/QR/FC
Distributed in the United States by IDG Books
Worldwide, Inc.
Distributed by CDG Books Canada Inc. for Canada;
by Transworld Publishers Limited in the United
Kingdom; by IDG Norge Books for Norway; by IDG
Sweden Books for Sweden; by IDG Books Australia
Publishing Corporation Pty. Ltd. for Australia and
New Zealand; by TransQuest Publishers Pte Ltd. for
Singapore, Malaysia, Thailand, Indonesia, and Hong
Kong; by Gotop Information Inc. for Taiwan; by ICG
Muse, Inc. for Japan; by Intersoft for South Africa;
by Eyrolles for France; by International Thomson
Publishing for Germany, Austria, and Switzerland;
by Distribuidora Cuspide for Argentina; by LR
International for Brazil; by Galileo Libros for Chile;
by Ediciones ZETA S.C.R. Ltda. for Peru; by WS
Computer Publishing Corporation, Inc., for the
Philippines; by Contemporanea de Ediciones for
Venezuela; by Express Computer Distributors for
the Caribbean and West Indies; by Micronesia
Media Distributor, Inc. for Micronesia; by Chips
Computadoras S.A. de C.V. for Mexico; by Editorial
Norma de Panama S.A. for Panama; by American
Bookshops for Finland.

For general information on IDG Books Worldwide's
books in the U.S., please call our Consumer
Customer Service department at 800-762-2974.
For reseller information, including discounts and
premium sales, please call our Reseller Customer
Service department at 800-434-3422.
For information on where to purchase IDG Books
Worldwide's books outside the U.S., please contact
our International Sales department at 317-572-3993
or fax 317-572-4002.
For consumer information on foreign language
translations, please contact our Customer Service
department at 800-434-3422, fax 317-572-4002, or
e-mail rights@idgbooks.com.
For information on licensing foreign or domestic
rights, please phone +1-650-653-7098.
For sales inquiries and special prices for bulk quan-
tities, please contact our Order Services department
at 800-434-3422 or write to the address above.
For information on using IDG Books Worldwide's
books in the classroom or for ordering examination
copies, please contact our Educational Sales department at 800-434-2086 or fax 317-572-4005.
For press review copies, author interviews, or other
publicity information, please contact our Public
Relations department at 650-653-7000 or fax
650-653-7500.
For authorization to photocopy items for corporate,
personal, or educational use, please contact
Copyright Clearance Center, 222 Rosewood Drive,
Danvers, MA 01923, or fax 978-750-4470.

Library of Congress Cataloging-in-Publication Data
Smith, Eric A., 1970-
    Active server pages 3 weekend crash course /
Eric A. Smith.
        p.   cm.
    Includes index.
    ISBN 0-7645-4756-9 (alk. paper)
    1. Active server pages.   2. Web sites--Design.
3. Web publishing.   I. Title.
TK5105.8885.A26 S6397   2001
005.2'76--dc21   00-054072

 ® is a registered trademark under exclusive
license to IDG Books Worldwide, Inc.,
from International Data Group, Inc.

**IDG
BOOKS**
WORLDWIDE

ABOUT IDG BOOKS WORLDWIDE

Welcome to the world of IDG Books Worldwide.

IDG Books Worldwide, Inc., is a subsidiary of International Data Group, the world's largest publisher of computer-related information and the leading global provider of information services on information technology. IDG was founded more than 30 years ago by Patrick J. McGovern and now employs more than 9,000 people worldwide. IDG publishes more than 290 computer publications in over 75 countries. More than 90 million people read one or more IDG publications each month.

Launched in 1990, IDG Books Worldwide is today the #1 publisher of best-selling computer books in the United States. We are proud to have received eight awards from the Computer Press Association in recognition of editorial excellence and three from Computer Currents' First Annual Readers' Choice Awards. Our best-selling ...For Dummies® series has more than 50 million copies in print with translations in 31 languages. IDG Books Worldwide, through a joint venture with IDG's Hi-Tech Beijing, became the first U.S. publisher to publish a computer book in the People's Republic of China. In record time, IDG Books Worldwide has become the first choice for millions of readers around the world who want to learn how to better manage their businesses.

Our mission is simple: Every one of our books is designed to bring extra value and skill-building instructions to the reader. Our books are written by experts who understand and care about our readers. The knowledge base of our editorial staff comes from years of experience in publishing, education, and journalism — experience we use to produce books to carry us into the new millennium. In short, we care about books, so we attract the best people. We devote special attention to details such as audience, interior design, use of icons, and illustrations. And because we use an efficient process of authoring, editing, and desktop publishing our books electronically, we can spend more time ensuring superior content and less time on the technicalities of making books.

You can count on our commitment to deliver high-quality books at competitive prices on topics you want to read about. At IDG Books Worldwide, we continue in the IDG tradition of delivering quality for more than 30 years. You'll find no better book on a subject than one from IDG Books Worldwide.

John J. Kilcullen

John Kilcullen
Chairman and CEO
IDG Books Worldwide, Inc.

Eighth Annual
Computer Press
Awards ≥1992

Ninth Annual
Computer Press
Awards ≥1993

Tenth Annual
Computer Press
Awards ≥1994

Eleventh Annual
Computer Press
Awards ≥1995

IDG is the world's leading IT media, research and exposition company. Founded in 1964, IDG had 1997 revenues of $2.05 billion and has more than 9,000 employees worldwide. IDG offers the widest range of media options that reach IT buyers in 75 countries representing 95% of worldwide IT spending. IDG's diverse product and services portfolio spans six key areas including print publishing, online publishing, expositions and conferences, market research, education and training, and global marketing services. More than 90 million people read one or more of IDG's 290 magazines and newspapers, including IDG's leading global brands — Computerworld, PC World, Network World, Macworld and the Channel World family of publications. IDG Books Worldwide is one of the fastest-growing computer book publishers in the world, with more than 700 titles in 36 languages. The "...For Dummies®" series alone has more than 50 million copies in print. IDG offers online users the largest network of technology-specific Web sites around the world through IDG.net (http://www.idg.net), which comprises more than 225 targeted Web sites in 55 countries worldwide. International Data Corporation (IDC) is the world's largest provider of information technology data, analysis and consulting, with research centers in over 41 countries and more than 400 research analysts worldwide. IDG World Expo is a leading producer of more than 168 globally branded conferences and expositions in 35 countries including E3 (Electronic Entertainment Expo), Macworld Expo, ComNet, Windows World Expo, ICE (Internet Commerce Expo), Agenda, DEMO, and Spotlight. IDG's training subsidiary, ExecuTrain, is the world's largest computer training company, with more than 230 locations worldwide and 785 training courses. IDG Marketing Services helps industry-leading IT companies build international brand recognition by developing global integrated marketing programs via IDG's print, online and exposition products worldwide. Further information about the company can be found at www.idg.com.   1/26/00

Credits

Acquisitions Editor
Greg Croy

Project Editor
Barbra Guerra

Technical Editor
David Hillman

Copy Editors
S.B. Kleinman
Luann Rouff

Proof Editor
Patsy Owens

Project Coordinators
Joe Shines
Danette Nurse

Graphics and Production Specialists
Bob Bihlmayer
Rolly Delrosario
Jude Levinson
Michael Lewis
Victor Peréz-Varela
Ramses Ramirez

Quality Control Technician
Dina F Quan

Permissions Editor
Laura Moss

Media Development Specialist
Megan Decraene

Media Development Coordinator
Marisa Pearman

Book Designer
Evan Deerfield

Illustrator
Ronald Terry

Proofreading and Indexing
York Production Services

Cover Image
© Noma/Images.com

About the Author

Eric A. Smith is an author, consultant, and trainer specializing in Active Server Pages, Visual Basic, and SQL Server. He is a Microsoft Certified Solution Developer and Microsoft Certified Systems Engineer. He has written, edited, or contributed to ten books covering Visual Basic and Web technologies. He is also a frequent contributor to industry magazines, such as *Visual Basic Programmers Journal*.

Eric also runs a series of Web sites devoted to his favorite technologies: VB Techniques (vbtechniques.com), ASP Techniques (asptechniques.com), and SQL Techniques (sqltechniques.com). He also maintains sites for several of the books he's written, including this one (aspcrashcourse.com). He is also the creator of the *Ask the VB Pro* site, currently part of the DevX.com site.

Eric volunteers as an Emergency Medical Technician and is currently active with the Fairfax County Fire and Rescue Department. If you have comments, questions, or suggestions about this book, you can reach him via e-mail at info@aspcrashcourse.com.

To my wife, Jodi

Preface

*A*ctive Server Pages 3 Weekend Crash Course teaches ASP in one admittedly busy weekend — 30 sessions of a half-hour each between Friday evening and Sunday afternoon. At the end of each part of the book, you'll get a chance to pause, reflect, and review what you've just learned before pushing on through the rest. Good luck!

Programming for the Web

In case you've been living under a rock the past few years, nearly every type of application has become available on the Web. Free e-mail programs, personalized search engines, shopping sites that let you buy everything from road salt to CDs, and nearly everything else are now available for you to use.

The best thing is that if you're a programmer interested in this technology, work abounds and is quite profitable. However, you have to get up to speed on this technology quickly, since you don't have the time to learn by building poorly designed Web sites — the venture capitalists have gotten a bit more picky about whom they give their millions to.

One of the leading technologies in this new world is Active Server Pages from Microsoft. ASP's key advantage is that it's free with Windows 2000. You can create applications in any plain-text editor, even Notepad. There aren't any complicated programming concepts to learn initially, but when you're ready, you can add a whole world of tools and features to your repertoire. ASP is also powerful enough to run commercial Web sites, and many of the most popular sites are built using this technology.

What's in the Book

This book is intended for the beginner or intermediate reader. The book doesn't assume any previous programming knowledge; however, any previous knowledge you might have can only help you learn this new technology.

I'll start out slow, giving you the information in small, manageable bites. You'll see lots of small, simple examples throughout the first 20 chapters. Once you've got all the tools and building blocks, you'll build a real-world application through which you will learn to put all the information together and be able to can continue to build.

Even if you've learned ASP on your own, you might not know what each line of code does. Once you're done with this book, you'll have of better understanding of what the code you might have acquired does, and more importantly, you'll have learned to expand and maintain your programs.

How to Use the Book

Active Server Pages 3 Weekend Crash Course follows a one-weekend format. You'll get started on Friday evening and finish up on Sunday afternoon or evening. This format is ideal for:

- The student who wants to catch up with the rest of the class
- The developer who needs to add to his or her skill base for future work
- Anyone who needs a more structured way to learn new technology

Of course, you don't have to fit all the material into a weekend. You might want to do a little bit at a time, work on your own project, come back to the book, and so on. The book is divided into six parts, each part containing four to six lessons. Each lesson is designed to be completed in 30 minutes. There are time markers in the margin to help keep you on track. As with any programming language, you'll want to write code as you read to help it sink in better.

Each lesson is followed by a set of review questions to allow you to judge your comprehension of the material. A set of more involved problems is provided at the end of each part to help drive home knowledge that you've gained in the part's lessons.

Overview

ASP3 Weekend Crash Course presents its lessons in groups of four to six chapters, organized in six parts as follows:

Friday Evening — Introduction to ASP

Part I helps you get the necessary tools installed on your Windows 2000 machine. You'll then get an introduction to the structure and architecture of Active Server Pages.

Saturday Morning — HTML and ASP Basics

Part II shows you how to get data from and send data back to the user. You'll also learn a bit about HTML, since that's the format you'll be using for your application's output.

Saturday Afternoon — VBScript

Part III teaches you VBScript, which is the primary language most ASP developers use to write server-side code.

Saturday Evening — ASP Features and Active Data Objects

Part IV will show you how to perform common tasks in ASP. You'll also learn to read database information from databases like Microsoft Access and SQL Server.

Sunday Morning — Designing the eOrganizer Application

Part V will introduce the design for the eOrganizer Personal Information Manager application that you'll be building, and then you'll build key pieces of the application.

Sunday Afternoon — Finishing the eOrganizer Application

Part VI shows you how to add the other features to the application and to put the finishing touches on it. You'll also see how to expand the application with additional features.

Layout and Features

Don't try to power through this material without a break — you'll hurt your brain. After each session, and at the end of each part, you'll find some review questions to test what you've learned. Take a break, grab a snack, and get away from the computer for a while. After a short break, you'll be ready to take on the next session.

Along the way, you'll find some features of the book to help you keep track of how far along you are and point out interesting and important bits of information that you shouldn't miss. First, as you're going through each session, check for something like this in the margin:

This icon and others like it let you know how much progress you've made through each session as you go. There are also several icons to point out special tidbits of information for you:

**20 Min.
To Go**

 This is an important piece of information that you should file away in your head for later.

 This is helpful advice on the best way to do something or a neat little technique that can help your programming go better.

 Don't do this! Bad things will happen! Danger, danger, Will Robinson!

 This mentions information that you'll find on the CD-ROM included with this book.

I also occasionally highlight text passages that explain key concepts of ASP and VBScript syntax, like so:

SYNTAX ▶ A function is a logically separate block of VBScript code. The function has this form:

```
Function DoSomething(parametervalue)
    ...
End Function
```

Conventions Used in This Book

Aside from the icons you've just seen, such as Tip, there are only three conventions used in this book:

- To indicate a menu choice, I'll use the ⇨ symbol, as in:

  Choose File ⇨ Save to save your work.

- To indicate programming code within a paragraph, I'll use a special font, like this:

  If you need to add a positive or negative value to a date/time value, you can use the DateAdd function.

- To show a programming example that is more than a keyword or two, I'll use this typeface:

  ```
  Function DoSomething(parametervalue)
      ...
  End Function
  ```

- To show the continuation of a line of code that breaks due to the limitations of the page size, I'll insert a continuation character (underline) at the end of the line: _

What's Left

Nothing. Open your book to the first lesson and have some fun!

Acknowledgments

First and foremost, I thank God for giving me the talent and strength to do this and everything else in my life. All of my efforts on this book and everything else are for his glory and not my own.

I want to thank my wife Jodi for keeping me on track in getting this book done. Max, my dog, kept my feet warm as he sat under my computer desk while I typed late into the night.

Dave Hillman (technical editor) did a great job making sure that my code all worked correctly. Thanks for the good work, Dave. Greg Croy (acquisitions editor), Barb Guerra (project editor), and S.B. Kleinman and Luann Rouff (copy editors) did a great job turning my bits into a book. I appreciate all their hard work on my behalf.

Margot Maley Hutchison and Waterside Productions did their usual great job in taking care of the administrative and financial details of writing books.

And to you, my readers, thank you for your input and feedback about my books. Your questions turn into my chapters and books, so keep them up!

Contents at a Glance

Contents

Active Server Pages 3
Weekend Crash Course™

☑ **Friday**

☐ Saturday

☐ Sunday

Part I — Friday Evening

PART

I

Friday Evening

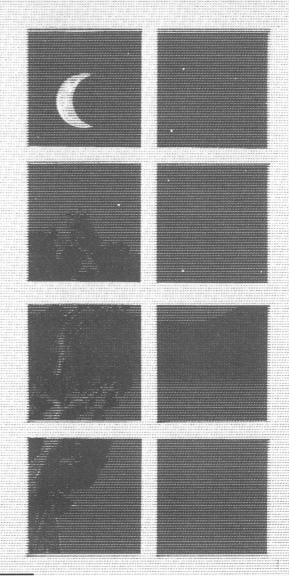

Introduction to Web Programming and Active Server Pages

Session Checklist

✔ Learn what Active Server Pages is and where to use it

✔ Understand how the server processes ASP files

✔ Understand how to program in ASP

✔ Use databases with ASP

✔ Learn about add-ons for ASP applications

30 Min. To Go

This chapter gives you an overview of how Active Server Pages works, where you can use it, and how you can write programs with it. You'll also learn about how expandable ASP is and how you can use it with other programs and databases to build really cool applications.

What Is Active Server Pages?

Early Web sites were just a collection of plain, HTML-formatted text files. Every time you viewed them they were exactly the same. Someone had to change the files manually in order to make new content available. Without automated tools, running a Web site like this was a real pain. On a site I was running, I got tired of having to build pages by hand so I wrote a program to generate plain HTML pages based on the contents of a database. It had some nice features, but it wasn't generating truly dynamic content, since I had to run the program to create the pages each time.

The introduction of Active Server Pages (ASP) solved this problem. ASP is designed to let you create pages that can change each time a user loads them. You write code in the page that is run on the Web server before the user ever sees the page. For instance, let's say you wanted to put today's date on the Web page. There's no way you could do that with static HTML pages, unless you edited the page every single day. With ASP, however, you write a piece of script to show the current date in the page. The server evaluates the script every time the page loads, no matter what day it is, and the code generates the current date.

ASP files can be written to perform a variety of tasks. Many commercial Web sites use ASP technology to run the major functions on their sites. For instance, I've seen ASP files doing all of the following (and more!):

- Stock portfolios
- Store catalogs and shopping carts
- Discussion boards
- Advertising management software

You can create ASP files in any text editor, since they are all just plain text. You can also use tools such as:

- Allaire HomeSite — http://www.homesite.com
- Microsoft FrontPage — http://www.microsoft.com/frontpage
- Macromedia Dreamweaver — http://www.macromedia.com
- Microsoft Visual InterDev — http://www.microsoft.com/vstudio
- Helios Software's TextPad — http://www.textpad.com

There are new tools coming out all the time to create ASP files. Some of these tools provide some intelligence to automatically create ASP code and files for you. However, if you rely on these "crutches" to learn ASP, you won't learn how the code really works.

To build the examples in this book, I recommend either using HomeSite or TextPad, because both programs will let you get right to the code. If you don't have either of those tools, you can use any plain text editor such as Notepad or WordPad. No matter which tool you choose, make sure that it is able to save plain text files without any extra formatting.

For the Windows environment, the files must be saved using carriage return/line feeds to break each line. This is different from UNIX files, which use only a line feed to break each line. If your editor doesn't understand the difference, you'll run into problems when you start editing your files.

Where Can I Use ASP?

Active Server Pages is a server-side technology. That means that the user's browser is not involved in processing your ASP code. I'm often asked whether there is a component or other tool that can process ASP code without a Web server. The short answer is no. You have to use a Web server to process the ASP code.

The good thing is that you have a number of options for running your ASP applications. All versions of Windows have either Internet Information Server or Personal Web Server available. You'll see how to install these in the next chapter.

If you're not on a Windows platform, you can still use Active Server Pages through an innovative product called ChiliSoft (http://www.chilisoft.com). (This company was purchased by Cobalt Networks in March 2000, which was purchased by Sun Microsystems in September 2000.) This product allows you to run ASP on virtually any operating system platform, including UNIX, Linux, Sun Solaris, and more.

Because ASP is so easy to learn, it is becoming a popular platform on which to build Web applications. The primary language is English-based and doesn't have lots of strict spacing and formatting rules, which makes it even easier to learn. When you visit your favorite Web sites, take a look at the extensions of files that your links point to. Chances are you'll see at least a few ASP files in use.

**20 Min.
To Go**

How Does the Server Process ASP Files?

As I mentioned before, ASP code is processed on the server. None of your server-side code ever gets sent to the user's browser. The only thing the user sees is HTML and any client-side script you may have included in your page.

Here's how ASP files are processed, step by step:

1. The user requests an ASP file through a Web browser.
2. The Web server gets the request and loads the ASP file.

3. The server processes all the ASP code in the file. Any output from the ASP code is in HTML format. This output will be evaluated by the user's browser.

4. The server sends the remaining HTML content to the user's Web browser.

This system has a number of advantages:

- The code you write in your ASP files never leaves the server. This provides a measure of security for your code and doesn't reveal to the user how the page was built.
- The ASP file can use databases or other sources of information available on the server to create the page without requiring a connection from the user's browser.
- On a large site, the page requests can be handled by multiple servers, each one handling the database activity or the Web publishing requests. This makes the system scalable to large applications, such as those run by some of the largest e-commerce sites on the Internet.

The other major benefit of using ASP for your Web sites is that if you have purchased Windows NT or Windows 2000, the ASP software is free. Other tools, such as Allaire ColdFusion, have both client and server costs involved, so ASP provides a built-in advantage from that point of view.

Another major benefit of using ASP is that it is a stable, mature technology with wide support from Microsoft, third-party vendors of tools and components, and the support of many book publishers and developers. There are yearly conferences covering ASP and related technologies, put on by several different companies.

Programming in ASP

ASP can use any language, including VBScript, JavaScript (JScript on Microsoft platforms), Perl, and more. VBScript is the default ASP language and is what we'll be focusing on in this book. Most other books on the market also focus on VBScript for the server-side code you write. However, since VBScript is not supported on Netscape as a client-side language, you'll usually only see JavaScript for client-side script code.

VBScript is a variant of Microsoft's popular Visual Basic development tool. Here's a sample of the code you'll soon be writing:

```
<%
    Dim objDB          ' As NCSBackOffice.Database
    Dim rsSites        ' As ADODB.Recordset

    Set objDB = Server.CreateObject("NCSBackOffice.Database")
    Set rsSites = objDB.Execute("sp_RetrieveClientSites")

    Response.Write "<ul>"
    Do Until rsSites.EOF
       WriteLine rsSites("WebSite")
       rsSites.MoveNext
    Loop
    rsSites.Close
    Set rsSites = Nothing
    Set objDB = Nothing
    Response.Write "</ul>"
%>
```

If you'd like to see it running, this particular page is located at this URL:

```
http://www.northcomp.com/res_clients.asp
```

These few lines of VBScript code do the following:

- Open a database connection.
- Run a SQL Server stored procedure to return a list of URLs.
- Print each URL out to a page.

As you can see, the code is English-based and you can basically read through it to learn what it does. You should also see that it doesn't take much code to do some cool stuff.

**10 Min.
To Go**

Using Databases with ASP

ASP was developed primarily to make it easier to create database-driven Web sites. In conjunction with ASP, Microsoft developed ActiveX Data Objects technology (ADO) to connect to your database, retrieve data, make changes if necessary, and manipulate that data in ASP files. ADO technology is quickly spreading across the Microsoft development platform. It is available throughout Visual Studio 6.0 and is now the database technology that Microsoft will be supporting and enhancing in the future. This is a great improvement over the data access "alphabet soup" that existed before ADO was released. Microsoft has created a Web site devoted to Universal Data Access, its strategy for accessing any type of data on any server from any client. The Web site is located at http://www.microsoft.com/data.

Through ADO, Active Server Pages can access any database. ADO uses a technology called OLE DB to access data sources. You use a *provider* with OLE DB to access certain types of data. For instance, there is an OLE DB provider for SQL Server, one for Access, and one for Oracle. A provider understands how to talk to a particular brand of database. This allows you, the ADO programmer, to not have to worry about how the connection is made. You just have to focus on how to get the data you need.

If you are using another type of database, you will probably not have an OLE DB provider available. If you don't, don't worry. ADO still supports Open Database Connectivity (ODBC), which your database probably does support. In this case, you'll use the OLE DB provider for ODBC instead of one specific for your database. You'll learn how to do this starting in Chapter 21 when you start building your Personal Information Manager.

Add-ons for ASP

One of the benefits of ASP is that it is expandable. ASP can use DLLs created with Visual Basic. This enables you to use code located in a DLL in both a Visual Basic application and an ASP application. You can also use third-party products to provide services like e-mail, credit-card validation, and more through this method.

ASP can also take advantage of Microsoft Transaction Server (MTS), which is designed for high-performance Web sites and sites with a high number of simultaneous users. It enables you to pool objects and share them among all your users. For instance, you might create a database object that is shared by anyone who hits the site. The benefit of this is that the object makes and holds open a database connection, instead of making your page create a new connection each time. This dramatically increases the speed of the pages and allows for more concurrent users.

ASP can also work with Java applets and Java servlets, just like any other object. If you're writing Java applets that download to your users' browsers, you can write client-side script to control them and include that code in an ASP file. ASP can also work with ActiveX controls that you might put in your Web pages. Although ActiveX controls don't work in Netscape, you can still use them in intranet environments where you know what browsers are in use.

The other "add-ons" that are available are not products, but support. There is a wide range of Web sites, books, online tutorials and courses, and more covering ASP. You'll find free products, samples, and more through these sites. I personally maintain an ASP site called ASP Techniques (`http://asptechniques.com`) where you can get updates for this book and other books I've written. You can also get links to other excellent sites from ASP Techniques, or you can use any search engine to get the information you need.

Done!

REVIEW

Active Server Pages is a great platform with which to develop your Web-based applications. It's widely supported and has great expandability through both your own custom components and third-party components. Talking to databases is a piece of cake and gives you enormous power in building dynamic, rich experiences for your users. You also have the support of thousands of other developers, hundreds of books, and lots of other online resources. In short, you're joining an active community building the next generation of applications for the Internet. Welcome aboard!

QUIZ YOURSELF

---

1. What platform does ASP run on? (See "Where Can I Use Active Server Pages?")
2. What tools can I use to build ASP files? (See "What Is Active Server Pages?")
3. What technology do I use to connect to my database? (See "Using Databases with ASP")

Setting up the Environment

Session Checklist

✔ Learn the basic requirements for ASP 3

✔ Install IIS on Windows 2000 Professional

✔ Install IIS on Windows 2000 Server

**30 Min.
To Go**

Before you can write ASP code, you have to have a place to run it. ASP files don't run in your browser like HTML files do. As you learned in the last chapter, ASP code is evaluated on the server before you ever see it in your Web browser. For this to work, you have to have Internet Information Server (IIS) installed on your machine. IIS version 5.0 ships with Windows 2000 and is a free product, as long as you've paid for the operating system. This is one of the benefits that have helped make it a popular platform for building Web sites.

Configuring Active Server Pages

Since IIS 5.0 runs as part of the operating system, the only documented requirements for IIS are the same as those for Windows 2000. As usual, the more memory you have, the better. However, the following information is the official "party line" information as to the recommended machine configuration you should use.

For more information on the differences between the editions of Windows 2000, visit this Microsoft site:

http://www.microsoft.com/windows2000/guide/platform/

Windows 2000 Professional

Windows 2000 Professional runs exactly the same software as any of the Server editions of Windows 2000. The difference is that, by default, Windows 2000 Professional has the Personal Web Manager console installed, as well. This console is for users who aren't comfortable using the IIS Console that we'll be using in this book. Here are the hardware requirements for IIS to run on Windows 2000 Professional:

- 133 MHz or higher Pentium-compatible CPU
- 64 MB of RAM recommended minimum; more memory generally improves responsiveness
- 2 GB hard disk with a minimum of 650 MB of free space
- Single or dual CPU system

Windows 2000 Server

Windows 2000 Server looks identical to Windows 2000 Professional, with the exception of some additional tools and services that don't run at the Professional level. Server requires a bit more memory, but can support more processors in the machine. Here are the requirements for Windows 2000 Server to run IIS 5.0:

- 133 MHz or higher Pentium-compatible CPU
- 256 MB of RAM recommended minimum (128 MB minimum supported; 4 GB maximum)
- 2 GB hard disk with a minimum of 1.0 GB free space (additional free hard disk space required if you are installing over a network)
- Up to four CPUs on one machine

Windows 2000 Advanced Server

Windows 2000 Advanced Server is designed for systems that require higher reliability and scalability. Here are the requirements for Windows 2000 Advanced Server to run IIS 5.0:

- 133 MHz or higher Pentium-compatible CPU
- 256 MB of RAM recommended minimum (128 MB minimum supported; 8 GB maximum)
- 2 GB hard disk with a minimum of 1.0 GB free space (additional free hard disk space is required if you are installing over a network)
- Up to eight CPUs on one machine

Windows 2000 Datacenter Server

Windows 2000 Datacenter Server, as its name suggests, is designed for heavily loaded, high traffic systems. Here are the requirements for Windows 2000 Datacenter Server to run IIS 5.0:

- Requires 8-way capable or higher server (supports up to 32-way); fault-tolerant system configurations required to have at least eight processors within the hardware solution
- Pentium III Xeon processors or higher
- 256 MB of RAM recommended
- 2 GB hard disk with a minimum of 1 GB free space (additional free hard disk space required if you are installing over a network)
- CD-ROM or DVD drive
- VGA or higher resolution monitor

**20 Min.
To Go**

Installing IIS 5.0 on Windows 2000 Professional

IIS is not installed with Windows 2000 Professional if you accept the default settings during the installation process. If you change the installation settings, you can add the Web services as you install Windows 2000 Professional. You can also add IIS once you've got Windows 2000 Professional installed. Either way, you'll see the same set of dialogs that you see here.

If you're installing IIS after completing the Windows installation, go to Control Panel ⇨ Add/Remove Programs, and pick the Add/Remove Windows Components button. The dialog that will appear is shown in Figure 2-1.

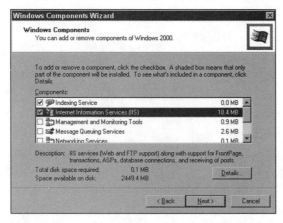

Figure 2-1
Add/Remove Windows Components dialog

There are a number of components in Internet Information Server that you can choose to add or leave out. If you click Internet Information Server in this dialog and then click the Details button, you will see the components that are available to you. The dialog is shown in Figure 2-2, and the list of components in Table 2-1.

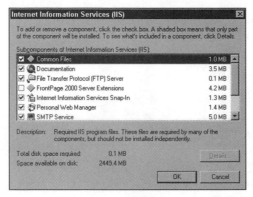

Figure 2-2
Details for Internet Information Server component

Table 2-1
Internet Information Server Components for Windows 2000 Professional

Component Name	Description
Common Files	These are files required by the server to operate.
Documentation	This includes sample Web sites as well as online documentation for the Web server.
FTP Service	This service enables you to set up file upload and download services for other users.
FrontPage 2000 Server Extensions	This component enables you to deploy Web sites from FrontPage directly to your Web server.
IIS Snap-In	This component enables you to administer the Web server from Microsoft Management Console.
Personal Web Manager	This is a simplified version of the IIS Snap-In.
SMTP Service	This service enables you to send e-mail from the server.
Visual InterDev RAD Support	This support works with Visual InterDev to enable you to deploy Web sites remotely.
World Wide Web Server	This service handles the actual Web services.

You may be wondering where the ASP component is. It's already included with the Web server and isn't a separate component you need to install.

If you're short on memory, stick with this minimum set of features:

- Common Files
- IIS Snap-In or Personal Web Manager
- World Wide Web Server

The other services aren't necessary for what you're going to be doing in this book. If you have enough disk space, add the documentation component so that you have some additional samples to work with.

**10 Min.
To Go**

Installation on Windows 2000 Server

You should install IIS when you install Windows 2000 Server. However, if Windows 2000 is already installed, you can add IIS after installation by going to the Add/Remove Programs applet on the Control Panel. The Add/Remove Windows Components section will allow you to add IIS.

Whether you install it before or after Windows is installed, the dialogs shown in this section will look the same. The first dialog shows all the components you can add to Windows 2000 Server, and it's shown in Figure 2-3.

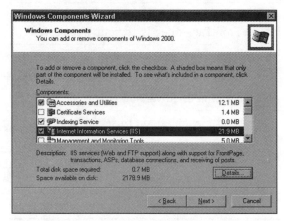

Figure 2-3
Windows 2000 Server components

You can pick all the components, or you can click the Details button and pick individual parts of IIS to install. Figure 2-4 shows the dialog that enables you to do this, and Table 2-2 shows the list of components available to Windows 2000 Server.

Table 2-2
Internet Information Server Components for Windows 2000 Server

Component Name	Description
Common Files	These are files required by the server to operate.
Documentation	This includes sample Web sites as well as online documentation for the Web server.

Component Name	Description
FTP Service	This service enables you to set up file upload and download services for other users.
FrontPage 2000 Server Extensions	This component enables you to deploy Web sites from FrontPage directly to your Web server.
IIS Snap-In	This component enables you to administer the Web server from Microsoft Management Console.
Internet Services Manager (HTML)	This is a Web-based server administration tool that gives you access to your Web server's configuration.
NNTP Service	This service allows your server to host Usenet-style newsgroups that can be accessed by Outlook Express and other newsreader applications.
SMTP Service	This service enables you to send e-mail from the server.
Visual InterDev RAD Support	This support is used with Visual InterDev to allow you to deploy Web sites remotely.
World Wide Web Server	This service handles the actual Web services.

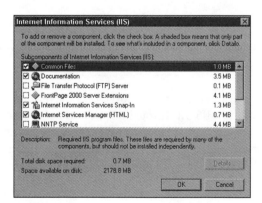

Figure 2-4
IIS components for Windows 2000 Server

You may be wondering where the ASP component is. It's already included with the Web server and isn't a separate component you need to install.

If you're short on memory, stick with this minimum set of features:

- Common Files
- IIS Snap-In or Personal Web Manager
- World Wide Web Server

The other services aren't necessary for what you're going to be doing in this book. If you have enough disk space, add in the documentation component so that you have some additional samples to work with.

If you're using a version of Windows other than 2000 — including 95, 98, Millennium (Me), or NT 4.0 — you can run ASP, too. However, you won't be running ASP 3. Depending on the edition of Windows you have, you will have ASP 2 (or below) available. The good thing is that there aren't really that many new features in ASP 3. Most of the improvements are in performance. In addition, most of the examples in this book will work fine on other versions of ASP. The best thing to do is to refer to your system documentation to install Personal Web Server (95, 98, Me) or Internet Information Server 4.0 (Windows NT 4.0). If you have questions about installing these pieces of software, there are a number of links up at the ASP Techniques Web site (asptechniques.com) that will show you how to install these pieces of software.

Done!

REVIEW

In this chapter, you configured and installed Internet Information Server 5.0 on your Windows 2000 machine. You will use IIS 5.0 throughout the rest of the book to run your ASP files. IIS is one of the most popular Web servers used for commercial Web sites today. As you saw, it only took a few steps to install it, and it comes pre-configured and ready to run. All you have to do now is learn to write ASP code and you'll be all set.

QUIZ YOURSELF

1. Where is ASP code evaluated — on the client or on the server? (See chapter introduction)

2. What version of Windows does ASP 3 run on? (See "Configuring Active Server Pages")

3. What does IIS stand for? (See chapter introduction)

4. What is an SMTP server used for? (See "Installation for Windows 2000 Server")

5. What is an NNTP server used for? (See "Installation for Windows 2000 Server")

Creating Your First Web Site

Session Checklist

✔ Learn to use the Internet Service Manager

✔ Create a virtual directory on your server

✔ Pick a text editor to use for your editing

**30 Min.
To Go**

N ow that you know some of the background of ASP, let's put some of the basics to use. In this chapter, we'll create your first Web site.

Using the Internet Services Manager

Now that you've got IIS installed on your machine, you have a new icon in your Administrative Tools folder called Internet Services Manager. If you use Windows 2000 Professional, you'll also have something called Personal Web Manager. The Web Manager is a simplified and somewhat crippled tool for managing your Web server. Instead, we're going to focus on the Internet Services Manager, which gives you access to all the Web server's features.

When you start Internet Services Manager, you'll see the window shown in Figure 3-1.

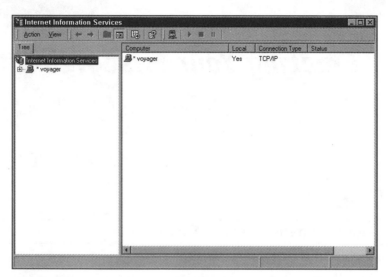

Figure 3-1
Internet Services Manager

You'll see the name of your machine on the left at the top of the screen. When you click the plus sign next to it, you'll see the sites currently configured on your server. Depending on the services you installed, you may have a different view from the one shown in Figure 3-2.

The site we're going to be focusing on is the Default Web Site, which you can view by typing this URL into your browser:

```
http://machinename/
```

Supply your machine name and you'll see the starter Web site supplied with IIS. To view details about this Web site, right-click it and select Properties from the popup menu. The dialog shown in Figure 3-3 will appear.

While you won't be using many of these properties in this book, you can look through the various tabs and use the Help dialog to get information about each dialog. A few key tabs are:

- The Home Directory tab, which enables you to configure the home directory for your Web site, as well as security permissions for each Web site.

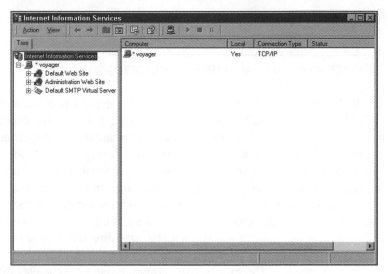

Figure 3-2
Sites and services currently installed on the machine

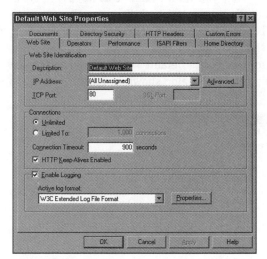

Figure 3-3
Web Site Properties dialog

- The Documents tab, which enables you to specify other documents to be
  handled as default documents for your directories. For instance, you might
  want to add index.html or index.htm to the list.

We'll cover some of the other tabs later in the book.

**20 Min.
To Go**

Building Directories and Virtual Directories

When you installed your Web server, the installer created a default Web site and set of directories for you. By default, these are located in C:\InetPub. The default Web directory is wwwroot in that directory. Besides the wwwroot directory, there will also be a number of additional directories there, based on the services you install. However, the wwwroot directory is the one we'll be focusing on for now.

Many Web sites will start building their applications right in that root Web directory. However, as the sites get bigger, you'll need to have a structure that allows the site to expand. For instance, you might have a subdirectory for your pictures, one for your movies, and so on. You might create directories to divide your content by functional area, by department, or by other criteria.

Any directories you create in the root Web directory are immediately available through the Web browser. However, you may want to create another directory that isn't in the same directory as everything else. For instance, if you have created a directory called files on your server that you want available as `http://server/ files`, you have to create a virtual directory. A virtual directory allows you to reference a directory in the Web browser but have it point to another directory or drive, or even a directory on another machine.

To create a virtual directory, right-click the Default Web Site and select New ⇨ Virtual Directory from the popup menu. The dialog shown in Figure 3-4 will appear.

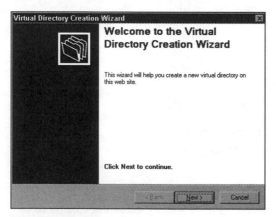

Figure 3-4
Virtual Directory wizard

As with most tasks in Windows, you create a virtual directory through a wizard. Figure 3-5 shows the next step, wherein you specify the name (also known as an *alias*) that you want to use in your Web browser.

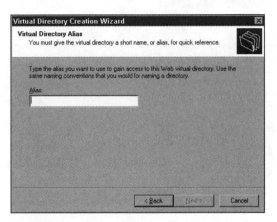

Figure 3-5
Enter an alias in this dialog

In the next dialog, you specify the directory to use for this alias. Figure 3-6 shows this dialog. Clicking the Browse button will enable you to pick the directory instead of having to type it in.

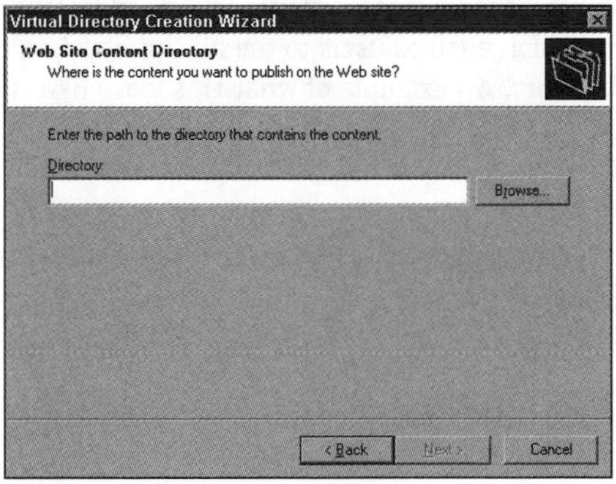

Figure 3-6
Select a directory to use for your virtual directory

The last step is to specify the security settings for the directory in the dialog shown in Figure 3-7.

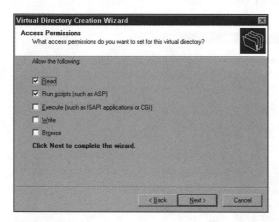

Figure 3-7
Access Permissions dialog

By default, you have read and script permission, which enable you to see HTML, image, and ASP files. You have to have both permissions checked. If you don't mark the script permission box, ASP files won't be able to run. If you don't mark the read permission box, nothing can be viewed. You can also add on execute permission, which enables you to run applications within your directory. You can also write permission for a directory, which allows special Web components to save files. Finally, you can set the browse permission, which enables users to see all the files in a directory if no default page is in the directory. An example of what this looks like is shown in Figure 3-8.

Once you click Next for the last time, you'll be able to use your virtual directory in your Web browser.

**10 Min.
To Go**

Picking a File Editor

To get started building Web sites, you'll need a text editor of some sort. There are a number of Web page editors, including Microsoft FrontPage and Macromedia Dreamweaver. However, I would suggest, for now, sticking to a basic text editor that doesn't try to do too much work for you. FrontPage and Dreamweaver will create the page for you, but you won't understand how to build the pages yourself.

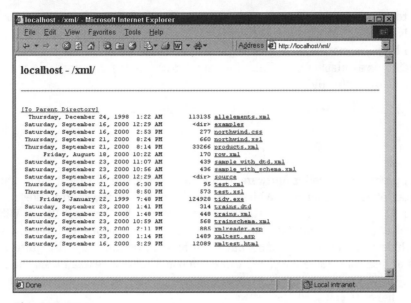

Figure 3-8
Directory browsing in Internet Explorer lets you pick files to view

Since Active Server Pages relies on your ability to integrate ASP code and HTML code, the best way to learn (in my opinion) is to write the code yourself. It's really not that hard and knowing the code will let you more easily debug code created in any of those tools.

There are a number of fairly inexpensive tools that you can use to build these Web pages. While you can create files in a simple text editor like Notepad, there are tools that provide a good compromise between doing everything for you and doing nothing for you. This section will cover some of these tools and where you can go to find more.

Allaire HomeSite

HomeSite, now produced by the makers of ColdFusion, is my favorite editor. It has a number of tools that make it easier to write HTML, ASP, and other types of code. For instance, there are dialogs that help you build tables, lists, frame sets, and more. There are wizards for JavaScript, ASP code, and ColdFusion. HomeSite will validate your HTML and provide immediate assistance and reminders about what parameters are available for tags. It also includes lots of keyboard shortcuts for entering HTML tags, which speeds up your typing.

This tool is also able to highlight the syntax for ASP, which means that your keywords will be marked in one color, literals in another color, and so on. This feature can help you notice when you've got errors in your code.

HomeSite is available from Allaire for around $90 (30-day downloadable trial available also) at this URL:

```
http://www.allaire.com/products/homesite/index.cfm
```

TextPad

TextPad, produced by Helios Software, is similar to HomeSite in that it understands the syntax of many languages. While it doesn't include as many shortcut keys for entering HTML, it does include a Macro Recorder, much like Microsoft Office. With this feature, you can memorize your own keystroke combinations for later use. It does include more language support but fewer built-in features. It's also quite a bit cheaper at less than $30 a copy. You can download a copy of TextPad from the following URL. You can install it and use it as shareware; it will simply remind you to register whenever you start the software.

```
http://www.textpad.com
```

Visual InterDev

For those of you who have purchased Visual Studio, Visual InterDev is the tool you'll want to use. Microsoft has bundled Visual InterDev as part of Visual Studio, making it more economical to buy the bundle if you're going to use more than one piece of software. Visual InterDev has a number of features that were originally designed to help you create ASP code; however, I'm not a big fan of this feature. The code it creates is not always perfect and is difficult to sort out. Visual InterDev also does pages in one way and doesn't allow you to build the features I show you later in the book. For that reason, I use it as a file editor only.

One disadvantage of Visual InterDev is that, by itself, it's quite expensive. A full retail copy of just Visual InterDev costs over $500. If you didn't get it with VB or VC++, don't buy it: you won't be getting your money's worth out of it.

More choices

There are a number of sites that provide reviews and downloads of additional text and code editors. Here are a few sites for you to visit:

CNet   http://www.cnet.com

ZDNet	http://www.zdnet.com
DevX	http://www.devx.com
ASP 101	http://www.asp101.com

You can also get more information about editors at the support site for the book:

http://www.aspcrashcourse.com

Done!

REVIEW

In this chapter, you learned a bit about the tools that you installed and how to use them. You also learned to create virtual directories and regular directories within IIS 5.0. Finally, you learned about some of the text editors available to help you build your pages later in the book.

QUIZ YOURSELF

1. What tools are available for administering your Web sites?
2. If your server name were GALAXY, how would you view the default Web site on the machine? (See "Using the Internet Service Manager")
3. Where are virtual directories located on your computer's hard drive? (See "Building Directories and Virtual Directories")
4. What permissions are available for a Web site? (See "Building Directories and Virtual Directories")
5. What permissions are available for a virtual directory? (See "Building Directories and Virtual Directories")
6. What permissions must be set for ASP pages to run properly? (See "Building Directories and Virtual Directories")
7. What permission must be set in order to browse a Web directory? (See "Building Directories and Virtual Directories")

Writing Your First Code

Session Checklist

✔ Create an HTML page on your server

✔ Make the page available on your Web server

✔ Create a simple ASP page on your server

I n the next two chapters, you'll learn how to craft an HTML page using all sorts of tags.

**30 Min.
To Go**

Creating an HTML Page

To begin you need to learn about putting files into your Web server's directories. Here are the steps you should follow to build this page:

1. In your text editor, enter the following code:

   ```
   <html>
   <head>
   <title>ASP Crash Course: Hello World!</title>
   ```

```
</head>
<body>
<h1>Hello, world!</h1>
</body>
</html>
```

2. Save the file to the root directory of your Web server under a name of your choosing. For this example, this file is called ch04_helloworld.html.

3. In your Web browser, type in the following URL, substituting the name of your server for *servername*:

    ```
    http://servername/ch04_helloworld.html
    ```

If you want to view a page running on a Web server on your local machine, you can use the name "localhost" in place of the machine name. This reserved name is configured to refer to the current machine.

The page, when shown in Internet Explorer, will look something like Figure 4-1.

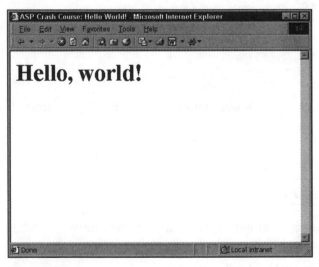

Figure 4-1
Results of ch04_helloworld.html

Congratulations! You just created your first Web page on your server. A couple of things to note:

- If you want to connect to your Web server, you can't simply double-click the filename to open it. If you do this with your file, your URL might look something like this:

  ```
  D:\Web\ASP Crash Course\ch04_helloworld.html
  ```

- If you see a drive letter or the prefix `file:` in your URL, it means you're not using your Web server. This is fine for HTML files, but it won't work for the ASP pages you'll be creating in rest of the book.

Creating an ASP Page

20 Min. To Go

Now that you've gotten a "crash course" in building an HTML page, let's do the same thing with an ASP page. Follow these steps to build this page:

1. Create a new file in your text editor.
2. Enter the following code into your browser.

   ```
   <html>
   <head>
   <title>ASP Crash Course: Hello World with ASP!</title>
   </head>
   <body>
   Hello World!<br>
   The current date and time are <% = Now %>
   </body>
   </html>
   ```

3. Save the file to your Web server. For this example, this file is named ch04_helloworld.asp.

If the Web server is not on your local area network, you'll need to FTP your file to the server. For specific instructions on how to FTP to your server, you'll need to contact the owner/administrator of the server.

**10 Min.
To Go**

If everything is configured correctly, you will be able to open the file in your browser with the URL `http://servername/ch04_helloworld.asp`.

When you load this page into your browser, you'll see something like the page shown in Figure 4-2.

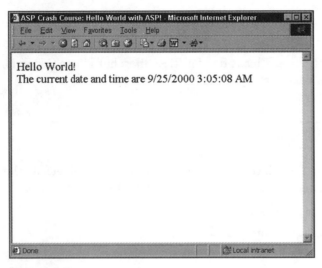

Figure 4-2
Results of ch04_helloworld.asp

Done!

Again, make sure that your URL has an `http://` prefix. If you don't, the ASP code won't execute properly. In this particular example, the ASP code is generating the current date and time. The <% and %> tags are called the ASP delimiter tags. They mark the beginning and end of ASP code. You'll be adding these tags many more times throughout the rest of the book.

REVIEW

In this quick chapter, you learned how to create HTML and ASP pages. There's not much else to building pages themselves in either language. Unlike with other languages, you don't have to compile the files, assemble them in any other way, or do anything else. All the files throughout the rest of the book are built in exactly the same way, so make sure you have your tools installed and can run these examples.

QUIZ YOURSELF

1. Create the URL to view a page named `test.html` running on `asp techniques.com`. (See "Creating an HTML Page")

2. What characters are used to mark the beginning and end of ASP code? (See "Creating an ASP Page")

3. What tool do you need to use to compile your ASP page? (See "Review")

4. What prefix must every URL have that accesses an ASP page? (See "Creating an ASP Page")

PART

I

Friday Evening
Part Review

Define the following terms:

1. IIS
2. ASP
3. ADO
4. ODBC
5. MMC

Using the Internet Information Server console, identify where the following actions begin:

6. Creating a new Web site
7. Changing the home directory for a Web site
8. Changing the information logged for a Web site

☑ Friday

☑ **Saturday**

☐ Sunday

PART

II

*Saturday
Morning*

Session Checklist

✔ Learn the basic structure of an HTML page

✔ Learn how to space text in a page

✔ Create headings in a page

✔ Use text-formatting tags around your text

✔ Learn how to add pictures and links to your page

**30 Min.
To Go**

All of the output that your ASP files will generate is going to be in HTML format. For that reason, we're going to start off with a review of HTML syntax. There are a number of good books that cover HTML in much greater depth than we have the space for here. However, this chapter will give you a good introduction to all the important syntax elements of HTML.

HTML Page Structure

No matter what you learn with Active Server Pages, the end result is generally going to have some HTML in it. As XML gains in popularity, HTML may eventually go away, but it's all we've got for now. In this chapter, you'll learn the basics of creating HTML pages, formatting data, and using some of the built-in text-formatting tags.

The <HTML> and </HTML> tags

To start with, every page must start with the <HTML> tag and end with the </HTML> tag. This marks the beginning and end of the content in the page. You don't have to put these tags in for the page to show properly; however, it's best to get in the habit of always including them. As the formats change and start using XML or whatever the Next Big Thing is, the browser will need to know what it's looking at. Using the correct HTML tags will ensure that your code is handled properly.

The HTML page heading

Every page has two parts: the heading and the body. Just as a letter has a heading, where you put the address, date, and so on, an HTML page has a heading. For an HTML page, the heading can contain information like this:

- Page title
- Information for search engines to use, such as keywords and page descriptions
- Style sheets for formatting text
- Client-side scripting

While we're not going to be covering everything you can put in the heading in this book, you can refer to other books available from Hungry Minds and other publishers for more details on these features.

A key difference between the heading and the body is that most of the heading is not shown to the user. The title of the page is usually shown in the browser's title bar, but information such as style sheets, client-side scripting, and search engine information is not visible on the screen. However, the information is in the page, and you can see it by viewing the source code for the page.

In Internet Explorer, you can view the source code for a page by selecting View ⇨ Source from the menu or by right-clicking on the text and selecting View Source. If you're using Netscape, you can view the source code for the page by selecting View⇨ Page Source. If you look at the source of my site, ASP Techniques, here's part of what you'll see:

```
<html><head><title>ASP Techniques: Your Source for Active Server
Pages Tips, Articles, Reviews, and more!</title>
<style type="text/css" title="ASP Techniques Style Sheet">
    .itemlink            { font-size : 12pt;
                            font-family: Arial, Helvetica;
                            font-weight: bold;
                            color: #990000;
                            text-decoration: none}

    .
    .
    .
</style>
<SCRIPT LANGUAGE="JavaScript">
<!--
  function LinkHighlight(objLink)
  {
      if (isMsie4orGreater()) {
         objLink.style.color = 'ffff00';
      }
  }
  function LinkClear(objLink)
  {
      if (isMsie4orGreater()) {
         objLink.style.color = 'ffffff';
      }
  }
  .
  .
  .
-->
</SCRIPT>
<meta name="description" content="ASP Techniques is a site devoted
to developers who can't find enough good technical material on the
web. You'll get original technical articles here that actually
explain Active Server Pages without using lots of buzzwords.
You'll also get unbiased reviews of books and products, as well
as links to the best ASP sites on the web.">
```

```
. . .

</head>
<BODY Background="/pics/bkgd_stripe_red.gif" link=#0000FF
vlink=#0000FF alink=#0000FF>

. .
```

The dots mark where there is more code than I'm showing here. This particular sample has all of the elements of a page header.

The <TITLE> tag specifies the page title. Any text between <TITLE> and </TITLE> will be put in the browser's title bar. In addition, when a user saves a page's URL to his/her favorites or bookmarks, the title of the page will be used. One thing to note: if you don't specify a title, the URL of the page will show up in the title bar.

The code within the <STYLE> tags is used with Cascading Style Sheets (CSS), an advanced text-formatting feature supported by the latest version of both major browsers.

The SCRIPT tags mark the beginning and end of some client-side script I'm including in the page. You can use any scripting language you want, as long as the browser supports it. Internet Explorer, as of version 4.0, supports both VBScript and JScript (a variant of JavaScript) as client-side scripting engines. Netscape, as of version 6.0, still only supports JavaScript. As far as I can tell, the group supporting Netscape has dropped previously announced plans to support VBScript or any other Microsoft technology, such as ActiveX controls.

The META tag provides some descriptive information for search engines that index my site. This particular piece of text provides a description of the Web site. By specifying a name parameter (as in the description), you can specify different pieces of data that describe your page. Here are a couple of parameters you can use with the META tag:

DESCRIPTION　　Provide a description of your site. Many search engines will use this to provide a short summary of your page to people using the search engine.

KEYWORDS　　If your site focuses on a particular topic, you can use this parameter to specify important keywords to help search engines send users to your site. In general, the more relevant keywords, the better.

The HEAD and /HEAD tags surround all of this information and mark the beginning and end of the page heading.

The HTML page body

Once you get through the heading of the page, you get into the body of the page. This is where you put the content that you want to show to the user. The body of the page is marked by the BODY and /BODY tags. The BODY tag can take a number of attributes. Here are some of the more useful ones:

BACKGROUND
: Specifies a background image to repeat on the background of the Web page. Any image you specify will be "tiled" on the page, just as Windows enables you to tile an image on your desktop. The image will be repeated continuously across and down the page to fill the area. Here's an example of how to use this tag:
`<body background="stripe.gif">`

BGCOLOR
: Specifies the color to be used as the background of the page. Depending on the browser you're using, the background is typically either white or a darker gray. I prefer white as the background, but I often use a background image instead of the BGCOLOR tag. Read the sidebar to learn how to specify a color with HTML.

TEXT
: This attribute specifies the default color for text on your page.

LINK
: This attribute specifies the default color to show any links on your page. While you can change it from the default of blue, many people will try to click on text that is blue and underlined, and will ignore text that is some other color and underlined. The blue link has been around since the Web took off and it's not a good idea to use underlined blue text for anything but links.

ALINK
: If you want to change the color of a link that is being clicked, you can specify the new color in the ALINK attribute. Note that once the link has been clicked, it changes to the color specified in the VLINK attribute.

VLINK
: To show a different color for links that the user has visited, you can use the VLINK color. It's a good idea to provide a different color for visited links so that the user can remember what he/she visited from your site.

LEFTMARGIN   This is a tag specific to Internet Explorer. This value
                  specifies, in pixels, how much empty space to leave on
                  the left-hand side of the page. I prefer to set this value
                  to 0, since generally I have other formatting that aligns
                  the page properly.

MARGINWIDTH   This tag is specific to Netscape and does the same thing
                  that the LEFTMARGIN tag does.

TOPMARGIN   This is a tag specific to Internet Explorer. This value spec-
                  ifies, in pixels, how much empty space to leave on the
                  top of the page. I prefer to set this value to 0, as well.

MARGINHEIGHT   This tag is specific to Netscape and does the same thing
                  that the TOPMARGIN attribute does.

**If you want to make sure you set margins for both Netscape and
Internet Explorer, you can use both sets of margin-setting tags in
your BODY tag, as shown here:**

```
<body marginheight=0 marginwidth=0 leftmargin=0 topmargin=0>
```

You can specify any, all, or none of these parameters in the BODY tag for your
page, depending on what you want to accomplish. Just remember to include the
/BODY tag at the end of the content section of your page.

Specifying HTML Colors

Specifying colors in HTML is pretty easy to do. In HTML, a color is made
of three components: red, green, and blue. To specify a color, you create a
number that combines these three components. The trick is that the values
have to be hexadecimal; that is, using a base of 16 instead of the normal
base of 10. For instance, if you wanted to use bright yellow (which is a
combination of red and green, believe it or not), you would use the color
tag #FFFF00. The first two characters, FF, translate to 255 in decimal. This
is the highest red value you can pick. The second two characters are the
green value, also equal to 255. The third two characters represent the blue
component and have the value of zero. Picking these numbers together,
following a pound sign, specifies the color to be zero. Most HTML editing
tools will allow you to pick a color from a window and will then determine
what the number should be.

Besides specifying the number, you can also specify a name for the color. This function is supported by Internet Explorer and Netscape. Here is a list of the colors you can pick:

Aqua	Navy
Black	Olive
Blue	Purple
Fuchsia	Red
Gray	Silver
Green	Teal
Lime	White
Maroon	Yellow

For instance, to specify maroon as the background color for your page, you would write the following: `<body bgcolor="Maroon">`

Spacing HTML Text

20 Min. To Go

One interesting thing about HTML is that it tries to take some of the work off your hands. One way it does this is by spacing the text in your page automatically. For instance, if you have an HTML page whose code looks like the following—

```
<html><head><title>Test Page</title></head>
<body>
This
text
is
all
on
separate
lines.
</body>
</html>
```

—then the browser (either one) will show this text all on one line, with a space between each word, like this:

```
This text is all on separate lines.
```

Depending on what you wanted the code to do, this can be either a good thing or a bad thing. The point is that leaving the spacing completely up to the browser isn't a great idea. Luckily, there are a number of spacing tags you can use to format your data in the page.

P tag

The <P> tag (P for paragraph) is used to break paragraphs of text. There are a couple of different implementations of this tag, because the way it's used has changed over the years. Initially, the <P> tag was used by itself to break one paragraph from another, like this:

```
The May 2000 tips have been posted to the site. If you're not
already receiving these tips from Topica, you can subscribe and
get them delivered daily.
<p>
For the month's archive, you can use the toolbar on the left to
view the Tip Archive.
```

However, the officially sanctioned definition of the <P> tag requires the use of the </P> tag as well. Here is the same text using that syntax:

```
<p>The May 2000 tips have been posted to the site. If you're not
already receiving these tips from Topica, you can subscribe and
get them delivered daily.
</p>
<p>
For the month's archive, you can use the toolbar on the left to
view the Tip Archive.
</p>
```

Instead of breaking paragraphs, the <P> tag is used to surround and mark each paragraph. This is the way you should use the tag, since that is the use that is "officially" supported by both major browsers. They support the first method as well, but I would expect to see that change in future releases.

Using the second method gets you a couple of extra features, since the P tag can take a parameter to specify how to align the text. The ALIGN parameter can be left, center, or right. Any text between the <P> and </P> will take on the alignment you specify, which defaults to left-aligned.

The P tag will also add, by default, about a line of white space between paragraphs. If you don't need the extra space, use the BR tag (coming up next).

BR tag

The <BR> tag (BR for break) is used to break one line from the next without adding extra white space. A good example of this is an address, like so:

```
Eric A. Smith<br>
123 Main Street<br>
Anytown, VA 12345<br>
```

This will break the text like this:

```
Eric A. Smith
123 Main Street
Anytown, VA 12345
```

Non-breaking spaces

If you want to keep two words together, you can use a non-breaking space. The non-breaking space will force the two words to stay together and the browser will wrap them to the next line, if necessary. For instance, you might have this text:

```
For more information, please call (800) 555-1234.
```

In this case, I wouldn't want to have the phone number broken up on two different lines. To prevent this, I add a non-breaking space character:

```
For more information, please call (800) 555-1234.
```

The   entity must contain both the ampersand (&) and the semicolon (;) to work properly. In this case, if the page is such that this statement has to wrap onto multiple lines, the entire phone number will stay together.

Creating Headings in a Page

Just as you create headings in an outline, you can create various levels of headings in HTML. These tags (six in all) have gradually decreasing font sizes and are a good way to format data without having to worry too much about the other attributes currently being used in formatting the text, such as the size or color of the text.

These tags are in the format Hx, with x being a number from 1 to 6. H1 is the largest font, and H6 is the smallest. Each of these tags will add white space after the /Hx tag. Each browser, based on the settings you've specified, will use a different font size for each level. Figure 5-1 shows an example of each heading as shown in Internet Explorer 5.0.

Figure 5-1
Six headings in IE 5.0

Here's the code for the page:

```
<html><head><title>Heading Test</title></head>
<body>
<h1>Heading Level 1</h1>
<h2>Heading Level 2</h2>
<h3>Heading Level 3</h3>
<h4>Heading Level 4</h4>
<h5>Heading Level 5</h5>
<h6>Heading Level 6</h6>
</body>
</html>
```

Both browsers have a way to control the relative size of all the fonts on the page. In Internet Explorer, the View ⇨ Text Size menu shows five sizes: Largest, Larger, Medium, Smaller, and Smallest. In the previous figure, the text size was set to Medium in IE. In the next two figures (Figure 5-2 and 5-3), you can see the differences between the font sizes from Largest to Smallest.

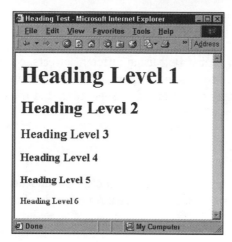

Figure 5-2
Text using the Largest font size in IE

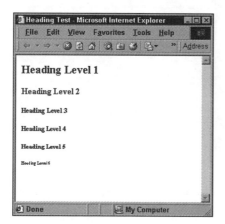

Figure 5-3
Text using the Smallest font size in IE

As you can see in Figure 5-3, the Smallest font size makes the H6 tag almost illegible. When you're picking fonts for your text, remember that if the user resizes the fonts on the page, some of your text may not be legible. The other bad thing about these tags is that you can't control the fonts once you've used a heading tag. The tags in the next section will give you more control over the fonts and styles available for use in HTML.

**10 Min.
To Go**

Text-Formatting Tags

HTML has a number of tags designed to format text using different effects, colors, and fonts. These tags are straightforward to use and in general, can be combined. For instance, you can use one tag to apply the color red to some text, and then use another tag to put part of that text in italics.

BLOCKQUOTE tag

The BLOCKQUOTE tag is used to mark a section of text as a quote from another source. The text is indented on both the left and right sides. An example of this is shown in Figure 5-4.

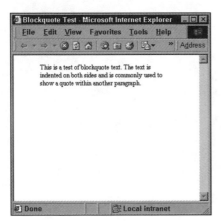

Figure 5-4
Text within the BLOCKQUOTE tag is indented on both sides

PRE tag

The PRE tag (PRE for preformatted) is used to show text in a monospace font. Any text surrounded by the PRE tag pair will be shown exactly as it is in the file. Figure 5-5 shows an example of preformatted text as shown in the browser. Listing 5-1 shows the source code for this example.

Figure 5-5
Preformatted text, as shown in the browser

Listing 5-1
Preformatted text example

```html
<html>
<head>
   <title>Preformatted Text Example</title>
</head>

<body>

This text is on
multiple lines
in the file but will
be automatically wrapped
in the browser.

<pre>
Text inside of the PRE
tags will show exactly
as it is in the file.
</pre>
</body>
</html>
```

One problem with the PRE tag, as shown in the previous example, is that it automatically adds a line break and extra space in between the lines of text. If you need to include code in the same line, use the CODE tag (covered next).

CODE tag

Like the PRE tag, the CODE tag shows text in a monospace font. However, it does not add a line break either before or after the text.

FONT tag

One of the more flexible text-formatting tags is the FONT tag. You can supply a number of parameters to change the look of the text. Table 5-1 lists the most common parameters.

Table 5-1
FONT Tag Parameters

Parameter	Description
COLOR	Specifies the color the text should be displayed in
FACE	Specifies the font name to use
SIZE	Specifies the relative size to use for the text

The FACE parameter can list multiple fonts, separated by commas. If you are using a font specific to a particular machine, be sure you specify a similar font as the second font in the tag. For instance, Tahoma is a font normally available with Windows. However, it's not normally available on other platforms. A good use of the FACE tag is shown here:

```
<font face="Tahoma, Arial, Helvetica">
```

If the Tahoma font is not available, the browser will look for Arial. If that isn't available, it will look for Helvetica. If that one is missing also, it will revert to the default font for the browser. If you're going to specify particular font names, remember that not everyone has all the fonts that you might have on your machine. In general, stick to formatting with these fonts:

- Courier New (fixed-width font)
- Arial

- Times New Roman
- Tahoma (comes with most Office and Windows products now)

These fonts are available on all Windows platforms, and most other systems have equivalents that often have similar or even identical names. You can also specify sans serif, serif, and fixed, which are often available on UNIX platforms as generic-sized fonts.

The SIZE parameter does not allow exact pixel or point sizes; rather, it uses relative values. You can specify values using two different methods. The first uses an absolute value of 1 through 7, as shown here:

```
<font face="Arial" size=3>
```

You can also specify a change in font size using the values -4, -3, -2, -1, +1, +2, and +3.

Miscellaneous formatting tags

There are several other tags that can provide quick formatting for your HTML. These tags are shown in Table 5-2.

Table 5-2
Formatting Tags

Tag	Description
B	Boldface text
I	Italic text
S	Strikethrough text
U	Underlined text

A quick example of boldfacing is shown here:

```
<b>This text will be shown in boldface text.</b>
```

You can follow this model for all of the tags shown in the previous table. Remember to close the tag pair or you could get unexpected formatting results.

Links and Images

In most Web sites — including the ones we build in this book — you will inevitably have to link to other pages, and you will often need to display images. This section is devoted to the tags you use to do these things.

Anchor tag

The anchor tag marks a link to another document or object. Anchor tags can also be used as relative links within a document. To add a link to another document, you can use code like the following:

```
<a href="http://www.hungryminds.com">Hungry Minds</a>
```

The text in the HREF parameter specifies the actual link. Any text that precedes the </A> tag will be shown as a link; that is, colored and underlined. If you want to use a link within a document (sometimes called a bookmark), you first mark the destination location with the tag shown here:

```
<A NAME="destination">
```

Replace the word *destination* with the name of the location you wish to use. To provide a link in the document to the destination, use the code shown here:

```
<A HREF="#destination">
```

The pound sign indicates that the browser should go to a relative location in the page.

Image tag

The image tag is used to show a graphic within a page. Typical graphic formats supported by most browsers include CompuServe Graphics Interchange Format (GIF) and Joint Photographic Experts Group (JPEG) format. A newer format, the Portable Network Graphic (PNG), is slowly gaining acceptance and support as an alternative to the proprietary GIF format, which is owned by the Unisys Corporation. PNG supports features from both the GIF and JPEG formats.

To specify an image to use, use this code:

```
<img src="/pics/icon.gif">
```

The src parameter specifies the filename to use. Depending on the Web server you are using, the source will be either a relative link or an absolute one. A relative link begins with a slash and does not include a hostname. An absolute link includes the hostname where the file is located.

Done!

The image tag can include the WIDTH and HEIGHT attributes to specify the size of the graphic. If you use a height and width that are not the same size as the graphic, the graphic will be stretched or shrunk to fit the size specified.

REVIEW

This chapter showed you the basic structure of an HTML page and how to arrange your code in the page. You'll be using many of the text-formatting functions discussed in this chapter throughout the book, so be sure to play with them a bit to make sure you understand them.

For more HTML information, you can look at these Web sites:

- W3C Consortium: http://www.w3c.org
- Microsoft: http://www.microsoft.com
- Netscape: http://www.netscape.com

QUIZ YOURSELF

1. What tag marks the beginning of the page heading? (See "HTML Page Structure")
2. What tag makes text boldface? (See "Text-Formatting Tags")
3. What tag creates a line break without any white space? (See "Spacing HTML Text")
4. How do you center a paragraph in a page? (See "Spacing HTML Text")

HTML Lists and Tables

Session Checklist

✔ Learn how to create a bulleted list of data

✔ Learn how to create several types of numbered lists

✔ Learn to create tables for arranging data

**30 Min.
To Go**

When you start working with databases later in the book, you'll find that you need a good way to organize the data. In some cases, you'll want lists, and in other cases, you'll want grids. This chapter will show you the HTML required to make each of these features available on your pages.

Creating a Bulleted List

One of the things you'll be doing on Sunday is creating an application that reads from a database. When you get some of the data from the database, you'll need to show it in some sort of list. The easiest type of list to create is one known as a bulleted list. This list shows all the items with a small solid circle next to them, as shown in Figure 6-1.

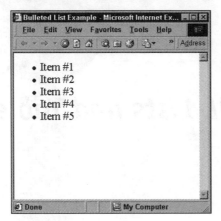

Figure 6-1
Bulleted list example

The source code for the page is shown in Listing 6-1.

Listing 6-1
Bulleted list example

```
<html>
<head>
    <title>Bulleted List Example</title>
</head>

<body>
<ul>
<li>Item #1</li>
<li>Item #2</li>
<li>Item #3</li>
<li>Item #4</li>
<li>Item #5</li>
</ul>
</body>
</html>
```

The UL tag stands for Unordered List, since we're using bullets instead of numbers. Each list item is prefixed with the LI tag, which stands for List Item. In this sample, we also end the item with the /LI tag. This is not required; however, it's a good habit to get into. If the /LI tag is not specified, everything up to the next LI tag is used as part of the list item.

There are three types of bullets you can use. To specify a different type, you add the TYPE parameter to the UL tag. Here are the three options you have:

☐ Square

● Disc (filled circle)

○ Circle (outlined circle)

You can also create a nested list of bullets, as shown in Figure 6-2.

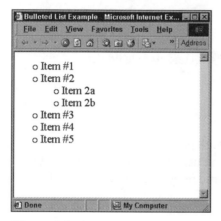

Figure 6-2
Nested bulleted list

The source code for this page is shown in Listing 6-2.

Listing 6-2
Two nested, unordered lists

```
<html>
<head>
   <title>Bulleted List Example</title>
</head>

<body>
<ul type="circle">
<li>Item #1</li>
```

Continued

Listing 6-2 *Continued*

```
<li>Item #2</li>
<ul>
<li>Item 2a</li>
<li>Item 2b</li>
</ul>
<li>Item #3</li>
<li>Item #4</li>
<li>Item #5</li>
</ul>
</body>
</html>
```

The browser takes care of indenting the second unordered list.

Creating Numbered Lists

While the bulleted list takes care of a lot, there are many cases in which you will want to have a numbered list. For this, you use the OL, or Ordered List, tag. The basic format of this tag is just like the basic format of the UL tag, as shown in Listing 6-3 and Figure 6-3.

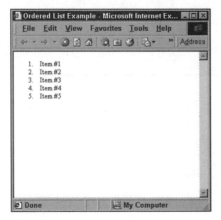

Figure 6-3
Ordered list example

Listing 6-3
Ordered list example source code

```
<html>
<head>
   <title>Ordered List Example</title>
</head>

<body>
<ol>
<li>Item #1</li>
<li>Item #2</li>
<li>Item #3</li>
<li>Item #4</li>
<li>Item #5</li>
</ol>
</body>
</html>
```

The browser keeps track of how many items it has shown and puts the appropriate number next to each item.

As with the UL tag, you can further configure the OL tag for different numbering schemes. By specifying the TYPE parameter, you can pick one of five different list-numbering types, shown in Table 6-1.

Table 6-1
Type Parameter Values

Value	Result
A	Capital letters (A, B, C, ...)
a	Lowercase letters (a, b, c, ...)
I	Large Roman numerals (I, II, III, ...)
i	Small Roman numerals (i, ii, iii, ...)
1	Arabic numerals (1, 2, 3, ...)

Using some of these list types, you can build an outline with several nested lists. Listing 6-4 shows the source code for this outline, and Figure 6-4 shows what it looks like in a browser.

Listing 6-4
Outline source code

```html
<html>
<head>
   <title>Ordered List Example</title>
</head>

<body>
<ol type="I">
<li>Introduction
   <ol type="A">
   <li>Key Point
   <li>Key Point
   <li>Key Point
   </ol>
<li>Body
<li>Conclusion
</ol>
</body>
</html>
```

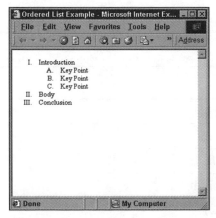

Figure 6-4
Showing the outline in a browser

You can also specify a different number to start with using the START parameter. For instance, if you needed to restart an outline in another page, you can say START=5 and the list will start with Item #5. If you are using letters, the list will start with the letter E. However, you should always specify the START parameter with a number if you're using it to create lists using letters or Roman numerals. HTML won't understand it, otherwise.

Table Formatting Tags

Tables are probably the most flexible of all the tags because of the unique way in which they can be combined. As you've probably seen by now, HTML evaluates from top to bottom and you don't have a lot of control over how the text is displayed. However, using tables can give you more control. While this section won't show you all of the ins and outs of using tables in unique ways, you will learn enough to build the basic tables used throughout this book.

TABLE tag

The TABLE marks the beginning of a table. It can take a number of optional parameters, the most common of which are shown in Table 6-2.

Table 6-2
TABLE Tag Parameters

Parameter Name	Description
ALIGN	Specifies whether the table should be aligned to the left or right side of the page
BACKGROUND	Specifies an image to be used as the background of the table
BGCOLOR	Specifies the color to be used as the background for the table
BORDER	Specifies the width of the border around the table cells; if you use 0, no border will be shown
CELLPADDING	Specifies the number of pixels between the border of each cell and the contents of that cell

Continued

Table 6-2 *Continued*

CELLSPACING	Specifies the number of pixels between the cells in the table
COLS	Specifies the number of columns in the table; this value is not required, as the table will count the number of columns you create
HEIGHT	Specifies, in pixels or a percentage, the height of the table
WIDTH	Specifies, in pixels or a percentage, the width of the table

A sample table is provided at the end of this section, using all the tags covered in the section. As with all table tags, be sure that you match the <TABLE> tag with a </TABLE> or the browser won't necessarily interpret the code properly.

Some of the parameters listed in the table do not always work consistently in Netscape. Depending on the version of Netscape you have, some of the parameters won't be available at all. Check Netscape's Web site for more details on the features they support and the ones they don't.

TR tag

The TR tag marks the beginning of a table row. This tag can take several optional parameters, some of which are shown in Table 6-3.

Table 6-3
TR Tag Parameters

Parameter Name	Description
ALIGN	Specifies whether the contents of the cells in the row should be aligned to the left side, center, or right side of the page
BACKGROUND	Specifies an image to be used as the background of the cells in the row
BGCOLOR	Specifies the color to be used as the background for the cells in the row

A sample table is provided at the end of this section, using all the tags covered in the section. As with all table tags, be sure that you match the <TR> tag with a </TR> or the browser won't necessarily interpret the code properly.

If you're using Internet Explorer, be sure to test your tables in Netscape. Netscape is much pickier on table structure and requires that all ending tags be included for the table to show properly. Internet Explorer is much more lenient (and intelligent, in my opinion) and will show the table in more cases than Netscape would.

TH tag

The TH tag marks a table heading. A table heading can be used at the top of each column. This tag can take several optional parameters, some of which are shown in Table 6-4.

Table 6-4
TH Tag Parameters

Parameter Name	Description
ALIGN	Specifies whether the contents of the cells in the row should be aligned to the left side, center, or right side of the page
BACKGROUND	Specifies an image to be used as the background of the cells in the row
BGCOLOR	Specifies the color to be used as the background for the cells in the row
COLSPAN	Specifies how many columns the heading should span
ROWSPAN	Specifies how many rows the heading should span
VALIGN	Specifies whether the contents should be aligned vertically to the top, middle, bottom, or text baseline of the cell
WIDTH	Specifies the width of the cell; the largest width used for the column will be used for all cells in the column

Any text within the table heading will be shown in boldface. You can add other tags such as italics and underline, if you wish. A sample table is provided at the end of this section, using all the tags covered in the section. As with all table tags, be sure that you match the <TH> tag with a </TH> or the browser won't necessarily interpret the code properly.

TD tag

The TD (table definition) tag marks the contents of a cell. The tag can take several optional parameters, some of which are shown in Table 6-5.

Table 6-5
TD Tag Parameters

Parameter Name	Description
ALIGN	Specifies whether the contents of the cells in the row should be aligned to the left side, center, or right side of the page
BACKGROUND	Specifies an image to be used as the background of the cells in the row
BGCOLOR	Specifies the color to be used as the background for the cells in the row
COLSPAN	Specifies how many columns the heading should span
ROWSPAN	Specifies how many rows the heading should span
VALIGN	Specifies whether the contents should be aligned vertically to the top, middle, bottom, or text baseline of the cell
WIDTH	Specifies the width of the cell; the largest width used for the column will be used for all cells in the column

Any text within the table heading will be shown in boldface. You can add other tags such as italics and underline, if you wish. A sample table is provided at the end of this section, using all the tags covered in the section. As with all table tags, be sure that you match the <TD> tag with a </TD> or the browser won't necessarily interpret the code properly.

Table example

The code in Listing 6-5 shows a complete table, including table headings and examples of the most common properties. Figure 6-5 shows how the table appears in Internet Explorer.

Listing 6-5
Table example code

```html
<html>
<head>
   <title>Table Example</title>
</head>

<body>
<h2>Product List</h2>

<table cellpadding=3>
   <tr>
      <th colspan=2>Item</th>
      <th>Quantity</th>
      <th>Price</th>
      <th>Extended</th>
   </tr>
   <tr>
      <td>127250</td>
      <td>PC Hard Drive</td>
      <td align=center>3</td>
      <td align=right>$150.00</td>
      <td align=right>$450.00</td>
   </tr>
   <tr>
      <td>199240</td>
      <td>Modem</td>
      <td align=center>1</td>
      <td align=right>$75.00</td>
      <td align=right>$75.00</td>
   </tr>
   <tr>
```

Continued

Listing 6-5 *Continued*

```
        <td colspan=4 align=right><b>Total:</b></td>
        <td align=right>$525.00</td>
    </tr>

</table>
</body>
</html>
```

Figure 6-5
Table example, as seen in Internet Explorer

Done!

If you want to see how the cell structure is built, you can add border=1 to the TABLE tag. The result will look like Figure 6-6.

REVIEW

You can use the tags presented in this chapter to present data in several different ways. There are lists that can be useful for certain types of data. If you need a tabular format, the HTML TABLE tag and its relatives are quite versatile. There are cases that you'll find where one format is better than another for formatting data, but it often comes down to personal preference. Like the tags presented in the last chapter, these tags will be used throughout the rest of the book for formatting data.

Figure 6-6
Table example shown with borders around the cells and table

QUIZ YOURSELF

1. How do you create a bulleted list using an outlined circle as the bullet character? (See "Creating Bulleted Lists")
2. Which tag is used to create a table heading? (See "Table Formatting Tags")
3. Which tag is used to mark an item in either an ordered or unordered list? (See "Creating Bulleted Lists")
4. Which tag is used to specify data that goes into a table? (See "Table Formatting Tags")
5. How do you create a table border? (See "Table Formatting Tags")

Processing User Input

Session Checklist

✔ Learn how data gets from the user to the server

✔ Create a form and handle input data

✔ Link one page to another using several different methods

✔ Learn how to get data from various types of input controls

**30 Min.
To Go**

I n the previous chapters, you learned how to create HTML to send to the user's browser. Many Web sites don't get beyond this point. They are made up of static HTML pages that don't change based on the visitor or any other input. However, the more interesting and feature-rich Web sites change based on a variety of factors. This chapter will show you how to get data from the user, which can be used to control what the page does.

Getting Data from the User

Anytime you visit a Web page, there is a "conversation" going on between your computer (the client) and the computer providing you the Web page (the server). There are times when you specifically send data to the server, such as when you enter your address into a form. There are other times where you send data just by visiting a page. In this chapter, you'll learn different ways to look at all the data being submitted. You'll use these techniques throughout the rest of the book to build a complex Web site made up of many Web pages that all work together.

Using the command line

The first way you're sending data is through the address line, or the URL (Uniform Resource Locator). At a minimum, you send in the name of the page you want. For instance, you might use the following URL:

```
http://www.asptechniques.com/default.asp
```

This URL gives quite a bit of information to the server. HTTP indicates that the browser wants to use HyperText Transfer Protocol. This indicates to the server that it needs to provide data from the Web server to the requestor. Data comes across the network to a particular port on the server. When we talk about a *port,* that doesn't mean a physical port, like a network or serial cable port. Instead, we're talking about a network concept called a *socket*. You can think of this as a phone number that the server answers. Anytime data comes across port 80 (which is the one that HTTP uses by default), the Web server answers and works with the data.

The next part of the URL is the name of the machine you're connecting to. In this case, the URL specifies that you are going to www.asptechniques.com, which is a Web site running on a server I own. The text name of the Web site is translated to a numeric address, known as an IP address, by way of a service known as the Domain Name Service (DNS). DNS translates into a special type of number in the format N.N.N.N. Your request comes into my server, which looks at the name of the server (www.asptechniques.com) and uses the appropriate settings for that Web server.

The last part of the URL is the name of the page you want to see: in this case, default.asp. On my server, default.asp is one of the default pages for a directory. This means that if your URL had just been

```
http://www.asptechniques.com/
```

the Web server would look for a default page in the root directory of that particular site's home directory.

As you can see, even sending a short URL tells the Web server a lot about what you want to do. The next version of the URL we're going to cover looks something like this:

```
http://asptechniques.com/content.asp?a=rs&sID=3
```

In this URL, you still have the same domain name and protocol name, but following the page name, you have a bunch of extra data. These values together are called the query string. At the end of content.asp (which is the file you want to load), there is a question mark. This starts the query string. Next, there is a letter *a*, an equals sign, and the letters *rs*. This is the basic syntax for a query string attribute; that is, name = value. The ampersand (&) separates name/value pairs, so the next pair is sID = 3. You'll be learning how to use this structure later in the book.

You'll be using the URL to send requests to the Web server in several different instances as you build the applications throughout this book. There are several limitations on the URL. First of all, the URL is limited in size. In general, a URL has to be less than 2K (2048 characters) in size. Don't worry—not everything has to be sent via the URL. In the previous example, the series of parameters specifies database record IDs for the ASP page to look up while it builds the page. This saves you from having to pass lots of data on the URL. The second limitation is on the characters you put in the URL. For instance, you can't use spaces or parameter names. Later in the book, you'll learn about a way to automatically encode text so that it can safely be put in the URL.

Using data input forms

This is the method that most people think of when they think of sending user data to a Web server. A form can be as simple as a single text box for searching, or as complex as a mortgage application that you fill out online. There's really no limit to what you can do with forms.

Here's an example of a simple, single-box form from the ASP Techniques Web site:

```
<form action="content.asp?a=s" method="post">
<input type="text" size="20" name="txtKeywords">
<input type="submit" name="cmdSubmit">
</form>
```

Some of the extra HTML tags have been removed for clarity. This is a simple form. The form is started with a FORM tag and ended with /FORM. When the user submits the form, all the fields between FORM and /FORM will be considered part of the form data and will be submitted to the server.

The FORM tag has several parameters that are important to us. First, the ACTION parameter specifies the page on which server should handle the data input. In this case, the content.asp page on the same server (asptechniques.com, that is) will handle the data being sent from this form. Note that the ACTION parameter can use any valid URL. In this case, you are using a relative URL, which means that content.asp will be searched for in the same directory as the current page where this form is located. If you needed to, you could create an ACTION parameter that was "fully qualified"; that is, that contained a domain name too, like this:

```
<form action="http://asptechniques.com/content.asp?a=s"
method=post>
```

This is helpful if you are sending data from one server to another by way of a form. You can see this method in action at this URL:

```
http://links.northcomp.com
```

I've duplicated input forms to my favorite search engines on the home page to save myself a few clicks. Each one of these forms' ACTION parameters is a fully qualified URL since I'm sending data from one server to another.

The second parameter you see is the METHOD parameter. This parameter specifies how the data should be sent to the receiving page. You have two options here: GET and POST. If you use GET, any data from the form is put on the URL as a series of parameters. This is fine, but remember the 2 KB limit on the size of the URL. If you are trying to submit your mortgage application via the Web, you're probably going to have too much data to fit on the URL. In addition, the user is going to see all the data in the URL, which is not aesthetically pleasing.

The alternative and more popular approach is to use POST. In this case, all the data values are sent to the receiving page in the request header. This method gives you a virtually unlimited page size to work with. However, the more data you have to push to the server, the longer the request will take. At the time of this writing, most users are still using slow connections (56 Kbps or less, generally), so this is still an issue. As broadband connections (cable, DSL, satellite, and so on) become more commonplace, it will become less of one.

Other ways to send data

Even when you aren't putting parameters on your URLs or sending data through forms, you may still be sending data to Web servers as you surf. Ever wonder how a site knows that you're using a particular browser? Or how it figures out you are coming from a particular company's domain? All of this information, and more, is passed to the Web server each time you make a request. The data come up by way of the request header (the data going across the socket indicating what page you want) and are made available to the Web page you request. The server also makes data available, such as where the ASP page is located on the hard drive of the computer, what version of software the server is running, and so on. These pieces of data are helpful in several different instances, as you'll see later in this chapter and throughout the book.

Another type of data that is sent to the server is somewhat confusing and sometimes controversial: *cookies*. The basic concept behind cookies is this: each time you visit a Web site, the Web site has absolutely no idea who you are or what you may have been doing on the site before. As far as the server is concerned, your second visit functions identically to someone else's first visit. In techie-speak, the server does not maintain any *state*.

In some cases, not maintaining state is fine. If you have a Web site with your company's brochure as static HTML pages with some graphics, it doesn't matter whether the user saw the first page or the last page. The pages work fine without anyone having to worry about this information. However, if you have a site that requires a login, you have to maintain the fact that the user logged in successfully between page requests. If you don't, you will have to prompt the user for his/her login information on every page. That would get annoying after the second request for most people.

To solve this problem, Web servers tell your browser to create a small text file on your computer with some data in it. Depending on which browser you're using, the format may differ. However, the idea is that once the server tells you to save these data, your browser will automatically send them back to the server on every successive request. As before, the server doesn't know that it's you making a second request after you've logged in. However, when it looks at the contents of the cookie, it can say, "Oh, I remember you, and you've already logged in successfully."

The controversy surrounding cookies is pretty much unfounded. There were cases in the past in which Web servers were unwisely storing personal information, such as credit card information, in cookies on your computer. Because the cookie files were unencrypted, this was a major security risk. Someone else could start your computer, look at the cookie files, and get your credit card numbers. Instead, most servers are now storing that sensitive information in a secure location and giving you a customer number in the cookie. The customer number is used in conjunction with a database to look up your information when it is needed.

Building a Simple Form

20 Min. To Go

Now that you understand how data comes into the server, you're ready to build a simple form and respond to the data that was submitted. For this example, you'll need to create two text files: one for the form, and one to handle the response.

The first form is just plain HTML, as shown in Listing 7-1.

This file is on the CD-ROM and is called ch7_basicform.html.

Listing 7-1
A simple HTML form

```
<html>
<head>
   <title>Chapter 7: Basic Form</title>
</head>
<body>
<h1>Basic Input Form</h1>

<form action="ch7_basicform_process.asp" method=post>
Keywords: <input type="Text" name="txtKeywords" size="20"><p>
<input type="Submit" name="cmdSubmit" value="Submit">
</form>
</body>
</html>
```

This code shows a simple form with a text box and a submit button on it. When the user clicks the submit button, the data in the page is sent to the ASP page specified in the ACTION parameter of the FORM tag. Each control on the form has a name specified in the NAME parameter. What you use for the value of the NAME parameter doesn't matter at all. However, it's often helpful to create a naming scheme for your form controls so that you know what you're looking at when you write the code to process the data. For a text box, we'll be using a prefix of txt for all the text boxes on the forms.

The next step is to create the page to respond to the user. If you submit this form as is, nothing will happen. For the form's data to be processed, you have to specify a page in the FORM tag. In this case, you're simply going to repeat what the user typed into the box. This is known as echoing a response. Since you'll be using a little bit of ASP code, this file has to have an .asp extension. The code for the response is shown in Listing 7-2.

This file is on the CD-ROM and is called ch7_basicform_ process.asp.

Listing 7-2
The ASP code to respond to the user

```
<html>
<head>
    <title>Chapter 7: Basic Form Response</title>
</head>
<body>
<h1>Basic Form - Response</h1>

You entered these keywords:
<% = Request.Form("txtKeywords") %>
<p>
</body>
</html>
```

When you have both of these files on your Web server, clicking Submit on the form will send the text box's data to this page. When you look at the code in Listing 7-2, you'll see that the page is mostly HTML. The difference is in this line:

```
<% = Request.Form("txtKeywords") %>
```

This is your first bit of ASP code. The <% and %> are called delimiters. They mark the beginning and end, respectively, of the ASP code. This particular statement causes a value to be printed out. The equals sign, when preceded immediately by <%, causes the value that follows the equals sign to be printed.

The first keyword following the equals sign, Request, is a built-in object in Active Server Pages. An object is a way to organize data and the corresponding actions for that data. The Request object holds all the data that came from the user. This includes form, URL, cookie, and server variable data. In this case, you want data from the form, so you specify **Form** following the Request object, using a period to separate the two. The Form collection contains all the data submitted in the form. A collection is like a bag. If you look through the bag, you can see all the items in it, but the items aren't in any particular order. To retrieve a particular piece of data, you specify the name of the piece of data within parentheses after the name of the collection. In this case, you want the field named txtKeywords, so you put that name within double-quote characters. Finally, end the line of code with another ASP delimiter.

When you run the first page, it looks like Figure 7-1 below.

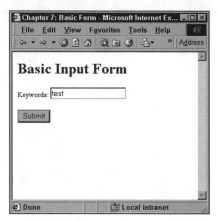

Figure 7-1
The input form

In this case, you've entered the word **test** in the text box. Once you click the Submit button, the response will be as shown in Figure 7-2.

Figure 7-2
The response to the form

The HTML for the response form is shown in Listing 7-3.

Listing 7-3
The output from the response form

```
<html>
<head>
    <title>Chapter 7: Basic Form Response</title>
</head>
<body>
<h1>Basic Form - Response</h1>

You entered these keywords:
test
<p>
</body>
</html>
```

Note that the word "test" is on the line following the prompt. Essentially, the word "test" was substituted for the ASP code you wrote. All the ASP processing is done before the HTML response is sent to the user. The rest of this chapter builds on this basic concept and shows you how to respond to data coming in via other types of input controls.

Reading Data from the URL

You've already got a little experience reading data from the form, and this section will show you how to use the URL to pass data from one page to the next. The first file you need to create is shown in Listing 7-4.

 This file is on the CD-ROM and is called ch7_url.html.

Listing 7-4
An HTML file with two links to another file

```
<html>
<head>
    <title>Chapter 7: Reading a URL</title>
</head>
```

```
<body>
<h1>Reading a URL</h1>

<p><a href="ch7_url_process.asp?link=First">Click here</a>
to use the first link.</p>

<p><a href="ch7_url_process.asp?link=Second">Click here</a>
to use the second link.</p>

</form>
</body>
</html>
```

This page is shown in Figure 7-3 below.

Figure 7-3
A page with two links on it

The links you created both use a parameter called link. Again, the name of the parameter isn't particularly important. For this particular example, you do need to use the same parameter name for both links because of the way you're going to display the data. The result page is shown in Listing 7-5.

This file is on the CD-ROM and is called ch7_url_response.asp.

Listing 7-5
Response page to handle the link clicks

```
<html>
<head>
    <title>Chapter 7: URL Response</title>
</head>
<body>
<h1>URL - Response</h1>

<p>You clicked the <% = Request.QueryString("link") %> link.

</body>
</html>
```

In this case, you want to get the value from the URL, so you have to use the QueryString collection instead of the Form collection. You print out the value of the link parameter, which is what you specified on the URL to be passed.

Clicking on the first link passes the word "First" to this page: the result is shown in Figure 7-4 below.

Figure 7-4
This is what happens when you click the first link

Handling Other Controls' Input

Besides the simple text box, there are a number of other controls you can use on your input forms. You access all of them by way of the Request.Form collection; however, the values you get vary based on the control you're using. In this section, we'll cover the main input types. We will cover dropdown lists later in the book when we discuss databases, and after you've had a bit more code, since they require more code to be able to interpret the values. This will be enough to get you started using the forms you'll be building in the book.

The TEXTAREA tag

The simple text box we used earlier in the chapter is ideal for small amounts of data. However, if you need a box with more capacity, the TEXTAREA tag is the one to use. Listing 7-6 shows an example of a TEXTAREA tag in use.

Listing 7-6
An example of a TEXTAREA tag

```
<textarea wrap=virtual name="txtTitle" rows=2 cols=60>
</textarea>
```

Unlike a regular text box, the text area has to have both TEXTAREA and /TEXTAREA tags. This particular text area is named txtTitle and has two rows (height) and 60 columns (width). Depending on the font being used by the client, you may get more or less than 60 characters wide in a text area. The other parameter here is the WRAP parameter. This parameter handles what happens when the user hits the Enter key. With the VIRTUAL value, hitting Enter causes the cursor to add a new line within the text area. These line breaks are sent along with the data that are entered. This is the best approach to use since it enables the user to enter more than one line of text and the Enter key will add line breaks within the text. There are other values you can specify for WRAP, but they are not used nearly as often.

If you need to show a value in a regular text box, you can add a VALUE parameter and put the value to be shown in double quotes following the parameter, as shown here:

```
<input type="text" name="txtKeywords" size="20" value="data">
```

For a text area, however, the data to be shown in the box goes between the TEXTAREA and /TEXTAREA tags, as shown here:

```
<textarea wrap="virtual" name="txtTitle" rows="2" cols="60">
data
</textarea>
```

The best part about this tag is that from an ASP standpoint, this control looks just like a regular text box. To access the data in this box, you use Request.Form with the name of the text area and the data print out just like a regular box. For instance:

```
You typed: <% = Request.Form("txtTitle") %>
```

Using a checkbox

Checkboxes are used for choices that can be either on or off. A checkbox is an independent control, which means that checking a box doesn't affect whether another box can be checked. A radio button (covered next) is mutually exclusive; that is, only one radio button can be selected from a group at a time.

SYNTAX ▶

To create a checkbox, use this syntax:

```
<input type=checkbox name=chkPizza value="Y"> I like pizza.
```

This code generates a box that looks like the one shown in Figure 7-5.

A checkbox doesn't automatically add a "prompt" next to itself. You have to add this with an extra bit of HTML, as you did in the line above. When the form is submitted, if the box is checked, the value of chkPizza will be whatever is in the VALUE parameter of the checkbox; in this case, the value will be Y. The value doesn't matter, but when you're checking the value, be sure you're looking for the same value that you specified in the form.

If the checkbox isn't checked and you look for Request.Form("chkPizza"), ASP will give you an empty string and won't generate an error. This little twist makes programming easier and at the same time more difficult. You'll see how this comes into play as you go further into the book.

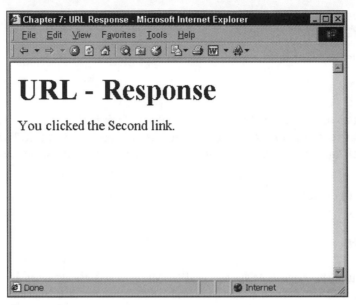

Figure 7-5
An example of a checkbox

Using a radio button

A radio button (also known as an option button) is named that because it allows only a single choice from a group at any one time. For instance, if you are ordering a single pizza, that pizza can only be one size. A radio button forces you to pick only one of a group of choices. It's named after the old radio buttons from the mechanical radios. If you pushed in a button, all the others popped back out. That's the same way this control works. If you click a radio button, any others that were selected in the same group are cleared.

Listing 7-7 shows an example of where you might use a radio button group.

This file is on the CD-ROM and is called ch7_radio.html.

Listing 7-7
Radio button example

```
<html>
<head>
    <title>Chapter 7: Radio Buttons</title>
</head>
<body>
<h1>Radio Button Example</h1>
What size pizza would you like?

<form action="ch7_radio_process.asp" method=POST>
<input type="radio" name="optSize" value="S">
Small<br>
<input type="radio" name="optSize" value="M">
Medium<br>
<input type="radio" name="optSize" value="L" CHECKED>
Large<br>
<input type="radio" name="optSize" value="XL">
Extra Large<br>
<input type=submit name=cmdSubmit value=Submit>
</form>
</body>
</html>
```

In this case, you have a group of four radio buttons. These buttons function as a group because they all have the same NAME property. The difference is in the VALUE parameter. In addition, when the form first displays, you default the choice to be Extra Large by adding the CHECKED parameter to the end of the INPUT tag. When you run this page, the results are as shown in Figure 7-6.

The response page for this file is shown in Listing 7-8 and uses the same syntax you've been using all along.

This file is on the CD-ROM and is called ch7_radio_response.asp.

Figure 7-6
Radio buttons in action

Listing 7-8
This page shows how much pizza you ordered

```
<html>
<head>
    <title>Chapter 7: Radio Buttons</title>
</head>
<body>
<h1>Radio Button Result</h1>
<p>You selected this size pizza:
<% = Request.Form("optSize") %></p>
</body>
</html>
```

Done!

The result prints out whatever was in the VALUE parameter of the radio button you picked.

REVIEW

This chapter introduced forms, a number of different input controls, and the method by which data is submitted to the server. You also wrote your first ASP code to echo back input from your forms. In later chapters, you'll be using the Request object extensively to read submitted data and to process it.

QUIZ YOURSELF

1. Which attribute specifies the page to send a form's data to? (See "Getting Data from the User")

2. What character separates the name of the file from its parameters in the URL? (See "Getting Data from the User")

3. What character separates parameter pairs on the URL? (See "Getting Data from the User")

4. What is a collection and how is it used? (See "Building a Simple Form")

5. Which collection contains data submitted in the URL? (See "Building a Simple Form")

Responding to the User

Session Checklist

✔ Learn how to send output to the user's browser

✔ Learn about data buffering and how it affects the output of a page

✔ Learn how to redirect a browser to another page

**30 Min.
To Go**

I n previous chapters, you've learned how to create HTML blocks that will be sent to the user's browser. However, you haven't had much control over how that output is sent. In this chapter, you'll be introduced to the Response object, which gives you more control over the data, or response, you send to the user from your ASP files.

Sending Data to the User

In the last chapter, you built some simple input forms and echoed back the input to the user. In this section, you'll build on those skills and learn some additional methods of sending data back to the user.

The method you used in the last chapter to print data used syntax like this:

```
<p>You clicked the <% = Request.QueryString("link") %> link.
```

This method writes out a value to the result page without your having to do anything else. Unfortunately, this method has some limits. First of all, the value you're printing can't wrap onto more than one line. If you have a really long piece of HTML with lots of these values being printed in it, a line can easily stretch well beyond where you can see it in your editor. The other problem is that it can only be used in conjunction with embedded HTML; that is, HTML placed directly in an ASP file. This creates some performance problems that have been alleviated somewhat in ASP 3; however, as you'll see later in the book, there's a better way to write ASP code.

The better method that you'll be using to print output uses the Write method of the Response object. A method is an action that is part of an object. In this case, you Write data to the user's browser. The previous statement is shown in Listing 8-1 using Response.Write.

Listing 8-1
Using Response.Write to generate output

```
<%
Response.Write "<p>You clicked the " _
& Request.QueryString("link") & " link.</p>"
%>
```

There are a couple of new things going on here. First of all, note that you're printing HTML tags using the Write method. Because all the ASP code is evaluated on the server, the end user sees only the resulting HTML.

The next thing you should notice is the underscore character at the end of the first line. This is called a *continuation character*, and it enables you to break a long line into multiple lines within the ASP delimiters.

The ampersand (&) character enables you to glue two pieces of text together to create one bigger one. For instance, the text that immediately follows Response. Write is going to be prepended to whatever is in Request.QueryString("link"). Then the text "link.<p>" will be added to the end of that. The end result is printed out as one line to the user's browser. This is called *string concatenation*. You'll be using it extensively throughout the book to generate output for the user.

The end result is basically the same from the browser's point of view. The difference is in how you put the text together.

Another example of using this method produces some side effects that might not be immediately visible through your browser. Look at Listing 8-2.

Listing 8-2
Four Response.Write statements together

```
<html><head><title>Test Page</title></head><body>
<%
Response.Write "This is line 1.<br>"
Response.Write "This is line 2.<br>"
Response.Write "This is line 3.<br>"
Response.Write "This is line 4.<br>"
%>
</body></html>
```

When you look at this code in a browser you don't see anything strange. The BR tags add in line breaks so the four lines follow each other, as shown in Figure 8-1.

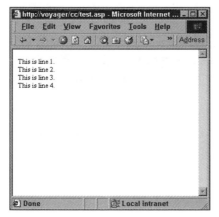

Figure 8-1
The four lines print out, each one on a separate line

However, when you look at the source code for the page by selecting View ⇨ Source, you'll see that it isn't quite as pretty. All four lines printed on the same line in the file. HTML can interpret this correctly since you included BR tags; however, this makes it difficult to read, especially when you have a lot more HTML and ASP code in your files.

The solution is to manually add a line break to the output file, in addition to the BR tags you're already using. You do this using the built-in vbCrLf constant.

This constant represents a carriage return/line feed combination, which will cause the output to be put on different lines in the file. HTML ignores the extra characters and follows the BR tags to see where the breaks should be. Listing 8-3 presents the same code with the extra character added to it:

Listing 8-3
Four Response.Write statements together, with line breaks

```
<html><head><title>Test Page</title></head><body>
<%
Response.Write "This is line 1.<br>" & vbCrLf
Response.Write "This is line 2.<br>" & vbCrLf
Response.Write "This is line 3.<br>" & vbCrLf
Response.Write "This is line 4.<br>" & vbCrLf
%>
</body></html>
```

This makes the HTML much easier to read and debug, if necessary. Note that the vbCrLf constant is case-insensitive; that is, you can use either uppercase or lowercase to specify it in your ASP code.

In addition, there's no reason you can't use Response.Write statements to print all the HTML in your page. In fact, the ASP code is much easier to read if you follow this technique. Listing 8-3 would become the following, using all Response.Write statements:

```
<%
Response.Write "<html><head><title>Test Page</title></head><body>"
Response.Write "This is line 1.<br>" & vbCrLf
Response.Write "This is line 2.<br>" & vbCrLf
Response.Write "This is line 3.<br>" & vbCrLf
Response.Write "This is line 4.<br>" & vbCrLf
Response.Write "</body></html>"
%>
```

If you were to use some of the code in the last chapter when building forms, you could use Response.Write with them, as well. However, there's a catch. In Chapter 7, there was this listing:

```
<html>
<head>
   <title>Chapter 7: Basic Form</title>
</head>
```

```
<body>
<h1>Basic Input Form</h1>

<form action="ch7_basicform_process.asp" method=post>
Keywords: <input type="Text" name="txtKeywords" size="20"><p>
<input type="Submit" name="cmdSubmit" value="Submit">
</form>
</body>
</html>
```

This listing can be converted to a series of Response.Write statements. The first six lines are easy:

```
<%
Response.Write "<html><head>" & vbCrLF
Response.Write "<title>Chapter 7: Basic Form</title>" & vbCrLF
Response.Write "</head><body><h1>Basic Input Form</h1>" & vbCrLF
%>
```

However, the FORM tag has double-quote characters within it. This is a problem since Response.Write uses double-quote characters to mark the beginning and end of the text that it prints. The solution? For every double-quote character you want to print, you print two double-quote characters next to each other. Here's the FORM tag as a Response.Write statement:

```
Response.Write "<form action=""ch7_basicform_process.asp""" _
& " method=post>"
```

Don't let this line scare you. The code was too long to print on one line in the book, so I used a continuation character to wrap it to a second line. In the first line, I put two double-quote characters after the ACTION parameter. At the end of the name of the ASP file, I use two more double-quote characters, and then a third to mark the end of the text before using a continuation character. On the next line, I pick up again with another double-quote character to print the rest of the FORM tag.

The rest of the form converts pretty easily:

```
<%
Response.Write "Keywords: "
Response.Write "<input type=""Text"" name=""txtKeywords""" _
    & " size=20><p>" & vbCrLF
```

```
Response.Write "<input type=Submit name=cmdSubmit value=Submit>" _
   & vbCrLf
Response.Write "</form></body></html>"
%>
```

Note that I removed some of the double-quote characters from the original form. As long as the value following an equals sign does not have any spaces, the double quotes are not required. I tend to leave all the double-quote characters in, but you can choose your favorite method.

In addition, note that whenever I broke a line into two, any piece of text was terminated and restarted with double-quote characters. You can't break a piece of text in the middle without doing it this way.

You'll be using this technique exclusively throughout the rest of the book to generate HTML output. The ASP code looks cleaner, and there are some minor performance gains over having the embedded HTML code in your ASP pages. Note that all your files have to have ASP extensions if you use this method.

Data Buffering

**20 Min.
To Go**

When ASP evaluates the code in a page, it may generate some HTML along the way. If your page takes a long time to run and no output is generated for a while, your users might wonder if the page has broken. Most Web users have a short attention span, and if your page doesn't load within about 10 to 15 seconds, the user is going to either reload the page or leave your site.

As the page is built, one of two things will happen. Either the HTML will be immediately sent to the user as it is generated, or the page will be sent when the server is completely done evaluating the page. The latter is known as *buffering*. You can think of a buffer as a temporary holding pen. As soon as the HTML is complete, the pen is opened and all the data dumps down to the user at the same time.

Generally, you don't have to worry about how the data is buffered. If you have a bunch of small pages, they will run the same either way because the data gets to the user fairly quickly.

However, if you're using a lot of database calls with complex queries, the user may find it frustrating to see nothing for a while. In IIS 5 on Windows 2000, buffering is turned on by default, but in IIS 4 in Windows NT 4, buffering is turned off. If you've moved to Windows 2000 from NT 4 and are expecting your pages to buffer, you're going to be unpleasantly surprised when it doesn't work.

To turn off buffering for a single page, you can use this statement:

```
Response.Buffer = False
```

To turn on buffering, you can use this statement:

```
Response.Buffer = True
```

For the Response.Buffer statement to work properly, it should be at the beginning of the ASP file.

You can also change this setting for your entire Web site by changing the properties of your Web site. Here are the steps for Windows 2000 Server:

1. Right-click the Web site whose setting you want to change.
2. Select Properties from the popup menu that appears.
3. Click the Home Directory tab and click the Configuration button at the bottom of the dialog shown in Figure 8-2.

Figure 8-2
The Home Directory tab of the Properties dialog

4. In the Configuration dialog, click the App Options tab. In the dialog shown
in Figure 8-3, the Enable Buffering will turn buffering on or off by default.
To turn buffering off, clear the box. To turn it on, check the box. When
you're done, click the OK button on this dialog and the Properties dialog
to close them.

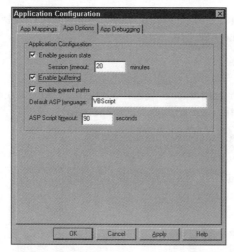

Figure 8-3
The App Options dialog

There are a few other methods of controlling buffering. First, if you need to
clear the buffer while the page is running, you can call this method:

```
Response.Clear
```

This will wipe out the buffer as if you had just started the page from scratch. If
you want to send the data to the user at some point during processing, you can
call this method:

```
Response.Flush
```

This will send whatever is in the buffer so far to the user.

**10 Min.
To Go**

Redirecting the Browser

Something you'll often do as you build applications in this book is move the user from one page to the next. This is a fairly common thing to do, but in fact the technology came out of what is essentially an error message.

One of the problems with the Internet and the World Wide Web is that pages are constantly appearing and disappearing. This isn't such a big deal if you give out your home page as your address. However, if a person is linking to pages within your site (which they inevitably do) and the page moves or is removed, the visitors are rewarded with a 404 File Not Found error. The 404 is called the *response code*. If you know the page is still on the site, you or your administrator can set up a page that redirects the user to the new page. For that to happen, the response code is 302. The browser receives this code along with the new URL and changes to that page.

The thing to remember is that the response code comes in the header and that the header is sent before any HTML content is sent to the browser. What this means to you is that you have to write your redirection instructions before you send any HTML or flush the buffer. When you send HTML to the browser and haven't already sent a response code, the Web server automatically sends a valid page code, which is code 200.

If you try to change the response code (which is what Response.Redirect does), you will get an error message indicating that the headers have already been written to the browser. Since that has happened and the Web server already sent a response code (200 for a valid document), you can't send another one. If you understand how the redirection works, the somewhat cryptic error message will make more sense in the future.

To redirect to another page, add this code:

```
Response.Redirect "secondpage.asp"
```

This can be any valid URL, so this version is also valid:

Done!

```
Response.Redirect "http://asptechniques.com/content.asp?a=s"
```

REVIEW

This chapter introduced some of the key features of the Response object. This object lets you send HTML output to a user's browser. You can also control how output is kept in memory using the buffering features of the Response object. You can also move the user from one page to another using the Redirect method. With the ability to control buffering and redirection, you have some helpful tools for building your Web applications.

QUIZ YOURSELF

1. Which method sends data to the browser? (See "Sending Data to the User")
2. What code do you add to add a new line to the HTML output? (See "Sending Data to the User")
3. What property do you set to turn buffering on or off? (See "Data Buffering")
4. What response code is returned for a File Not Found error? (See "Redirecting the Browser")
5. What character concatenates two pieces of text? (See "Sending Data to the User")
6. What character breaks a long line into two lines? (See "Sending Data to the User")

Understanding Variables and Data Types

Session Checklist

✔ Learn how to use a constant

✔ Learn what a variable is for

✔ Learn how data types work in VBScript

✔ Learn what arrays are for and how they work in VBScript

**30 Min.
To Go**

I n this chapter, you're going to get your first taste of writing code in the VBScript language. VBScript is the most popular language used to write server-side ASP code. There aren't lots of funny characters in the language; instead, all the keywords are simple English. This chapter introduces constants, variables, data types, and arrays, and gives you some examples of how they are used.

Creating and Using Constants

One of the easiest things you can do (and already have done) in VBScript is use constants. There are two types of constants that you can use in VBScript. The first is also known as a *literal*. This type of constant is simply entered right into the page. In Listing 9-1, each piece of text following Response.Write is considered a literal.

Listing 9-1
Samples of text literals

```
<%
Response.Write "This is line 1.<br>"
Response.Write "This is line 2.<br>"
Response.Write "This is line 3.<br>"
Response.Write "This is line 4.<br>"
%>
```

You can also use numeric literals, such as these:

```
Response.Write 5
Response.Write 3.14
```

While there are many cases in which you'll use literals in this way, there are also cases in which you need to define a constant. For instance, in the last chapter, you used the built-in constant vbCrLf, which is a carriage return/line feed combination.

To define a constant, you use the Const keyword, as shown in Listing 9-2.

Listing 9-2
Examples of constants

```
Const TAXRATE = 0.045
Const PI = 3.1415926
Const NAME = "Eric Smith"
Const HOLIDAY = #07/04/2000#
```

You have to provide a name for the constant, which can be any combination of letters, numbers, and underscore characters, as long as the first character is not a number. I prefer to keep my constant names all uppercase so they stand out in the rest of the code. If you use numbers as part of the variable name, the only restriction is that the first character of your variable name can't be a number.

You can list numbers after the equals sign. Text constants, also known as *strings*, are surrounded by double-quote characters. For the HOLIDAY constant, pound signs (#) surround date and time values. You can use constants anywhere that you use literals in your VBScript code. Constants are also subject to the scope rules covered later in this chapter.

Creating and Using Variables

So far, you've been operating on constants and literals. In most cases, you'll be performing operations on different values each time your code runs. Instead of operating on literals, you'll be operating on *variables*. Variables are essentially placeholders for real values. Variables follow the same naming conventions as constants; that is, any combination of numbers, letters, and underscores, as long as the first character is a letter. You create a variable like this:

```
Dim MyVariable
```

The Dim statement stands for Dimension, which is a holdover from the old BASIC language. This statement creates a variable named MyVariable. This variable can be used in calculations just as literals can be.

Data types

In most languages, a variable can hold only a single type of data, whether it is numeric, text, or date/time information. VBScript is different in this aspect. VBScript only has a single data type: the Variant. A Variant is able to hold any type of data, which can cause some problems since VBScript can't verify types. For instance, you can write an expression that adds a number to a date. VBScript will attempt to add the values but won't necessarily get a valid result. For this reason, I always make sure to prefix my variables with text to tell myself what type of data I intend to put in it. Table 9-1 shows the prefixes and data types you can use.

Table 9-1
Data Types and Prefixes

Prefix	Data Type
bln	Boolean
byt	Byte
int	Integer
str	String
lng	Long Integer

Continued

Table 9-1 *Continued*

Prefix	Data Type
sng	Single Precision
dbl	Double Precision
cur	Currency
dat	Date and Time data
obj	Object data
var	Variant (when being used for multiple types)

When variables are initialized, a numeric variable is initialized to 0, and a string is initialized to a zero-length (empty) string. To store a zero-length string in a variable, follow this example:

```
Dim strTest
strTest = ""
```

When using the Dim statement in a procedure or function, it is good programming practice to put the Dim statement at the beginning.

While declaring variables is optional, you can run into all sorts of problems when, for instance, you misspell a variable name when you're using it. Upon a variable's first use, VBScript will create the variable. This can be a problem if you misspell a variable's name. To avoid this problem, add this statement at the top of your file:

```
Option Explicit
```

This will force you to declare every variable you use, which will eliminate the problems you run into if a variable is misspelled. VBScript will flag an undeclared variable as an error when the page is run. All of the examples throughout the rest of the book will use Option Explicit, so you should get into the habit of using it.

Naming variables

One way to make your code easier to read is to be consistent in how you name your variables. VBScript allows for extremely long (255 characters) variable names, so why are you naming everything temp1 and temp2? There are a number of naming schemes available, and if you're working for a company where a lot of VBScript development is going on, they probably already have a scheme. The particular scheme you use doesn't really matter. What does matter is that you use it consistently and correctly. In my opinion, the best scheme is one that is memorable and easily taught to new programmers.

The thing to remember when you're naming a variable is to make the name as descriptive as possible without being wordy. Sure, you can create a variable name like TheAmountOfTaxPaidOnTheOrder, but imagine using it in a calculation:

```
TheAmountOfTaxPaidOnTheOrder = _
    TheCurrentSalesTaxRate * TheOrderTotal
```

At the same time, you can't use names so short that they aren't obvious to other programmers:

```
A = ST * OT
```

However, you can easily strike a balance between the two extremes. Use enough key terms (or abbreviations) to make it clear what the variable is used for. For instance, you might use OrderTax as the variable name for the amount of tax on an order.

The other thing you have to add to your name (which I'll call a *base name*) is information describing the data type being stored in the variable. While OrderTax might imply a Currency data type, the variable name PartNumber doesn't tell us much of anything. It could be a number or a combination of numbers and letters. For this reason, I always add a prefix (as shown in previous section) to the front of the variable to indicate what data type is in use. Our OrderTax variable, since it is holding a financial value, would become curOrderTax instead of just OrderTax. Anyone looking at the code will be able to tell what code you used because you will have declared your variable like so:

```
Dim curOrderTax      ' As Currency
```

I also add on a comment after the Dim statement indicating the type of data being stored in the variable. For simple variables, it's not as useful, but for objects (you'll learn about them later), the information following the Dim statement can indicate the type of object being stored in the variable.

The final piece of information you have to put on some variables is a prefix indicating the scope of the variable. Most variables have procedure scope, which means that they can't be used outside of the procedure where they were declared. However, there are cases in which you have to use variables declared at the page level. These variables can be used throughout all the subroutines in the page, and I prefix them with m_, which stands for module-level variable. It's a holdover I use from Visual Basic, but you can use p_, for instance, for page-level variables. The idea is to make these variables stand out from the others in the page.

**20 Min.
To Go**

Using Arrays

All of the variables we've been talking about so far will hold a single value of some type of data. However, there are cases in which you need to have multiple values. You could create a number of separate variables, but there are also cases in which you won't know how many values you need, so separate variables won't always work. In these cases, you can use an array. An array allows you to hold multiple values in a single variable and access the values through the use of indices.

There are many ways to think of arrays. The first is like a row of boxes, as shown in Figure 9-1.

```
| 1 | 2 | 3 | 4 | 5 | 6 | 7 | 8 | 9 | 10 | 11 | 12 |
```

Figure 9-1
A one-dimensional array is like a row of boxes

Each box in this diagram and in an array is identified by a number, which is called an index. In this particular diagram, the index values go from 1 to 12. You can create an array like this in VBScript like so:

```
Dim a_intValues(12)
```

This array is known as a *one-dimensional* array, since it only has one dimension: 12. The Dim keyword creates the variable. For an array, I always prefix the variable name with a_, but this is not required. The number in the parentheses indicates how many items, or elements, should be in the array. In this case, you would think that there would be 12 elements in the array, since the number 12 is in the parentheses. However, VBScript starts all arrays at 0. In this particular case, you will actually have 13 elements — 0 to 12. Since you can always just ignore the first element, this usually won't affect what you're doing. However, you'll learn about some built-in functions later in the book that return arrays and actually use the element whose index is zero.

Besides the simple one-dimensional array, you can also create arrays with multiple dimensions — up to 60, in fact. A two-dimensional array can be thought of as a grid, as shown in Figure 9-2.

1,1	1,2	1,3	1,4	1,5	1,6
2,1	2,2	2,3	2,4	2,5	2,6
3,1	3,2	3,3	3,4	3,5	3,6
4,1	4,2	4,3	4,4	4,5	4,6
5,1	5,2	5,3	5,4	5,5	5,6
6,1	6,2	6,3	6,4	6,5	6,6

Figure 9-2
A two-dimensional array is like a grid

In the diagram, each cell is represented by two index values. In this case, the first value represents the row, and the second represents the column. To create this particular array, you would declare it like so:

```
Dim a_intValues(6, 6)
```

Again, there are actually seven rows and seven columns, for a total of 49 cells. It really doesn't matter which index you consider the row and which you consider the column, but you do need to keep it straight mentally or you'll get confused when you start manipulating the array.

Once you have an array created, there are a number of functions that will provide information about the array and the number of elements in it. These functions, LBound and UBound, return the lower and upper bounds of the array, respectively. For the previous variable, a_intValues, you can call the functions like so:

```
Response.Write LBound(a_intValues, 1)     ' prints 0
Response.Write UBound(a_intValues, 1)     ' prints 6
```

The first parameter to this function is the name of the array variable, and the second is the index that you want to check. This value goes from 1 to the number of dimensions in the array. If you have a one-dimensional array, this parameter is optional since it defaults to 1.

You'll use these functions again in Chapter 12 when we discuss how to use looping structures to perform repeated operations.

*10 Min.
To Go*

Checking Data Types

While there is only one variable type, remember that the Variant type can hold any type of data. In addition, a variable can determine (to a point) what type of data you put in it. For instance, if you assign the number 5 to a variable, it will "know" that it is holding integer data. This feature is helpful if you're validating user input. For instance, if you know that a field needs to be in the form of a date, you can use the VarType function to determine if the data is actually date/time format.

There is a built-in function called the VarType function that will return the data type being held in a Variant. Here's how you use it:

```
Dim MyVariable
MyVariable = 502
Response.Write VarType(MyVariable)
```

This will print out a number indicating the type of data in the variable. Table 9-2 shows the return values that `VarType` will generate.

Table 9-2
VarType Return Values

Value	Variable Type Description
0	Empty (uninitialized)
1	Null (no valid data)
2	Integer
3	Long integer
4	Single-precision floating-point number
5	Double-precision floating-point number
6	Currency
7	Date
8	String
9	Automation object
10	Error
11	Boolean
12	Variant (used only with arrays of Variants)
13	Non-Automation object
17	Byte
8192	Array

There are a few important things to note about this function:

- When you assign a value to a variable and it's not immediately clear what type of data it is (5.4, for instance), VBScript will take its best guess. For instance, if you assign 5.4 to a variable and then check the `VarType` on the variable, VBScript will assume a Double, even though this value could be a Currency, Single, or Decimal. VBScript is a bit smarter about integers, but it isn't always perfectly reliable.

- If you have an array of a particular data type, the value 8192 will be added to the base data type. An array of integers will return the value 8194 (8192 + 2).

- If you don't want to have to decode the values, you can use the TypeName function and it will convert the data type to a text representation.

Converting Data Types

There are many cases in which you will have to change data from one type to another. For instance, if you are accepting data from a Web form, it will generally come in as text. However, if you need to do a calculation with that data, you'll have to convert the data to a different data type. You can use a number of conversion functions to convert data from one type to another. In most cases, you can convert any data type to any other. However, there are some obvious cases where you can't use these functions. For instance, you can't convert a sentence to a number. While the function will work, the result will be a 0 on a piece of text. Table 9-3 lists the conversion functions and their uses.

Table 9-3
Data Conversion Functions

Function	Use
CBool	Converts a value to a Boolean
CByte	Converts a value to a Byte
CCur	Converts a value to a Currency
CDate	Converts a value to a Date
CDbl	Converts a value to a Double
CInt	Converts a value to an Integer
CLng	Converts a value to a Long
CSng	Converts a value to a Single
CStr	Converts a value to a String

Note that you can use the functions that convert values to numbers on string values. You'll get a valid result if the string vaguely resembles a number. Here are some examples:

```
Response.Write CDbl("$5.60")        ' Prints 5.6
Response.Write CLng("5,142,233")    ' Prints 5142233
Response.Write CInt("$8.30")        ' Prints 8.3
```

The conversion functions are pretty flexible about punctuation during conversion.

Done!

A common error is to try to convert an empty string with a numeric conversion function. This will cause a Type Mismatch error. While the error might not make sense to you at first, check the line where the error occurred. It's more than likely that you'll find a conversion function there. Print out the value and you'll probably find that the value you tried to convert was empty. The solution is to always verify that the data in the variable is valid and not empty (check against an empty string) before attempting a conversion. You'll eliminate a lot of errors with this simple check.

REVIEW

In this chapter, you learned about constants and how they can be used to write cleaner code in your ASP applications. You also learned about variables and how to declare and use them. Arrays can often come in handy when you have many values that you need to organize into manageable packages. Later in the book you'll learn about some cool functions that use arrays for their output, and you'll need the skills you learned in this chapter to manage them.

QUIZ YOURSELF

1. Which keyword do you use to declare a constant? (See "Creating and Using Constants")

2. What data type would be used to hold the following types of data? (See "Checking Data Types")

   Phone number

   Birth date

Yes/No responses

Product price

3. Which keyword is used to create a variable? An array? (See "Creating and Using Variables")

4. What rules must you follow when you create a variable name? (See "Creating and Using Variables")

Working with Strings

Session Checklist

✔ Learn about functions that manipulate strings

✔ Work with arrays of strings and functions to manipulate them

✔ Learn to combine function results

**30 Min.
To Go**

One of the best features of VBScript is its rich function library. While you can easily recreate these functions using some basic VBScript code, you won't have to do this in most cases. This chapter is devoted to manipulating strings using the various functions that are available. You'll also learn about the functions that work on arrays of strings instead of individual strings.

Manipulating Strings

One of the most common things you'll be doing in your Web applications is manipulating text entered by your users. All data, when submitted from Web forms, will look like text to VBScript. This text, when put in a variable, is called a string. There are lots of functions that allow you to look at and manipulate the data in string variables. This section covers these functions and shows you how to use them.

Editing strings

There are a number of built-in functions that help you to edit the contents of your strings. These functions enable you to change the contents of your string in various ways. Each of these functions operates on a single string at a time. This doesn't mean that you can't use them with arrays; rather, you use the function with one array element at a time.

String function

In cases where you need a string to be made up of all one character, such as dashes or other punctuation, you need a quick way to create the string without having to resort to code involving loops or other structures you don't know yet. The String function will create a string of any one character and of any length you specify. Here's an example:

```
Dim strSeparator
strSeparator = String(20, "-")
Response.Write strSeparator
```

This creates a string of 20 dashes in the strSeparator variable. The preceding snippet of code then prints out the string to the browser window. If you were to specify more than one character, like this,

```
strSeparator = String(20, "#-")
```

the resulting string would only duplicate the first character — in this case, the pound sign. Any other characters in the second argument would be ignored.

LCase and UCase functions

When comparing strings, it's often helpful to be able to convert each string in the comparison to uppercase or lowercase, so that you're comparing "apples to apples," so to speak. The reason for this is shown in the following example:

```
Response.Write "Word" = "WORD"        ' Prints False
```

When you're comparing strings, the case of the letters matters. A lowercase letter is not the same as its uppercase sibling. For this reason, you should always make sure that you are comparing uppercase to uppercase or lowercase to lowercase. Here's a quick example of how to use these simple functions:

```
Response.Write UCase("My phone number is 212-555-1212")
```

This statement prints:

```
MY PHONE NUMBER IS 212-555-1212
```

Note that the UCase function (and the LCase function) doesn't affect non-letter characters in the string. The LCase equivalent produces this result:

```
my phone number is 212-555-1212
```

There aren't any other options for use with these functions. . . they do one thing, and they do it well.

White space functions

There are several functions designed to create and remove white space characters in your strings. The trimming functions are especially helpful when you're dealing with database records. Some databases will return fields packed with spaces at the end. For instance, if the field can hold 40 characters and there are 10 non-space characters in the field, you'll get 30 spaces at the end. This is highly annoying, especially if you're trying to put strings together, such as a last name and first name. For example, let's say that your database has two 20-character fields: one for the first name, and one for the last name. If my name, Eric Smith, is stored in the database, there will be 16 spaces at the end of Eric and 15 spaces at the end of Smith. If I concatenate these two strings, I will end up with this value. Note that a pound sign represents the spaces in the values.

```
My name is Eric################Smith###############.
```

This isn't really practical. Note that HTML ignores the amount of white space between words, so that if you actually printed this to a Web page, the source code would look like the line above, but the result would look normal:

```
My name is Eric Smith.
```

The solution to this problem is to trim the spaces from your data before attempting to perform concatenations or other operations on them. Each of these functions is smart enough to remove only the spaces and not any non-space characters from the string. This means that you can use these functions in most cases without having to worry about side effects.

There are three functions: LTrim, RTrim, and Trim. LTrim removes spaces starting at the first character and stopping at the first non-space character. RTrim starts at the last character and works to the beginning of the string. Trim is a combination of both functions. It removes spaces from both the left and right ends of the string and stops at either end when it reaches a non-space character. Note that any invisible control characters, such as carriage returns or linefeeds, are considered non-space characters and won't be removed from the string. This can be helpful if you're working with large free-form text fields.

One last white space function that doesn't really fit anywhere else is the Space function. This function, given a number, will create a string with that many spaces in it. It's a specialized form of the String function we covered earlier. Since HTML ignores repeated white space anyway, you probably won't find much of a use for this in formatting your output. However, it's good to know it's there.

StrReverse function

The StrReverse function is included here for completeness' sake. This function takes a string and reverses the characters in it. I'm not quite sure what useful purpose it serves and have never used it in any coding I've ever done. The only rule is that the string you give the function can't be Null, such as a result from a database. If it is, you'll get an error.

Substring functions

The next group of functions is designed to help you extract substrings from your strings. You can combine these functions with the search functions in the next section in order to extract bits of data required for your program to operate.

**20 Min.
To Go**

Len function

The Len function returns the length of a string. Here's a quick example:

```
Response.Write Len("This is a test.")    ' prints 15
```

This function includes all spaces, punctuation, and non-printable characters as well.

Left function

The Left function returns a selected number of characters from a string, starting at the first character. Here's an example:

```
Response.Write Left("This is a test.", 4) ' prints "This"
```

You can combine this function with others. For instance, let's say you wanted to return all but four characters of the string, but you didn't know what the contents of the string were. You could use the Len function to generate the length to return, as shown here:

```
Dim strInput    ' As String
strInput = "This is another test."
Response.Write Left(strInput, Len(strInput) - 4)
```

This statement prints the following value:

```
This is another t
```

Mid function

The Mid function can return a string from within another string. This function takes three arguments. The first is the string to look in. The second is the character position to start reading at, and the third is how many characters to return. Here's an example of how to use it:

```
Dim strInput    ' As String
strInput = "This is another test."
Response.Write Mid(strInput, 9, 7)    ' prints "another"
```

If the final parameter is bigger than the length of the string, everything until the end of the string will be returned but no error will be generated.

The Mid function has two uses. The first uses the syntax you just saw. The second eliminates the third parameter and returns everything from the selected position to the end of the string, as shown in this example:

```
Dim strInput    ' As String
strInput = "This is another test."
Response.Write Mid(strInput, 17)    ' prints "test."
```

Right function

The Right function returns a selected number of characters from the right side of the string. Here's an example:

```
Response.Write Right("This is a test.", 5)  ' prints "test."
```

You can use this function, in combination with the Len function, to replicate the effect of the Mid function in its second usage. Here's how you would do it:

```
Dim strInput    ' As String
strInput = "This is another test."
Response.Write Right(strInput, Len(strInput) - 17 + 1)
```

In this case, the string's total length is 21. In the previous example, we used the Mid function to start at character position 17 and return everything to the end of the string. To use the same value here, we have to add one to the result, since otherwise we would only return four characters instead of five. This sort of "string math" is very common and it's easy to find yourself off by one character if you're not thinking about what you're doing.

**10 Min.
To Go**

Search functions

VBScript includes several functions that will search a string for a substring. There are also some other functions that can find substrings and replace them with other substrings. These are extremely helpful functions, especially when combined with the others you've just learned about. This section will show you some common ways to combine the functions.

InStr function

The InStr function returns the position in which a string occurs within another. The function has options as to where to start searching the string and whether to match case or not. Here's the basic usage:

```
Response.Write InStr("This is a test.", "is")
```

This usage searches the first string for the second and returns the position in which the second string starts in the first string. In this case, the function returns 3, since the substring is is in the word This.

If you wanted to skip the first five characters and start searching after that, you would invoke the function like this:

```
Response.Write InStr(5, "This is a test.", "is")
```

In this case, the function returns the value 6, which is where the second instance of is begins. The final option for using this function is to indicate whether the case of the letters should be used or ignored. Using the vbTextCompare constant as the fourth parameter, you can tell the function to ignore the case of the letters, as shown in this example:

```
Response.Write InStr(5, "This is a test.", "IS", vbTextCompare)
```

If you want case to be matched, you use the vbBinaryCompare constant as the last argument, as shown here:

```
Response.Write InStr(5, "This is a test.", "IS", vbBinaryCompare)
```

In this case, the word IS is not in the string, so the function returns a 0. Note that if you're using the fourth parameter, you also have to supply the character to begin the search, even if that value is a 1. You also can't call the function like this:

```
Response.Write InStr( , "This is a test.", "IS", vbBinaryCompare)
```

Normally, leaving an argument blank will cause the default value to be supplied. For this particular function, that won't work.

Using the InStr function in combination with some of the other functions, you can do some more interesting manipulations. For instance, let's say you wanted to search a piece of test for an HTML <A> tag, which indicates that a link should be created. Here's the complete format for an A tag:

```
<a href=http://www.asptechniques.com>ASP Techniques</a>
```

In this particular example, let's say that you only wanted to see the site's address and not the rest of the formatting. There are several ways you could search for the URL in the text, but the way we're going to use works like this:

1. Search for http:// in the string.

2. Add 7 to the result of step 1 so that you are "pointed" to the first character of the site's address.

3. Using the result of Step 2 as the starting point, search for a > character.

4. Use the Mid function with the original string. Use the result of Step 2 (plus 7) as the starting point, and subtract the result of Step 3 from the result of Step 2 to determine how many characters to return.

Here's the code in action:

```
Dim strInput
Dim strDomainName
Dim intStart, intEnd
strInput = "<a href=http://www.asptechniques.com>" _
```

```
& "ASP Techniques</a>"
intStart = InStr(strInput, "http://") + 7
intEnd = InStr(intStart, strInput, ">")
strDomainName = Mid(strInput, intStart, intEnd - intStart)
Response.Write strDomainName
```

As you can see, the InStr function can be a useful tool in your programmer's toolbox.

InStrRev function

The InStrRev function works much like the InStr function, except that it starts at the end of the string and searches toward the beginning of the string. There's no easy way to replicate this behavior using the regular InStr function. Conveniently, when this function returns a position, it bases that position on the start of the string. Here's an example:

```
Response.Write InStrRev("This is a test", "is")
```

Since this function is working from the end of the string to the front, it finds the word is first and returns a value of 6.

This function takes the same optional arguments as the InStr function; however, they are at the end of the function instead of the beginning. In addition, if you choose to use a constant to control case sensitivity, you also have to provide the starting position. Remember that if you want to search the whole string, you have to start from the last character in the string. Here's an example of how you can do it:

```
Dim strInput = "This is a test."
Response.Write InStrRev(strInput, "IS", _
    Len(strInput), vbTextCompare)
```

By using the Len function, you don't have to manually count up the number of characters in the string.

Replace function

The Replace function finds a substring and then replaces it throughout a string. It has options to control where to start looking, how many times to replace the target string, and whether to be case sensitive or not. Here's the basic example:

```
Dim strInput = "This is a test."
Response.Write Replace(strInput, "test", "good test")
```

The result of this code will be:

```
This is a good test.
```

Note that once the Replace function has read through the string and changed text, it doesn't keep changing the same text over and over again. If it did, the function would never end and the result would be something like this:

```
This is a good good good good good good good ...
```

By adding a fourth argument, you can specify the character position (with the first character being 1) to start replacing data. Here's another example:

```
Dim strInput
strInput = "She sells sea shells by the sea shore."
Response.Write Replace(strInput, "s", "#", 20)
```

Specifying 20 as the third argument tells the Replace function to start replacing at position 20. However, a side effect of this function is that the first 19 characters are not included in the output. The result of this code is:

```
# by the #ea #hore.
```

The first pound sign is the last s in shells, which is position 20. In this case, you could use the Left function to return the first 19 characters, followed by the Replace function you just used, like so:

```
Dim strInput
strInput = "She sells sea shells by the sea shore."
Response.Write Left(strInput, 19) _
    & Replace(strInput, "s", "#", 20)
```

The last argument you can use is the same as in the InStr/InStrReverse function; that is, you can specify vbTextCompare or vbBinaryCompare as the last argument, as shown in these examples:

```
Dim strInput
strInput = "She sells sea shells by the sea shore."
Response.Write Replace(strInput, "s", "#", 1, -1, vbTextCompare)
```

This example prints the following:

```
#he #ell# #ea #hell# by the #ea #hore.
```

All the *s*'s, regardless of case, are replaced by pound signs. If you use the variation shown here

```
Dim strInput
strInput = "She sells sea shells by the sea shore."
Response.Write Replace(strInput, "s", "#", 1, -1, vbBinaryCompare)
```

this version prints the following:

```
She #ell# #ea #hell# by the #ea #hore.
```

In this case, the uppercase *s* is ignored and not replaced.

StrComp function

The StrComp function compares two strings, using either text or binary comparison, just as in the other functions in this section. Here's an example:

```
Response.Write StrComp("test", "TEST", vbTextCompare)    ' True
Response.Write StrComp("test", "TEST", vbBinaryCompare) ' False
```

The first usage of this function is equivalent to:

```
Response.Write (LCase("test") = LCase("TEST"))    ' True
```

The second is equivalent to just using the equals sign to compare the strings:

```
Response.Write ("test" = "TEST")  ' False
```

String Array Functions

All of the functions we've covered so far operate on single strings and perform various actions on them. The group of functions we'll cover in this section take arrays as input or generate arrays as output. They're helpful functions to have on your palette.

Filter function

The Filter function is designed to search through an array of strings and return the strings that either match or don't match another string. The strings that match (or don't match) are returned in another array. Here's an example of how to use this function:

```
Dim i                   ' As Integer
Dim a_strNames(5)       ' As Array of Strings
Dim a_strResults        ' As Array of Strings

a_strNames(0) = "Smith, Eric"
a_strNames(1) = "Jones, Bob"
a_strNames(2) = "Mitchell, George"
a_strNames(3) = "Andrews, Eric"
a_strNames(4) = "Gatewood, Andrew"
a_strNames(5) = "Reeves, Michelle"

a_strResults = Filter(a_strNames, "chell")

For i = LBound(a_strResults) To UBound(a_strResults)
    Response.Write a_strResults(i) & "<br>"
Next    ' i
```

The array is loaded up with six names, and then the Filter function returns only the names that have the substring chell in them. This matches names 2 and 5. The code at the end loops through the items in the array that is returned. Note the use of the LBound function and the UBound function to determine how many items are in the array. We'll come back to this code in Chapter 12.

The Filter function can be configured to return the names that don't include the search string, as well. If you change the Filter call to be the following:

```
a_strResults = Filter(a_strNames, "chell", False)
```

In this case, all names but 2 and 5 will be printed out.

The last argument you can add to this function specifies how to handle case sensitivity. Here's an example of this:

```
a_strResults = Filter(a_strNames, "eric", True, vbTextCompare)
```

In this case, names 0 and 3 will be printed. However, if this routine is changed to use vbBinaryCompare, no names will be printed, since the names use mixed case.

Join function

The Join function concatenates an array of strings, using a delimiter between the array elements. Here's an example using the name list from before:

```
Dim a_strNames(5)      ' As Array of Strings
Dim strResult          ' As String

a_strNames(0) = "Smith, Eric"
a_strNames(1) = "Jones, Bob"
a_strNames(2) = "Mitchell, George"
a_strNames(3) = "Andrews, Eric"
a_strNames(4) = "Gatewood, Andrew"
a_strNames(5) = "Reeves, Michelle"
strResult = Join(a_strNames, "<br>" & vbCrLf)
Response.Write strResult
```

This example takes all the names and puts them together with an HTML <BR> tag, as well as a carriage return/linefeed character. This generates a nicely formatted list of names that eliminates the need to loop through the array.

Split function

The Split function breaks up a string wherever a delimiter is found. The resulting words are placed into an array. Here's an example:

```
Dim strInput
Dim a_strResults      ' As Array of Strings
strInput = "She sells sea shells by the sea shore."
a_strResults = Split(strInput, " ")
Response.Write Join(a_strResults, "<br>" & vbCrLF)
```

This usage breaks up the string wherever a space is found, and puts each word into an array. You then use the Join function to put the words together with BR tags and CR/LF tags so that you can print it in a single step.

The Split function can take a third argument, indicating how many words should be returned. The last array item will contain all the remaining text in the string. If you don't want to use this functionality, you can specify -1 as the default value. The fourth argument is used for case sensitivity, using the same constants as the rest of the functions in this chapter. The case sensitivity is used for matching the delimiter within the string.

Done!

REVIEW

In this chapter, you learned many functions that can manipulate, edit, and search strings. You'll see them many times throughout the rest of the book, as they are used for quite a few different functions, some of which you've already seen in the chapter. Feel free to play with these functions to get a feel for how you can combine them to get the data you need.

QUIZ YOURSELF

1. Which function is interchangeable with both the Left and Right functions? (See "Manipulating Strings")

2. Which constant do you need to add to make the InStr function case-insensitive? (See "Manipulating Strings")

3. What two ways can you use to compare strings? (See "Manipulating Strings")

4. Given the following string, how can you replace only the first comma with a dash? (See "Manipulating Strings")

   strData = "This sentence, and the previous one, has two commas."

5. Write the code to create a string of 25 exclamation points. (See "Manipulating Strings")

PART

II

Saturday Morning
Part Review

Define the following HTML tags:

1. <HEAD>

2. <TD>

3. <B>

4. <TH>

5. <FONT>

Provide the HTML tag to start each of the following lists:

6. A bulleted list of items

7. A list of items, numbered using uppercase Roman numerals (i.e. I, II, III, and so on)

8. A list of items bulleted with a circle instead of the default character

Answer these questions about the Request object:

9. Which collection would contain data sent to the page on the URL?

10. Which method of the Request object allows you to create cookies for the user?

11. Which collection contains the name of the current ASP file?

12. If no collection is specified, which is read first? Last?

Answer these questions about the `Response` object:

13. How do you create a temporary cookie? A permanent one?

14. What formatting does `Response.Write` add to lines of text printed to the Web page?

15. If you receive an error indicating that the headers have already been written to the page, what does that typically indicate you've done?

16. How do you terminate processing of a Web page immediately?

PART

III

Saturday Afternoon

Working with Numbers and Dates

Session Checklist

✔ Learn the differences between the numeric data types in VBScript

✔ Learn about the operators used to manipulate numeric data

✔ Use date and time values within VBScript

✔ Use the built-in functions for manipulating date and time values

**30 Min.
To Go**

I n this chapter, you'll learn to work with both numeric and date/time data within VBScript. VBScript includes a rich function library for manipulating both types of data. If you're familiar with Visual Basic, many of these functions should look familiar. However, there are some key functions missing from VBScript that you may be used to from VB, and any key differences will be noted in the text.

Numeric Data Types

As you learned in an earlier chapter, there are quite a few data types that can hold numeric data. Each one of these data types has a maximum and minimum capacity. Once you've learned what the available data types are, you'll be better able to choose the right one for the task. Table 11-1 lists the available data types (that can be stored in a Variant) and their capacities.

Table 11-1
Numeric Data Type Capacities

Name	Capacity
Byte	0 to 255, positive values only
Integer	-32,768 to 32,767
Long	-2,147,483,648 to 2,147,483,647
Single	-3.40E38 to -1.401E-45 for negative values 1.401E-45 to 3.40E38 for positive values
Double	-1.79E308 to -4.94E-324 for negative values 4.94E-324 to 1.79E308 for positive values
Currency	-922,337,203,685,477.5808 to 922,337,203,685,477.5807
Decimal	+/-79,228,162,514,264,337,593,543,950,335 with no decimal point +/-7.9228162514264337593543950335 with 28 places to the right of the decimal; smallest non-zero number is +/-0.0000000000000000000000000001

There are a few things to note when using these data types. In general, you have to think big. If a number might be larger than 255, you should use an integer. If a number might be bigger than 32767, you should use a Long. While the Variant hides a lot of this from you, you have to be careful when using the conversion functions. If the value is more than 32767, you can't use CInt on the value. Always use the larger data type if there is a question about size.

The Currency data type is a good choice for currency and financial transactions because it only calculates using four decimal places. This eliminates the possibility of miniscule rounding errors. The other data types have far more capacity than what you'll probably ever need, but in general, I always use Double when I'm dealing with non-currency-related decimal numbers.

The Decimal data type does not have a conversion function, unlike Visual Basic, which has the CDec function. The rest of the functions are covered in Chapter 9.

Numeric Functions and Operators

VBScript has the usual cast of operators for doing math on your variables. It also has a fairly lengthy list of numeric functions that provide everything from trigonometry to logarithms. While these functions might not be useful to you unless you're building a calculator application of some sort, there are some numeric functions that do formatting of data and that can be helpful. We'll cover those in more depth since you'll probably be using them more often.

Numeric operators

In VBScript as in other languages, you have the normal set of operators for doing math with your constants and variables. Most of these operators should be familiar to you, but some are less common. Table 11-2 shows the operators and their meanings.

Table 11-2
Mathematical Operators

Symbol	Meaning
+	Addition
-	Subtraction
*	Multiplication
/	Division
\	Integer Division
^	Exponentiation
Mod	Modulus Division

The Integer Division operator functions like this: when you divide two integers, the result has its decimal digits truncated automatically. This means that 5\2 = 2, and not 3 as it would be with standard division.

The Modulus Division operator, or Mod, returns the remainder of a division. 5 Mod 2 returns 1, since 2 goes into 5 twice, with one left over. This can be helpful if you're figuring out how many full rows you can get from a set of records, for instance.

The Exponentiation operator raises a number to a power. For example, 3 ^ 2 returns 9 (3 squared). You can also use it with fractional powers. For instance, 4 ^ 0.5 returns the square root of 4, which is 2.

Trigonometric and mathematical functions

A group of functions in VBScript were designed to help you do higher math functions. As my typical programs don't involve geometry or trigonometry, I don't use these functions much. However, your situation may be different. Table 11-3 shows these functions and their uses in VBScript.

Table 11-3
Higher Math Functions

Function	Meaning
Abs	Absolute Value
Atn	Arctangent Function
Cos	Cosine Function
Exp	The value of the constant *e* raised to a number
Log	Logarithm
Sgn	Returns 1 if the number is positive, -1 if negative
Sin	Sine Function
Sqr	Square Root Function
Tan	Tangent Function

For more information on these functions, consult your documentation or view the documentation online at msdn.microsoft.com. This Web site includes the complete documentation for nearly every part of the Microsoft development platform, including the entire VBScript language.

Formatting functions

**20 Min.
To Go**

There are several functions in VBScript that help you format your numbers. Some of the functions are simple and others have quite a few extra options for your use.

Note

If you're coming from a Visual Basic background, you may be distressed to find that the Format function doesn't exist in VBScript. However, the functions that are provided will be able to do most of the same things that the Format function can do.

FormatCurrency function

This function, as its name suggests, is able to format variables that contain Currency data. Like the other Format functions, it is localized to your server's Regional Settings. The Regional Settings are generally set when the administrator configures the server. If you're showing currency values to a user, remember that the user might not be in the same country as your server, so be sure to indicate what currency you're displaying.

The FormatCurrency function's syntax is as follows:

```
FormatCurrency(Expression[,NumDigitsAfterDecimal
[,IncludeLeadingDigit [,UseParensForNegativeNumbers
[,GroupDigits]]]])
```

The first argument is the value you want to format. The next specifies the number of digits you want to have following the decimal point. Remember that a Currency value can only hold up to four decimal digits, so anything more than 4 will give you 4 as a result.

The next argument is used only if a 0 is to the left of the decimal point. This flag indicates whether or not to show a 0 for numbers between −1 and 1. The values for this argument are shown in Table 11-4. This is an optional parameter and can be omitted, as shown in the examples that follow.

The third argument specifies whether to use parentheses around negative numbers, which is a common practice in accounting. This parameter takes the same values as the previous parameter, which are shown in Table 11-4. This is an optional parameter and can be omitted, as shown in the examples that follow.

The final argument specifies whether the digits should be grouped with the regional number-grouping symbol. For large numbers, the United States uses commas between groups of three numbers, as shown here:

```
1,002,045
```

This parameter also takes the values shown in Table 11-4. This is an optional parameter and can be omitted, as shown in the examples that follow.

Table 11-4
Parameter Values

Value	Meaning
TristateTrue (-1)	Yes
TristateFalse (0)	No
TristateUseDefault (2)	Use the computer's regional settings (default)

You can specify either the named constant or the equivalent value. In the examples shown here, I've used the numeric values here to save space. Remember that the local currency and grouping symbols will be displayed instead of what is shown here if you are using a regional setting other than United States.

```
Response.Write FormatCurrency(5.232)                    ' $5.23
Response.Write FormatCurrency(1.622, 3)                 ' $1.622
Response.Write FormatCurrency(0.916, 2)                 ' $.92
Response.Write FormatCurrency(0.1121, 2, -1)            ' $0.11
Response.Write FormatCurrency(-52217.523, 2, , -1, -1)
   ' ($52,217.52)
```

FormatNumber function

FormatNumber takes exactly the same arguments as the FormatCurrency function. The only difference is that this function won't display the regional currency symbol in front of the resulting string.

FormatPercent function

FormatPercent takes exactly the same arguments as the FormatCurrency function. The only difference is that this function multiplies the value by 100 and then uses the decimal-place argument. For instance, .1543 would become 15.43% if you were using two decimal digits.

Fix and Int functions

Besides the CInt function that you learned about earlier, VBScript also provides the Int and Fix functions. Each of these functions truncates the number given and produces an integer result. However, the functions differ when you're dealing with negative numbers. Int removes the decimal portion and displays the first negative integer that is less than the input number. Fix removes the decimal portion and displays the first negative integer that is greater than the input number. The following examples illustrate this difference:

```
Response.Write Int(65.3)      ' Prints 65
Response.Write Fix(65.3)      ' Prints 65

Response.Write Int(65.6)      ' Prints 65 - does not round number
Response.Write Fix(65.6)      ' Prints 65 - does not round number

Response.Write Int(-10.5)     ' Prints -11
Response.Write Fix(-10.5)     ' Prints -10
```

Round function

This function, as its name suggests, rounds a number to a specified number of decimal places, as shown here:

```
Response.Write Round(1.21125, 2)    ' prints 1.21
Response.Write Round(1.5624, 0)     ' prints 2
```

The only restriction is that the number of digits has to be greater than 0. If you use a number less than 0, you might think the Round function doesn't exist since you'll get an Invalid Procedure Call message. If you see this message, double-check the value before you attempt to round it.

Random numbers

To obtain a random number for your program, use the Rnd function. This function returns a value greater than or equal to 0 but less than 1. However, if you enter the following code in a page, you see that the Rnd function is not necessarily random.

```
Response.Write Rnd()
```

Each time you reload the page, you expect to see a different number on the screen. Without any arguments, the Rnd function always displays the same initial number. Further calls to the Rnd function in the same code return successive numbers in the random number sequence.

Sometimes you want a truly random number. To ensure that you get one, follow the Randomize statement that uses the system timer to generate a sequence of random numbers. Under this process, reloading the page results in a different number each time.

```
Randomize
Response.Write Rnd()
```

In most cases, you'll need to generate a random number in a range, such as 1 to 10. Here's a formula you can use to generate these values:

```
intValue = Int((upper - lower + 1) * Rnd() + lower)
```

If you substitute a 1 for lower and 10 for upper, you get this:

```
intValue = Int((10 * Rnd()) + 1)
```

This will generate a random number from 1 to 10.

Miscellaneous math functions

There are several additional math functions that don't really fit in other groups, so we'll cover them here. These are the functions you should tuck in a back corner of your brain, since you'll find a use for them someday.

Eval function

The `Eval` function will evaluate a function stored in a string variable and return the value. The simple version works like this:

```
Response.Write Eval("5 + 4")
```

This prints out the value 9. However, the routine is a lot smarter than that. If you have a variable declared, you can use the variable within the `Eval` function and perform calculations with it. Here's an example:

```
Dim i
i = 20
Response.Write Eval(i + 20)
```

This prints out the value 40. `Eval` is a handy function to have since you can allow your users to type in calculations and then process the calculations automatically without having to parse them.

Hex and Oct functions

The `Hex` function converts a value to hexadecimal (base 16) notation, and the `Oct` function converts a value to octal (base 8) notation. Here's a quick example:

```
Response.Write Hex(12768)     ' Prints 31E0
Response.Write Oct(234)       ' Prints 352
```

If you need to specify an octal or hexadecimal number in your code, prefix the number with &0 or &H, respectively, as in these examples:

```
Response.Write &H1000     ' Prints 4096
Response.Write &0700      ' Prints 448
```

Part III—Saturday Afternoon
Session 11

Date and Time Functions

VBScript has an extensive list of date and time functions. You can add, subtract, and manipulate date and time values very easily with the functions covered in this section. If you're familiar with other Microsoft languages and tools, these functions are basically identical across the Microsoft products that use a Visual Basic derivative as their language.

Date function

This function returns the current date, plain and simple. For pages running on a server, the date is the date on the server at the time (includes any time zone or daylight savings time adjustments). If you are running this function in a client-side script, the date will be the date on the local machine. The return value of this function can be put into a variable and manipulated as a date, as well.

DateAdd function

This function adds dates together. It can also increment (or decrement) a date by an amount in any time or date unit. For instance, if you want to know the date 60 days from the current date, the DateAdd function can be used like so to do it:

```
Dim datCurrent
Dim datFuture

datCurrent = Date()
datFuture = DateAdd("d", 60, datCurrent)
Response.Write datFuture
```

This will print the date that is 60 days from the current date. The DateAdd function's first argument specifies the unit of time to use. Table 11-5 shows the valid strings that can be used with this and other functions in this section.

You can use the DateAdd function to decrement a date/time value, as well. Just use a negative number for the number of intervals you want, and the date/time will decrease accordingly. A common mistake is to use DateDiff when you really want to use DateAdd with a negative value.

Table 11-5
Date Function Codes

Code	Meaning
yyyy	Year
q	Quarter Year
m	Month
y	Day of year
d	Day
w	Weekday
ww	Week of year
h	Hour
n	Minute
s	Second

DateDiff Function

The DateDiff function gives the difference between two dates in the unit that you specify. Here is a simple example:

```
Response.Write DateDiff("m", #6/19/2000#, #6/19/2001#)
```

This, as you might guess, gives a result of 12. If you were to reverse the date values, the result would be –12 instead. The time interval codes used here are the same as in Table 11-5 in the previous section.

DatePart function

This function extracts part of a date/time value. The part can be any of the constants used for the DateAdd function shown in Table 11-5. Here's a quick example of the function:

```
Response.Write DatePart("ww", Date)
```

This will give the week number of the year to date. This function is similar to the Hour, Month, Second, and other functions that return a particular part of a date. This one is more generic and can handle all parts, including a few (like Quarter) that the individual functions can't deal with.

DateSerial function

This function creates a date value based on integer year, month, and day values. Here is an example:

```
datCurrent = DateSerial(2001, 6, 19)
```

The variable will hold the date June 19th, 2001 after this code executes. This is another way to create a date, instead of concatenating values together and then feeding the concatenated string through the CDate function. The end result is the same, but this method takes a little less code.

DateValue function

This function converts a string to a date, much like the CDate function. This function will make certain assumptions that the CDate function does not. For instance, if you provide a date without a year, the DateValue function assumes the date to be in the current year. It will also accept time values and simply not include them in the date that it returns.

FormatDateTime function

This function formats variables and values that represent times or dates. It is quite limited and can only show five formats: two for date, two for time, and one for both. The function's syntax is as follows:

```
FormatDateTime(Date[, NamedFormat])
```

The NamedFormat parameter is a number from 0 to 4, with each value being a different format. The format values are shown in Table 11-6.

Table 11-6
NamedFormat Parameter Values

Constant Name	Value	Meaning
vbGeneralDate	0	Displays a date and/or time
vbLongDate	1	Displays a date in long format
vbShortDate	2	Displays a date in short format
vbLongTime	3	Displays a time in long format
vbShortTime	4	Displays a time in short format

The default formats changed in Windows 2000 to always show four digits for the year, unlike previous versions that only showed four-digit years in the long date formats. Here are some examples:

```
Response.Write FormatDateTime(#6/19/2000 11:59 AM#, vbGeneralDate)
' 6/19/2000 11:59:00 AM

Response.Write FormatDateTime(#6/19/2000 11:59 AM#, vbLongDate)
' Monday, June 19, 2000

Response.Write FormatDateTime(#6/19/2000 11:59 AM#, vbShortDate)
' 6/19/2000

Response.Write FormatDateTime(#6/19/2000 11:59 AM#, vbLongTime)
' 11:59:00 AM

Response.Write FormatDateTime(#6/19/2000 11:59 AM#, vbShortTime)
' 11:59
```

If you don't care for these formats, you can use the functions covered in the section "Date/time parsing functions," later in this chapter, to create your own formats.

Now function

This function returns the current date and time together. It's the equivalent of concatenating the results of the Date and Time functions together with a space between them.

Time function

This function returns the current time. If you're using server-side VBScript code, it will return the time on the server, just as the Date function returns the date on the server's clock.

Date/time parsing functions

A number of related functions return a selected part of a date/time value. These functions are shown in Table 11-7.

Table 11-7
Date/Time Parsing Functions

Function	Use
Day	Returns the day in a date value
Hour	Returns the hour in a time value
Minute	Returns the minute in a time value
Month	Returns the month in a date value
MonthName	Returns the name of the month, given a value from 1–12
Second	Returns the second of a time value
Weekday	Returns the weekday of a date value (1–7)
WeekdayName	Returns the name of the day, given a value from 1–7
Year	Returns the year of a date value

The nice thing about these functions is that you can create your own date formats that might not be supported by the FormatDateTime function covered earlier in the chapter. For instance, if you wanted to create a date in the format:

```
The author's birthday is on day 19 of June.
```

You would do it with this code:

```
Dim datBirthday
datBirthday = CDate("6/19/1970")
Response.Write "The author's birthday is on day " _
    & Day(datBirthday) & " of " _
    & MonthName(Month(datBirthday)) & "."
```

Done!

REVIEW

In this chapter, you learned more about mathematical data and how VBScript can handle various sizes of data. You also got a taste of the vast function library that VBScript has for working with numbers and date/time values. You'll be using these functions throughout the book as you start checking, storing, and retrieving data for your users.

QUIZ YOURSELF

1. Create the code required to format the current date as follows: (See "Date and Time Functions"): `3 Nov 2000`

2. What is the difference between the Date and Now functions? (See "Date and Time Functions")

Which data type would be most appropriate for these values? (See "Numeric Data Types")

3. 542

4. 54.1

5. 50000

6. 13-Nov-2000

Decision Structures

Session Checklist

✔ Learn to use the If/Then/Else structure

✔ Learn to use Select/Case

**30 Min.
To Go**

Very few programs run from top to bottom without any logic along the way to "branch" or change the flow of the program. In this chapter, you're going to learn two structures that let you perform different actions based on values or conditions.

If/Then/Else Structure

If you have ever done any programming, you are probably very familiar with the If/Then/Else decision structure because it is one of the most common programming constructs used. Even if you are not a programmer, you are already familiar with the concept as it is used in language. For example, this sentence uses the If/Then/Else structure:

"If your car's gas tank is empty, you need to get gas. Otherwise, you do not have to stop at the gas station."

Three separate components make up these sentences:

- "If your car's gas tank is empty,"
- "You need to get gas."
- "Otherwise, you do not have to stop at the gas station."

The first clause is known as the *conditional expression*. If this condition is true, the second clause occurs. If the condition in the first clause is false, the third clause occurs. These three pieces of the statement correspond directly to the three keywords of the If/Then/Else construct. The conditional expression in the first clause follows the If keyword. The second clause follows the Then keyword. Finally, the third clause follows the Else keyword. If this sentence were formatted in a computer program, it would look like this:

```
If (Your car's gas tank is empty) Then
    You need to get gas
Else
    You do not have to stop at the gas station.
End If
```

This particular pair of sentences, since they show a condition and both results, converts easily to code. You'll get sick of If/Then structures by the end of the book, since you have to use them everywhere. If you don't use them, you end up with a program that runs from start to finish without any possibility for changes. Even batch programs, running on mainframes, have to use If/Then statements to handle the data being fed to them.

The basic syntax of the If/Then/Else construct is as follows:

```
If expression Then statement
```

In this case, the statement will be run if the expression is True. If the expression is False, nothing happens. You can also add an Else clause to this version, like so:

```
If expression Then statement1 Else statement2
```

If the expression is False, statement2 will run.

Using the End If statement

What if statement1 actually needs to be multiple statements? VBScript provides you with a way to format the If/Then/Else condition to enable multiple statements in a more readable format.

An example of the multiple-line format is as follows:

```
If A > B Then
   Response.Write "Variable A is greater."
   Response.Write "<BR>"
Else
   Response.Write "Variable B is greater."
   Response.Write "<BR>"
End If
```

In the preceding example, you see the addition of the End If statement. End If is used at the end of the final section of the If/Then/Else structure. If you are using the Else clause, End If follows the end of the Else code block. If the Else clause has been omitted, as in the following example, the End If statement follows the Then code block.

```
If A > B Then
   Response.Write "Variable A is greater."
   Response.Write "<BR>"
End If
```

Enhancing readability in If/Then/Else code

Notice that the code within the If/Then/Else block is indented in the preceding example. Typically, the code should be indented three or four spaces. The indents increase readability by showing which code is associated with which conditions. When you learn about nested If/Then/Else structures, you will see the need for this sort of formatting.

**20 Min.
To Go**

As you learned in the preceding chapter, logical expressions can be quite complex. Any valid logical expression can be used in the If/Then/Else statement, as in the following example that verifies a character is an uppercase letter:

```
Dim strCharacter
strCharacter = "E"
If Asc(strCharacter) >= Asc("A") _
   And Asc(strCharacter) <= Asc("Z") Then
   Response.Write "The letter is an uppercase letter."
Else
   Response.Write "The letter is not an uppercase letter."
End If
```

The continuation character, the underscore character (_), is used to split long lines into multiple small lines. The character can be in the same place as a space within a statement. Here's an example:

```
If Asc(strCharacter) >= Asc("A") [_]
    And Asc(strCharacter) <= Asc("Z") Then
```

In cases where you have long conditions or statements, the continuation character can make your code easier to read. This book uses the continuation character extensively since there isn't enough page width for long statements.

Nested If/Then/Else structures

Within an If/Then/Else structure, you can have other If/Then/Else structures. These structures are called *nested structures*. Here's an example that determines what you can do, based on your age:

```
Dim lngAge
If lngAge = 16 Then
    Response.Write "Get your drivers' license."
Else
    If lngAge = 18 Then
        Response.Write "Register to vote."
    Else
        If lngAge = 65 Then
            Response.Write "Time to retire!"
        Else
            Response.Write "There's nothing to do."
        End If
    End If
End If
```

Note the placement of the three End If statements. One follows the outside If/Then/Else construct at the very end of the sample. This End If closes the structure that began at the top of the sample. The second End If closes the structure within the Else clause of the first If/Then/Else structure. Formatting your code consistently makes reading the code much easier.

Even in this simple example, quickly finding the decision blocks is difficult. As your code becomes more complex, reading code formatted in this manner will become impossible.

Using the ElseIf keyword

The preceding example brings up a good question: What happens when the nesting goes too deep? The following example illustrates this question:

```
If condition Then
    If condition2 Then
        If condition3 Then
```

In some cases, using the ElseIf keyword can help you "flatten" this complex structure. If you are using mutually exclusive possibilities, as in the example that checked a character against several ranges, you can use ElseIf to create a much simpler structure. The structure in the preceding example changes as follows when you add the ElseIf keyword:

```
Dim lngAge
If lngAge = 16 Then
    Response.Write "Get your drivers' license."
ElseIf lngAge = 18 Then
    Response.Write "Register to vote."
ElseIf lngAge = 65 Then
    Response.Write "Time to retire!"
Else
    Response.Write "There's nothing to do."
End If
```

This type of structure is similar to a series of filters designed to trap smaller and smaller particles. The first If clause traps certain cases, the ElseIf clause traps others that didn't match the first, and so on. Finally, cases that didn't match any of the first conditions are handled by the final Else clause. In this example, the code traps letters and numbers. All other cases are handled by the final condition.

**10 Min.
To Go**

Select/Case Structure

In cases where you have a number of items that you want to match a variable against, you can write your code as an If/Then/Else or an If/ElseIf/Else structure. However, if you are performing the same action for more than one possible value, you end up with a lot of duplicated code. To eliminate the duplication, the Select/Case structure enables you to create a list of values to test against and perform various actions based on the results. An example of Select/Case structure follows:

```
Dim strValue
strValue = "B"
Select Case strValue
    Case "A":
    Response.Write "Letter is A"
    Case "B", "C":
    Response.Write "Letter is B or C"
    Case Else:
    Response.Write "I don't know what letter it is"
End Select
```

The equivalent code, using If/ElseIf/Else statements, is as follows:

```
Dim strValue
strValue = "B"

If strValue = "A" Then
    Response.Write "Letter is A"
ElseIf strValue = "B" Or strValue = "C" Then
    Response.Write "Letter is B or C"
Else
    Response.Write "I don't know what letter it is"
End If
```

In the previous section, you saw this code example:

```
Dim lngAge
If lngAge = 16 Then
    Response.Write "Get your drivers' license."
ElseIf lngAge = 18 Then
    Response.Write "Register to vote."
ElseIf lngAge = 65 Then
    Response.Write "Time to retire!"
Else
    Response.Write "There's nothing to do."
End If
```

Here's what it would look like with the Select/Case statement:

```
Dim lngAge
Select Case lngAge
    Case 16
        Response.Write "Get your drivers' license."

    Case 18
        Response.Write "Register to vote."

    Case 65
        Response.Write "Time to retire!"

    Case Else
        Response.Write "There's nothing to do."
End Select
```

The best part about the Select/Case structure is that you can easily add more cases to the check without having to enter lots of extra code. If you wanted to include something at age 25, such as the ability to rent a car, the change would be minimal:

```
Dim lngAge
Select Case lngAge
    Case 16
        Response.Write "Get your drivers' license."

    Case 18
        Response.Write "Register to vote."

    Case 25
        Response.Write "You can rent a car."

    Case 65
        Response.Write "Time to retire!"

    Case Else
        Response.Write "There's nothing to do."

End Select
```

Again, this structure eliminates the need to repeat the condition check for every single If/Then statement, which helps eliminate possible sources of errors. It's also much easier to see what values you're checking, in this case.

For short lists, you can use either structure. However, in cases where you are testing for multiple items to perform the same action (as in the preceding example for B or C), the Select/Case structure is much easier to use and change later. You can separate each of the items in the acceptable list with commas (as in the first example), and any matching value causes the statements below it to be executed. You can add items to any of the Case statements more easily than you can add additional ElseIf clauses to an already large If/ElseIf block.

Using the Case Else keyword

In cases where you are evaluating a user's input, you should assume that the user may type invalid characters. The Case Else keyword enables you to have a generic case that catches all values not handled in a previous case. Note that only one Case can be matched for any given value. In the following example, the first Case is matched and "Letter is A or B" is printed on screen. This event occurs even though the letter *B* can be matched by either of the first two Case statements.

```
Dim strValue
strValue = "B"

Select Case strValue
    Case "A", "B":
    Response.Write "Letter is A or B"
    Case "B", "C":
    Response.Write "Letter is B or C"
    Case Else:
    Response.Write "I don't know what letter it is"
End Select
```

You can use the Select/Case structure to match any valid values, not just string values.

Performing blank actions

In cases where you do not want to perform any statements when a value is matched, you can leave the statement section blank, as in the following example. If the letter is *A*, no action is taken. You should use this method when you're checking a large number of values. In these cases, you can add a blank action for the sake of completeness to show that you did consider the value but that no action was required.

```
Dim strValue
strValue = "B"

Select Case strValue
    Case "A":
    ' No action is required
    Case "B", "C":
    Response.Write "Letter is B or C"
    Case Else:
    Response.Write "I don't know what letter it is"
End Select
```

In cases where you use a placeholder, you should use a comment to explain your actions to anyone who might use your code later. Otherwise, users may think that you introduced an error into your code.

Done!

REVIEW

Decision structures help your program respond to user input. They allow the program to branch and perform different operations, based on input data or changes in conditions that occur when your ASP application is running. The If/Then statement enables you to make simple decisions as to what to do, based on values or conditions. The Select/Case statement enables you to select from a number of possible values and perform a different action for each. You'll be seeing lots of both of these structures as we continue through the book.

QUIZ YOURSELF

1. How can you match multiple values with a single Case in a Select/Case statement? (See "Select/Case Structure")

2. Rewrite the following code to use one less "End If" statement: (See "If/Then/Else Structure")

```
If x = 5 Then
    Response.Write "x = 5"
Else
    If x = 6 Then
        Response.Write "x = 6"
    Else
        Response.Write "x is not 5 or 6"
    End If
End If
```

3. What does Case Else mean? (See "Select/Case Structure")

4. Which character can be used to break a long line into multiple smaller lines? (See "If/Then/Else Structure")

Looping Structures

Session Checklist

✔ Learn the For/Next statement

✔ Learn the Do/Loop statement

✔ Learn to use Boolean math to reverse conditions

✔ Learn the While/Wend statement

✔ Learn the For Each/Next statement

**30 Min.
To Go**

One of the ideal tasks for a computer is to perform repetitive tasks. In this chapter, you'll learn the structures available in VBScript to repeat blocks of code. The structures you learn can handle cases in which you have a definite end point or a conditional end point. You'll be using a mix of these structures throughout the rest of the book.

Simple Looping with For/Next

One of the things you can rely on the computer to do well is to perform tasks over and over again. In cases in which you have a fixed starting and end point, such as when you're looping through an array, you can use the For/Next statement. This statement has some additional options for looping that you'll learn about in this section.

Here's the basic structure of the statement:

```
For variable = startvalue To endvalue
    <statements that should be repeated>
Next
```

Everything between the For and Next lines will be repeated as long as *intLoopiable*, which takes the values between *startvalue* and *endvalue*, until startvariable is equal to endvalue. The *variable* is incremented by 1 each time it gets to the Next statement. Once *variable* is equal to *endvalue* and hits the Next statement, it exits the loop. Here's an example:

```
Dim intLoop
For intLoop = 1 To 8
    Response.Write intLoop & "<BR>"
Next
```

The starting and ending values have to evaluate to be numbers, but they can be constants, variables, or expressions that are valid in VBScript. Here's an example that loops through all the uppercase letters in the alphabet and prints the letters out to the screen:

```
Dim intCharValue
For intCharValue = Asc("A") To Asc("Z")
    Response.Write.Write Chr(intCharValue) & "<BR>"
Next
```

The values for the loop's endpoints are generated through the use of the Asc function, which returns the ASCII value of the character provided. The Chr function accepts an ASCII value and prints out the corresponding character.

The For/Next structure enables you to use negative numbers as starting or ending values, as in the following example:

```
Dim intLoop
For intLoop = -5 To 5
    Response.Write intLoop & "<BR>"
Next
```

You can also use non-integers as your loop endpoints, as shown here:

```
Dim dblLoop
For dblLoop = 5.4 To 12.6
```

```
    Response.Write dblLoop & "<BR>"
Next
```

In this case, the results of the code will be:

```
5.4
6.4
7.4
8.4
9.4
10.4
11.4
12.4
```

Since 13.4 is bigger than the ending value, you will never actually see 12.6 printed as output. Generally, when you're using a For/Next statement, you'll be using integers, but this feature is available if you need it.

Using the Step keyword

In cases where you need to increment by a value other than 1, you can use the Step keyword to indicate how much to add to the counter each time. In this example, the loop will count from 0 to 30, by threes:

```
Dim intLoop
For intLoop = 0 To 30 Step 3
    Response.Write intLoop & "<BR>"
Next
```

You can also make a Step value negative to make the loop iterate backwards. To step backwards by one, for example, you would use a step value of –1. If you do this, you need to make sure that you reverse the order of the start and end values for the loop. If you accidentally did what is shown in this next example, you would get no results at all:

```
Dim intLoop
For intLoop = 0 To 30 Step -3
    Response.Write intLoop & "<BR>"
Next
```

The For loop keeps iterating as long as the counter variable is less or equal to the ending value given in the loop. In the preceding example, the value 30 is the last value printed because the next value in the sequence, 33, is greater than 30.

You don't have to end exactly on the ending value. For instance, in this example, the counter is never given the value 21, but will be given 22. Because 22 is greater than 21, the loop will terminate when it passes the ending value.

```
Dim intLoop
For intLoop = 0 To 21 Step 2
    Response.Write intLoop & "<BR>"
Next
```

Exiting For/Next loops prematurely

In certain cases, you may need to exit the For/Next loop before reaching the ending value. In these cases, you can use the Exit For statement to exit the loop and continue at the first line following the Next keyword. Although exiting a loop this way is considered by some to be poor programming style, it often simplifies the logic for the reader of your code. In the following example, the For loop exits when it matches the first letter of the string held in the strVar variable:

```
Dim intLoop
Dim strVar
strVar = "Components"

For intLoop = Asc("A") to Asc("Z")

    <statements>

    If Left(strVar, 1) = Chr(intLoop) Then Exit For

    <statements>
Next
```

Nested loops

For/Next structures, like all other programming structures, can be nested. For instance, to generate a grid, you can create code like the following:

```
Dim intX, intY

For intX = Asc("A") to Asc("Z")
    For intY = 1 to 10
        Response.Write Chr(intX) & intY & Space(1)
```

```
    Next  ' intY
    Response.Write "<BR>"
Next  ' intX
```

A few things about this example are worth mentioning. For each time that the outer loop is executed, the inner loop is completely executed: that is, it iterates through all the values from 1 through 10 before the next iteration of the outer loop. The resulting output appears as follows:

```
A1 A2 A3 A4 A5 A6 A7 A8 A9 A10

B1 B2 B3 B4 B5 B6 B7 B8 B9 B10

C1 C2 C3 C4 C5 C6 C7 C8 C9 C10

D1 D2 D3 D4 D5 D6 D7 D8 D9 D10

E1 E2 E3 E4 E5 E6 E7 E8 E9 E10

F1 F2 F3 F4 F5 F6 F7 F8 F9 F10

G1 G2 G3 G4 G5 G6 G7 G8 G9 G10

H1 H2 H3 H4 H5 H6 H7 H8 H9 H10

I1 I2 I3 I4 I5 I6 I7 I8 I9 I10

J1 J2 J3 J4 J5 J6 J7 J8 J9 J10
```

To move to a new line after the inner loop finishes executing, the first line outside of the inner loop generates a line break. Because the Response.Write function prints characters without any formatting, insert the <BR> tag and force a line break at the end of each logical row.

In nested loops, you can become confused about which Next keyword matches a given For keyword. In Visual Basic, you have to specify the variable name when you use the Next keyword. However, VBScript doesn't allow that, so I always add the variable name in a comment following the Next keyword. That helps me keep things straight in complex loops.

Using the Do/Loop Structure

As I mentioned in the preceding section, every For/Next loop can be written as a Do/Loop structure. However, the Do/Loop structure offers more possibilities than the For/Next loop. For instance, you can exit the loop based on a logical condition instead of just when the counter reaches an ending value that you previously specified. In the following example, which emulates the behavior of the For/Next structure, the loop iterates as long as the loop variable is less than a given value:

```
Dim intLoop
intLoop = 1
Do
    <statements>
    intLoop = intLoop + 1
Loop While intLoop <= 5
```

Just as the For/Next loop initializes the counter variable to the starting value, the value of intLoop is set to the starting value before entering the loop. In this case, the programmer has to write the initialization statement to set intLoop to 1. At some point within the loop, intLoop increments. Finally, at the end of the loop, the counter is checked by the While condition to determine whether the loop should continue.

You can also write a Do/Loop structure using the Until keyword. The Until keyword essentially reverses the logic in the condition. For example, you can rewrite the preceding example using the Until keyword:

```
Dim intLoop
intLoop = 1
Do
    <statements>
    intLoop = intLoop + 1
Loop Until intLoop > 5
```

Using this keyword is similar to reversing the logic when you have a complex If/Then/Else condition. As I mentioned before, your syntax is clearer when you use fewer symbols and keywords. Using a simpler condition makes the code easier to understand and easier to debug.

Reversing operators

In several examples, you needed to reverse the logic of a condition. All logical operators can be reversed. Table 13-1 contains several examples of reversing operators.

Table 13-1
Converting Logical Expressions

Original Condition	Converted Condition
If X < 5	If Not(X >= 5)
If X = 5	If Not(X <> 5)
If X > 5	If Not(X <= 5)
If X >= 5	If Not(X < 5)
If X <= 5	If Not(X > 5)
If X <> 5	If Not(X = 5)

In general, I prefer to keep my conditions as simple as possible. This means that I remove any double negatives and try to use as few symbols as possible in my conditions. It makes them easier to read — both for me and for the other programmers who maintain code I've written.

In these conversions, the original logic stays the same, but the condition can be used with a different keyword. If, for example, you want to change a While condition to an Until condition, you first follow the rules given previously. Then, because the Until keyword uses the opposite condition from the While keyword, you use the reversed condition without the Not keyword. Look at the following steps to see how a condition can be reversed:

1. The original code statement is as follows:

```
Do
    <statements>
    intLoop = intLoop + 1
Loop While intLoop <= 5
```

2. You can reverse the condition by using the information in Table 13-1. The condition now becomes the following:

```
Loop While Not(intLoop > 5)
```

3. Finally, you replace the `While Not` keywords with Until, as follows:

```
Loop Until intLoop > 5
```

Following these rules, you can reverse any condition to make it easier to read. In cases where you have a compound condition that uses the And or Or keywords, the conversion is slightly more difficult. However, you still follow the same steps. Look at these examples to see how to convert the keywords:

```
Do While (Asc(strVar) >= Asc("A")) _
    And (Asc(strVar) <= Asc("Z"))
```

To reverse this condition, follow these steps:

1. Change the And keyword to Or, or vice versa, as follows:

```
(Asc(strVar) >= Asc("A")) Or (Asc(strVar) <= Asc("Z"))
```

2. Reverse the conditions on either side of the And/Or operator, as follows:

```
Not(Asc(strVar) >= Asc("A")) Or Not(Asc(strVar) <= Asc("Z"))
```

3. Using the rules about reversing operators, simplify the condition. Each Not operator reverses the conditions on either side of the Or keyword. After the simplification has happened, the condition becomes the following:

```
(Asc(strVar) < Asc("A")) Or (Asc(strVar) > Asc("Z"))
```

At this point, you can use this condition in the Do Until clause, as follows:

```
Do Until (Asc(strVar) < Asc("A")) _
    Or (Asc(strVar) > Asc("Z"))
```

If you look at this condition logically, it still uses the same logic. The loop should continue until the ASCII value of `strVar` is outside the range bounded by the letters *A* and *Z*. In the unreversed condition, the character has to be between the letters. In the reversed condition, the letter has to be outside the range. Either way, the same effect is achieved.

The previous examples are designed to give you some good methods for converting and simplifying your logic. Boolean logic involves many other complex rules for converting expressions, but this is probably the main rule you'll need to use.

Exiting the loop

When the condition is checked at the end, use the Do/Loop structure so that the program enters the loop immediately without checking any condition first. Checking the condition at the end of the loop guarantees that the statements within the Do/Loop structure will be executed at least once. However, sometimes you will have statements that should not be executed at all. In these cases, you can reposition the logical expression following the Loop keyword to follow the Do keyword. Because the script checks the exit condition where the Until statement is located, the entire block of statements can be skipped when dictated by conditions in the program. In the following example, the preceding structure has been rewritten with the alternative method just described:

```
Dim intLoop
intLoop = 1
Do Until intLoop > 5
    <statements>
    intLoop = intLoop + 1
Loop
```

If intLoop is initially set to 6, the statements within the Do/Loop structure do not execute. The exit condition is met when the program flow reaches the Do Until statement. You can write this example by using the While keyword in place of the Until keyword. Again, when you make the replacement, you have to reverse the logic of the exit condition, as in the following example:

```
Dim intLoop
intLoop = 1
Do While intLoop <= 5
    <statements>
    intLoop = intLoop + 1
Loop
```

The previous two examples are programmatically identical. They both stop iterating when the counter reaches 6.

Nesting the Do/Loop structure

As with all the other looping structures, the Do/Loop structure can be nested. In the following example, the For/Next example has been rewritten to use two Do Until loops instead of the For/Next loops that were used before:

```
Dim xVar, yVar

xVar = Asc("A")
Do Until xVar > Asc("Z")
   yVar = 1
   Do Until yVar > 10
      Response.Write Chr(xVar) & yVar & Space(1)
      yVar = yVar + 1
   Loop ' yVar loop
   Response.Write "<BR>"
   xVar = xVar + 1
Loop ' xVar loop
```

The Loop keywords are commented to indicate which loop they match. The statements within each loop are also indented so that you can tell which loop they belong to. If you do not indent and comment this code, it will look something like this:

```
Dim xVar, yVar

xVar = Asc("A")
Do Until xVar > Asc("Z")
yVar = 1
Do Until yVar > 10
Response.Write Chr(xVar) & yVar & Space(1)
yVar = yVar + 1
Loop
Response.Write "<BR>"
xVar = xVar + 1
Loop
```

As you can see, you need several more lines to perform the same functions that the For/Next structure performs automatically. You have to manually initialize your counters to their starting values, manually increment them, and manually reset them (for the inner loop) each time you want to use them again.

Exiting the Do/Loop prematurely

Finally, as with the For/Next statement, there will be some cases where it is easier to exit the loop when a condition is met. For instance, you may be using a For loop and have multiple exit conditions. If one of the optional exit conditions is met, you can use Exit For to exit immediately instead of waiting until the end of the loop. In these cases, you can use the Exit Do statement to exit the current Do/Loop structure. The Exit Do statement exits the current loop. If you have nested loops, you must use one Exit Do statement for each Do/Loop structure you have to exit.

Using the While/Wend Structure

10 Min. To Go

The final looping structure supported by Visual Basic is the While/Wend structure. This structure is identical to the Do While *<condition>*/Loop structure variation. Wend stands for End While and takes the place of the Loop keyword in the previous examples. The following example uses the Do While keywords:

```
Dim intLoop
intLoop = 1
Do While intLoop <= 5
    <statements>
    intLoop = intLoop + 1
Loop
```

You can rewrite the preceding example using the While/Wend structure, as follows:

```
Dim intLoop
intLoop = 1
While intLoop <= 5
    <statements>
    intLoop = intLoop + 1
Wend
```

Done!

Unlike the Do/Loop structure, the While/Wend structure does not have an Exit keyword that enables you immediately to exit the currently iterating loop. For this and several other reasons, you should use the Do/Loop structure instead of the While/Wend structure. The While/Wend structure is included primarily for compatibility and consistency with Visual Basic.

REVIEW

In this chapter, you learned about the looping structures provided in VBScript. These structures are easy to learn and you'll use them in nearly every application you'll ever write. The trick is to use the right one for the job. The For/Next structure is great when you know the starting and ending points, and the Do/Loop (or While/Wend) structure is good when you have an exit condition. You also learned how to reverse conditions to simplify your code. This is an important skill overlooked by many programmers. Remember that you probably won't be the only person to maintain your code, so be kind to your fellow programmers when you write complex code — keep it simple.

QUIZ YOURSELF

Reverse the following conditions: (See "Reversing Conditions")

1. X < 5

2. X >= 10

3. X > 5 And X < 10

4. Not (X > 10)

5. Rewrite the following loop using a Do Loop instead of a For/Next Loop: (See "Using the Do Loop Structure")

```
Dim i
For i = 10 To 20 Step 4
    Response.Write i & "<br>"
Next    ' I
```

Subroutines and Functions

Session Checklist

✔ Learn how to create your own subroutines

✔ Learn the differences between subroutines and functions

✔ Learn how to create your own functions

**30 Min.
To Go**

A key component of modular programming is the ability to break up code into manageable, reusable portions. A block of code that is much more than a few screenfuls is too long, since you have to scroll too often. In this chapter, you learn how to create subroutines and functions that let you write code that's easier to maintain and expand.

Creating Subroutines

So far, the code you've written has been pretty simple. However, as your programs get longer, you'll find that you can't just put all the code in one big chunk. In addition, there are cases in which you'll have to reuse the same code several times throughout the program. There are also cases in which you'll want to break your code up into manageable chunks to make it easier to understand and document.

In these cases, you can use a coding structure called a *subroutine*. This structure allows you to create a self-contained block of code that you can reuse throughout your application. In the next chapter you'll learn how to use subroutines to structure your code more cleanly.

Creating a simple subroutine

Creating a subroutine is straightforward. Here's an example of a simple subroutine:

```
Sub DoSomething()
    Response.Write "Here's a message."
End Sub
```

The Sub and End Sub keywords mark the beginning and end of the subroutine. The name of the subroutine immediately follows the Sub keyword. The parentheses at the end of the subroutine name surround parameters being passed into the subroutine. In this case you don't have any parameters, so you follow the name with a left and right parenthesis.

Any statements between Sub and End Sub are executed when the subroutine is called, which can be done in two different ways:

```
DoSomething
```

or

```
Call DoSomething
```

You can use either of these two methods to call the subroutine; it's all personal preference. If I'm calling a subroutine with no parameters I'll often use the Call keyword, just to make the call stand out a little bit more.

Adding parameters

You can also design your subroutine to accept parameters. Parameters, once declared in a subroutine, operate just like other variables you declare in the subroutine, which means that you should not re-declare them as regular variables. Here's the previous example using a parameter:

```
Sub DoSomething(strMessage)
    Response.Write strMessage
End Sub
```

In this case, the routine is designed to print out the message being passed into the subroutine. Here's how you would call this message:

```
DoSomething "This is a message."
```

or

```
Call DoSomething("This is a message.")
```

Note that if you're not using the Call keyword, the parameters are listed following the subroutine name. If you use the Call keyword, the parameters need to be within parentheses following the subroutine name.

If you have more than one parameter, you specify them in the parentheses, separated by commas. Here's an example:

```
Sub DoSomething(strMessage, strMessage2)
    Response.Write strMessage
    Response.Write strMessage2
End Sub
```

You call this routine with the parameters separated by commas, as well. Here's an example:

```
DoSomething "This is a message.", "This is another message."
```

or

```
Call DoSomething("This is a message.", "This is another message.")
```

Variable scope

**20 Min.
To Go**

You can declare variables within subroutines just as you can anywhere else in your ASP applications. These variables are only available within the subroutine where they are declared and once the subroutine exits, the variables are destroyed and any data in them is lost. Here's an example that also can cause some confusion:

```
<%
Sub ModifyValue()
    Dim intValue    ' As Integer
    intValue = 5
    Response.Write "Inside subroutine, intValue = " _
        & intValue & "<br>"
End Sub
Dim intValue
```

```
intValue = 3
Response.Write "Outside subroutine, intValue = " _
    & intValue & "<br>"
ModifyValue
Response.Write "After subroutine, intValue = " _
    & intValue & "<br>"

%>
```

In this example, you create a subroutine called ModifyValue that has a variable declared in it called intValue. You assign a value to the variable and then print it. However, this subroutine won't run until it is called. The code outside the subroutine will run first. In this code, another variable called intValue is declared and assigned the value 5. You print the value of the variable before and after the call to ModifyValue, and here are the results:

```
Outside subroutine, intValue = 3
Inside subroutine, intValue = 5
After subroutine, intValue = 3
```

VBScript is able to distinguish between two variables at different levels of the application, even if they have the same name. The variable within the subroutine overrides the variable declared outside the subroutine. Changing the local variable to a new value doesn't affect the one outside the subroutine.

Here's a variation of the previous example:

```
<%
Sub ModifyValue()
    intValue = 5
    Response.Write "Inside subroutine, intValue = " _
        & intValue & "<br>"
End Sub

Dim intValue
intValue = 3
Response.Write "Outside subroutine, intValue = " _
    & intValue & "<br>"
ModifyValue
Response.Write "After subroutine, intValue = " _
    & intValue & "<br>"
%>
```

In this case you haven't declared a new variable within the subroutine, so the subroutine will use the variable declared outside the subroutine. When you run this version, the results are a bit different from the previous example:

```
Outside subroutine, intValue = 3
Inside subroutine, intValue = 5
After subroutine, intValue = 5
```

In this case, the subroutine is actually modifying the value stored in the intValue variable. For this particular example, intValue is considered to be a page-level or global variable, since it is declared outside of any subroutine.

Parameter usage

You've already seen how to call a subroutine with parameters. Subroutine parameters have some interesting behaviors that you haven't seen yet. When you learn about functions in the next section, you'll learn that a function is designed to return a single value when it is complete. A subroutine, on the other hand, doesn't return a value, but it does have the ability to modify parameter values that are sent in. Here's an example:

```
<%

Sub ModifyValue(intInput)
    intInput = 5
    Response.Write "Inside subroutine, intInput = " _
        & intInput & "<br>"
End Sub

Dim intValue
intValue = 3
Response.Write "Outside subroutine, intValue = " _
    & intValue & "<br>"
ModifyValue intValue
Response.Write "After subroutine, intValue = " _
    & intValue & "<br>"

%>
```

This version is basically the same as the previous example, except for the fact that the ModifyValue subroutine now accepts a parameter, and sets that parameter's value to 5. Again, you print out the value in all the same places as before. When this code runs, here are the results:

```
Outside subroutine, intValue = 3
Inside subroutine, intInput = 5
After subroutine, intValue = 5
```

Changing the value of the parameter within the subroutine changes the source variable as well. This is called *passing by reference*, and it is the default behavior. In many cases you won't need to or want to change the values passed into your subroutines. In these cases, you need to pass your variables by value. To do this, use the ByVal keyword when you list the parameters in the subroutine declaration, as shown here:

```
Sub ModifyValue(ByVal intInput)
    intInput = 5
    Response.Write "Inside subroutine, intInput = " _
        & intInput & "<br>"
End Sub
```

If you make this minor change in the previous example, the results are a bit different:

```
Outside subroutine, intValue = 3
Inside subroutine, intInput = 5
After subroutine, intValue = 3
```

If the parameter is passed by value, you can change it all you want and it won't affect the original value. To pass a parameter by reference you don't have to put a keyword in front of it, but if you want to, you can add the ByRef keyword to explicitly specify that the variable is being passed by reference.

10 Min. To Go

Creating Functions

Subroutines are designed to perform a task and exit. You call them just as you call other statements, and in certain cases you pass data to them. However, subroutines can't be used within expressions and calculations. For this, you need a *function*. A function is designed to accept input parameters and return a value. It does give you the option of changing the parameter values, just as a subroutine does.

Here's a simple function that does a math calculation:

```
Function CubeValue(intInput)
```

```
    CubeValue = intInput ^ 3
End Function

Response.Write CubeValue(10)
```

The result of this function is 10 cubed, which is 1000. The function begins with the Function keyword and ends with End Function. A common mistake I make is to start writing a subroutine, switch it to a function, and forget to change End Sub to End Function. VBScript normally catches this error pretty easily.

Any parameters to the function are listed within parentheses after the name of the function, just as with a subroutine. In Visual Basic you would also need to specify the return type of the function with an As statement following the function parameters. In VBScript you don't do that because the keyword following the As keyword is a data type, which VBScript doesn't have.

Once you're into the function, you do the calculation and set the result equal to the name of the function. This has the result of returning the value to the caller. In this case, the result is immediately dumped into the Response.Write statement and out to the page.

Functions aren't used just for numerical calculations. Look at the function shown here:

```
Function CleanString(strInput)
    CleanString = Replace(strInput, "'", "''")
End Function
```

This function takes a string as input and searches for the single-quote characters. Each single-quote character is replaced with two single quotes, and the resulting string is returned to the caller. You'll use this function when you start working with databases, since single quotes in data can cause your database actions to work improperly.

Done!

Functions are always called as part of an expression or as an assignment to a variable. You don't have the additional options with functions that you do with subroutines. If you have a function that doesn't return a value, it should really be a subroutine.

REVIEW

In this chapter, you learned the difference between subroutines and functions. Subroutines and functions can both accept and modify parameters, but only a function can return a value and be used in an expression or calculation. You also got a preview of some of the subroutines and functions you'll be using through the rest of the book.

QUIZ YOURSELF

1. What keyword is used to specify a parameter to be passed by reference? (See "Parameter Usage")

2. How do you specify that a subroutine or function is to accept parameters? (See "Parameter Usage")

3. What is the key difference between a subroutine and a function? (See "Creating Functions")

4. What are two ways that you can call a subroutine? (See "Creating Subroutines")

Creating Structured Code

Session Checklist

✔ Create modular and reusable code with subroutines and functions

✔ Learn good coding practices for use with ASP

✔ Share code with server-side include files

✔ Combine multiple files into a single file

**30 Min.
To Go**

One of the key points in any computer programming class is how to write modular and reliable code. Since most ASP developers started out just writing HTML, this point has been lost over the years. However, writing good ASP code using modular programming is important to do and is a topic that is omitted by most texts. This chapter will show you how to write reusable modular code that will make your applications easier to read, maintain, and expand.

Creating Modular Code

One of the first topics covered in most programming courses is the benefit of modular code and what is known as *black box programming*. In black box programming, each function is treated as an independent block with input and output, but the details of how the function is handled is hidden from the caller. This is also known as modular programming, since you break your code into independent blocks of code. The main benefit of this is that you can change the inner workings of the "box" without affecting any other code, as long as the input and output parameter lists stay the same. You'll learn later in this chapter how to create a common file that can be included in multiple applications so that other developers don't have to repeat the same code in lots of different places.

The first way to create a common file is to put all of your code into subroutines within your ASP files. While this might seem unnecessary for a simple page, it's important to get into the habit of always putting your code in modular form. It makes it easier when you decide to add more functions or combine multiple functions into your files. If everything is already modularized, it's much easier to put the blocks together.

Listing 15-1 shows a typical example of a login form that doesn't use modular programming. This particular file just shows the input form.

Listing 15-1
A typical data-entry form

```
<html>
<head>
   <title>System Login</title>
</head>
<body>
<h1>System Login</h1>
<form action="ch15_listing2.asp" method=post>
<table>
   <tr>
      <td>User ID:</td>
      <td><input type=text name=txtUserID size=20></td>
   </tr>
   <tr>
      <td>Password:</td>
      <td><input type=password name=txtPassword size=20></td>
   </tr>
   <tr>
      <td colspan=2 align=center>
         <input type=submit name=cmdSubmit value=Login>
      </td>
   </tr>
```

```
</table>
</form>
</body>
</html>
```

 You might have noticed that I didn't use a lot of double quote characters in the HTML around each value for every attribute. HTML will function fairly well without double quote characters, as long as the attribute value has no spaces or other special characters in it. However, you should be aware that some older browsers may not interpret the HTML correctly without the double quote characters.

In this particular form, the data will be sent to a second page called ch15_listing2.asp, which is shown in Listing 15-2.

Listing 15-2
Login form handling code

```
<%
If Request("txtUserID") = "USER" _
    And Request("txtPassword") = "PASSWORD" Then
        Response.Write "Login successful."
Else
    Response.Write "ERROR: Invalid user ID/password."
End If
%>
```

This is how many ASP developers build their pages, and it works fine. However, you have the basic problem of having to manage two files for a single function. This problem gets worse when you need the typical functions available for any given data type:

- Create and Save New Record
- Update and Save Changes
- Confirm Delete and Delete Record
- Retrieve Record Details

Without a better method in place, this one entity requires seven different files to handle all the code. Multiply this by the number of data types in your system, and suddenly you have an ugly mess on your hands.

This particular dialog and back-end processor converts nicely to the modular approach. The rest of the section will show you what to do to convert the code.

Create a new file

The first thing to do is to create a blank file, into which you'll put the converted code. This way you still have the originals to refer to. The beginnings of this file should always include the ASP delimiters and the Option Explicit directive, which forces you to declare any variables you want to use. Here's what you should start with:

```
<%
Option Explicit

%>
```

Create logical functions in the new file

The next step is to determine what the logical functions are for this part of the application. For a login dialog, you have two basic functions:

- Show the form and accept data
- Validate the data and send the user to the next page

With these conditions identified, you create two subroutines in the new file that will start as empty but will eventually contain code. Here's what you should create next:

```
<%
Option Explicit

Sub ShowForm

End Sub


Sub Validate

End Sub
%>
```

You can call the subroutines whatever you like, but make sure you don't use any VBScript or ASP keywords when you create the names.

Copy code into subroutines

You now have to take the code from the first file, called ch15_listing1.html, and put it into the ShowForm routine. Since ch15_listing1.html is all HTML, you have to add some additional ASP delimiters to the file you're building. You should also add the code from the second file, ch15_listing2.asp, into the Validate routine. Here's what you'll have when you're done with this step:

```
<%
Option Explicit

Sub ShowForm
%>
<html>
<head>
    <title>System Login</title>
</head>
<body>
<h1>System Login</h1>
<form action="ch15_listing2.asp" method=post>
<table>
    <tr>
        <td>User ID:</td>
        <td><input type=text name=txtUserID size=20></td>
    </tr>
    <tr>
        <td>Password:</td>
        <td><input type=password name=txtPassword size=20></td>
    </tr>
    <tr>
        <td colspan=2 align=center>
            <input type=submit name=cmdSubmit value=Login>
        </td>
    </tr>
</table>
</form>
</body>
```

```
</html>
<%
End Sub


Sub Validate
   If Request("txtUserID") = "USER" _
      And Request("txtPassword") = "PASSWORD" Then
      Response.Write "Login successful."
   Else
      Response.Write "ERROR: Invalid user ID/password."
   End If
End Sub
%>
```

You should note the placement of the ASP delimiter tags within the ShowForm subroutine. Since you are embedding a block of HTML, you have to "close" the ASP code first. Once you're done with the HTML, you "open" the ASP code again and continue.

Since the HTML is between the Sub and End Sub keywords, the HTML won't be displayed until the subroutine is called. If you want to test this, you can save your file with an ASP extension and run it. Since all the code (other than Option Explicit) is within one subroutine or the other, nothing happens. The page loads and runs, but there is no code to call the subroutines.

Build the dispatcher

Every major railroad in the country is controlled from a central location by a dispatcher. The dispatcher is responsible for making sure that trains go where they are supposed to when they are supposed to. You're going to be building a dispatcher for this file. The dispatcher is responsible for determining which of this file's two functions should run:

- Show the form and accept data, or
- Validate the data and send the user to the next page

You have to make several changes to the file in order to make the dispatcher code work properly. The first is to change what the form's ACTION parameter is. Since this one file is going to do the work of two, you don't need to reference ch15_listing2.asp any longer. This particular file, when completed, is going to be called ch15_listing3.asp, so you can use that name instead. However, there's a better way to do this. Since the file will always refer to itself, regardless of the name that you give it, you can use a server variable to determine the name of the file. Change this line:

```
<form action="ch15_listing2.asp" method=post>
```

to this:

```
<form action="<% = Request("SCRIPT_NAME") %>" method=post>
```

The SCRIPT_NAME value appears in the ServerVariables collection of the Request object. Since the Request object automatically searches all the Request object's collections when no collection name is specifically used, this code will find the SCRIPT_NAME in the ServerVariables collection automatically.

Making this change will cause the form to submit its data to "itself," since both functions are now in the same file. However, there is a way to determine if the page is being asked to show the form or process the data. To do this, create a flag that the dispatcher will look for. If the flag is present, the dispatcher will assume that the form data is being submitted. If the flag is missing, it will assume that the page is being loaded for the first time. Here's what you should change the FORM tag to:

```
<form action="<% = Request("SCRIPT_NAME") %>?a=v" method=post>
```

Adding the ?a=v following the script name will cause it to be added to the end of the URL. If this file is named ch15_listing3.asp and in the /web directory, the whole URL will look like this:

```
/web/ch15_listing3.asp?a=v
```

When you're building a URL, the question mark separates the name of the file from any parameters that you add. These parameters are in the following form:

```
name=value
```

If you need additional parameters, separate each pair with an ampersand (&), as shown here:

```
name=value&name2=value2&name3=value3
```

For this example, I chose to use a name of a and a value of v. Why these values? It doesn't really matter what you choose. In this case, I chose a for "action," and v for "validate." You don't have to use these choices, but you'll see them throughout the book.

Having created the tag, you can easily write the dispatcher routine at the top of the file. Add the code following the Option Explicit statement and before the ShowForm subroutine declaration, as shown here:

```
<%
Option Explicit

Call Main

Sub Main
    If Request("a") = "v" Then
        Validate
    Else
        ShowForm
    End If
End Sub

Sub ShowForm
%>
... code continues here ...
```

At this point, other than Option Explicit, only one line of code is outside a subroutine: Call Main. This is a call to the new Main subroutine that serves as the dispatcher for the page. Main is not a special name, but in many languages (including Visual Basic and C) it is a special subroutine marking the beginning of an application. The statement Call Main doesn't have to be written using the Call keyword — the Call keyword is optional.

The code inside the Main subroutine looks at the value of the action (value: a) parameter coming in through the Request object. The parameter will actually be in the QueryString, but just searching the Request object will find it. In addition, if at some point you decide to put the flag within the form as a hidden input field, you won't have to change this code.

As we discussed earlier, you either see the flag or display the form. That's exactly what this form does. When you run the page for the first time, there won't be a value for the action parameter, so the dispatcher will call the ShowForm routine. When you submit the data from the form, the action parameter will be there, and the Validate routine will be called.

The completed file is located in ch15_listing3.asp.

Wrapping up

As you can see, combining your pages into one isn't really that hard once you've got the appropriate structure in place. The best part about this structure is that it is infinitely expandable. You could, in theory, build your entire Web site in one ASP file. Would you want to? Probably not. However, you can easily combine all the typical entity functions into one page:

- Create and Save New Record
- Update and Save Changes
- Confirm Delete and Delete Record
- Retrieve Record Details

Each one gets a different "action" code and the Sub Main dispatcher routine simply calls one of seven subroutines in the page. If you're smart about how you design the page (which I'll teach you how to do later), you can combine the create, update, and even the retrieve functions into a single subroutine, and have separate ones for each of the save routines. That reduces the number of subroutines from seven to five, saving you even more work. You'll be seeing this structure throughout the rest of the book.

**20 Min.
To Go**

ASP Development Tips

So far, you've been writing a lot of small pages with small amounts of code in them. However, you're soon going to be writing very complex pages that have multiple functions in them and lots of lines of code. Once you start doing this, you'll need to write clean code or you're going to have a real mess on your hands. This section will outline some practices that I follow when I write my own applications. Many of these practices are based on my personal opinion and preference, so use them as you see fit.

Use subroutines and functions

The first, and probably most important, practice you can follow is to break your code up with subroutines and functions. Any time I see code that I might use more than once, it becomes a subroutine or function. I've created lots of subroutines and functions that I can share among applications, either by copying them or by using server-side includes (covered later in this chapter.)

The first function that you'll use is the WriteLine subroutine. This routine takes a piece of text, HTML or otherwise, and prints it to the page. It also tacks on a carriage return/line-feed character to the end.

```
Sub WriteLine(strData)
    Response.Write strData & vbCrLF
End Sub
```

The purpose of the vbCrLf constant is to add on a line break in the HTML source sent to the browser. HTML doesn't need the line breaks in the file, but if you need to debug the output you're generating, you'll end up with all your HTML on one line if you don't use the vbCrLf character.

Here's another function that writes an HTML comment to the output. I use it a lot when debugging my code. If I need to see the value of a variable when the page is actually running, I create a comment in the HTML. This comment is invisible to the user (unless the user looks at the source of the page) and doesn't disrupt any HTML structures or tables.

```
Sub WriteComment(strData)
    WriteLine "<!-- " & strData & " -->"
End Sub
```

Note that this subroutine uses the WriteLine subroutine used earlier.

Use comment blocks

When you're writing code that might be maintained by other developers, you need to document your work. This goes for every language that you might use, including the code you write in ASP files. I generally use comment blocks for each function or subroutine, in addition to placing a block at the top of the file explaining the changes and functions of a particular file. Even if I'm developing the application for myself, I still comment my work so that I remember what I was thinking when I wrote the code.

If you're concerned about increasing the amount of information that has to be transferred to the user, remember that server-side comments are removed when the ASP engine processes the file. This means that comments are "cheap" and you should use them profusely.

Here's an example of a function/subroutine block:

```
'''''''''''''''''''''''''''''''''''''''''''''''''''''''''''''''
'
' Sub WriteLine
'
```

```
' Prints a line of text to the Web page, followed by a
' CR/LF character.
'
,,,,,,,,,,,,,,,,,,,,,,,,,,,,,,,,,,,,,,,,,,,,,,,,,,,,,,,,,,
```

The single quotes are comment characters, as you already know. I simply list the name of the function or subroutine and its basic purpose. You can also add

- Parameter names and functions
- Calls to other subroutines or functions
- Anything else you want

The point is to make the header useful to you and other programmers who might have to maintain your work later.

Here's an example of a file block:

```
,,,,,,,,,,,,,,,,,,,,,,,,,,,,,,,,,,,,,,,,,,,,,,,,,,,,,,,,,,
'
' common.asp
'
' Includes commonly used subroutines and functions
' for the entire site.
'
,,,,,,,,,,,,,,,,,,,,,,,,,,,,,,,,,,,,,,,,,,,,,,,,,,,,,,,,,,
' Modification Log
,,,,,,,,,,,,,,,,,,,,,,,,,,,,,,,,,,,,,,,,,,,,,,,,,,,,,,,,,,
' 12/12/00   EAS   Created file.
' 01/15/01   EAS   Added TYPELIB declarations.
,,,,,,,,,,,,,,,,,,,,,,,,,,,,,,,,,,,,,,,,,,,,,,,,,,,,,,,,,,
```

The modification log can be helpful, especially when several programmers are working on the same files, so that you can determine what has been done to the file over time.

Don't embed HTML

In the example at the beginning of the chapter, you created a subroutine that looked like this:

```
Option Explicit

Sub ShowForm
```

```
%>
<html>
<head>
   <title>System Login</title>
</head>
<body>
<h1>System Login</h1>
<form action="<% = Request("SCRIPT_NAME")?a=v" method=post>
<table>
   <tr>
      <td>User ID:</td>
      <td><input type=text name=txtUserID size=20></td>
   </tr>
   <tr>
      <td>Password:</td>
      <td><input type=password name=txtPassword size=20></td>
   </tr>
   <tr>
      <td colspan=2 align=center>
         <input type=submit name=cmdSubmit value=Login>
      </td>
   </tr>
</table>
</form>
</body>
</html>
<%
End Sub
```

You surrounded a block of HTML with Sub and End Sub keywords so that it wouldn't run until called. The problem with this format is that if you look at the middle of the code, you can't see that it's between Sub and End Sub. In addition, you have to switch back to ASP code to print the value of the SCRIPT_NAME variable.

While this format works, in the next chapter you're going to be writing code that generates HTML tables on the fly while printing out database field data. Using this particular method makes for very messy code, in my opinion. In addition, this type of code has created performance problems in previous versions of ASP. The ASP engine had to switch gears back and forth to handle raw HTML code.

For these reasons, I don't embed HTML in my page. Instead, I use ASP code to print every line of HTML. The best part about this method is that I don't have to switch back and forth between ASP and HTML, and it's very easy to see that the code statements are within various coding structures, such as subroutines, if/then blocks, and so on.

If you're not an expert HTML developer, you can let someone else generate the HTML initially. You can then take the HTML and "encode" it into your ASP files using the WriteLine statement. When I'm initially developing a site, I will often work in plain HTML to generate the site design. Once I've got the design how I like it, I wrap the HTML with the ASP code required for the page to show up correctly.

Using the WriteLine subroutine you created earlier, I would convert the code above into the following, shown in Listing 15-4.

Listing 15-4
Using the WriteLine subroutine

```
<%
Option Explicit
Const DQ = """"

Call Main

Sub Main
   If Request("a") = "v" Then
      Validate
   Else
      ShowForm
   End If
End Sub

Sub ShowForm
   WriteLine "<html><head><title>System Login</title></head>"
   WriteLine "<body>"
   WriteLine "<h1>System Login</h1>"
   WriteLine "<form action=" & DQ & Request("SCRIPT_NAME") _
      & "?a=v" & DQ & "method=post>"
   WriteLine "<table><tr><td>User ID:</td>"
   WriteLine "<td><input type=text name=txtUserID size=20></td>"
   WriteLine "</tr>"
```

Continued

Listing 15-4 *Continued*

```
      WriteLine "<tr>"
      WriteLine "<td>Password:</td>"
      WriteLine "<td><input type=password " _
         & "name=txtPassword size=20></td>"
      WriteLine "</tr>"
      WriteLine "<tr><td colspan=2 align=center>"
      WriteLine "<input type=submit name=cmdSubmit value=Login>"
      WriteLine "</td>"
      WriteLine "</tr>"
      WriteLine "</table>"
      WriteLine "</form></body></html>"
  End Sub


  Sub Validate
     If Request("txtUserID") = "USER" _
        And Request("txtPassword") = "PASSWORD" Then
        Response.Write "Login successful."
     Else
        Response.Write "ERROR: Invalid user ID/password."
     End If
  End Sub

  Sub WriteLine(strData)
     Response.Write strData & vbCrLf
  End Sub

%>
```

Using the WriteLine statement consistently makes the code much easier to read, since all the statements are at the same "level" in the subroutine. Deciding what to put on a line is up to you. You can put every tag on a separate line, group similar tags, or do whatever else you want to do. The point is to break up the output so that when you need to look at the HTML source in your browser, it's easier to read.

There are a few things you added to the file. First of all, you added the WriteLine subroutine to the bottom of the file. ASP doesn't care where the subroutine is defined, as long as it's in the file somewhere. The other thing you added at the top was the DQ constant. *DQ* stands for double quote. When you print out the FORM tag in the ShowForm subroutine, you need to embed double-quote characters in the text you're printing. In order to print a double quote character, you print two double-quote characters. VBScript considers the double-quote character a special character and will attempt to interpret it if you don't use two of them. Using the DQ constant at the top of the page and then in the WriteLine statement simplifies the code a lot. Here's the line with the DQ constant:

```
WriteLine "<form action=" & DQ & Request("SCRIPT_NAME") _
    & "?a=v" & DQ & "method=post>"
```

Here's what the line would look like if you didn't use the constant:

```
WriteLine "<form action=""" & Request("SCRIPT_NAME") _
    & "?a=v"" method=post>"
```

All those double quote characters can get confusing, especially for new programmers. Concatenating the DQ constant makes it very clear that you want to embed a double-quote character at that position in the HTML.

**10 Min.
To Go**

Server-Side Includes

One of the biggest pains about maintaining a large Web site is that it's tough to make changes to the overall design of the site without a lot of manual work. Most sites I've worked on have had all "hand-crafted" pages with lots of duplication of common elements, such as toolbars, headers, footers, and so on. Even if you just need to update an item on a toolbar, you have to change every file containing the toolbar.

However, one of the early additions to the Web developer's palette were server-side include directives. These directives enabled developers to build a file from other files by including common elements. Changing the files the first time takes quite a bit of work, but once you've made the initial changes to use SSI directives, you can make a lot of changes without ever having to touch the rest of your pages.

Using the directives

Here's an example of what a server-side include directive looks like when in use:

```
<!--#include virtual="/class/include.asp" -->
```

This directive instructs ASP to look, starting at the Web site's root directory, for a directory (or Web share) called class and to read the file called include.asp. The name of the file to include isn't really important and doesn't have to be include.asp. I often name my own include files common.asp, util.asp, and so on.

If you want to include a file from the current directory, you can use a slightly different form of the #include directive:

```
<!--#include file="common.asp" -->
```

This form of the directive enables you to read a file from the current directory, or from a subdirectory of the current directory, as shown here:

```
<!--#include file="inc/common.asp" -->
```

This directive will read the common.asp file from the inc subdirectory in the current directory (of the page using the directive). When you use the file parameter, you can't specify a forward slash as the first character of the filename — ASP will generate an error.

Structuring your include files

It's important to set up your include files properly because these files will be shared throughout your entire application. Here are a couple of rules to follow:

1. Use as few include files as possible. I personally use a single include file for the application. This minimizes the number of directives required for each file in the site and prevents confusion as to the location of the code you want to use.

2. Add Option Explicit to the top of the include file so that it is included in all your other files. This will prevent the errors that you learned about in earlier chapters.

3. Declare any constants or global variables at the top of the file. This makes them easier to find later.

4. Put all code in your include files in subroutines or functions. This prevents it from running prematurely.

Some include files you'll see in use elsewhere are snippets of code that get included in other ASP files when needed. Here's an example of one of these files:

```
Dim cnDB        ' As ADODB.Connection
Set cnDB = Server.CreateObject("ADODB.Connection")
cnDB.ConnectionString = _
    "Provider=SQLOLEDB;" _
    & "Data Source=VOYAGER;" _
    & "Initial Catalog=Northwind;" _
    & "User ID=sa;" _
```

```
   & "Password=;"
cnDB.Open
```

This file is included in another file wherever the developer wants to open a database connection. There are a few problems with this approach. First of all, if the developer already has a variable named cnDB declared in the page (or subroutine, depending on where this file is included), an error will occur because you can't declare the variable more than once.

Another problem is that you will have lots of #include directives throughout the page. This makes it more difficult to change the included code, since you have to be aware that any changes you make will actually change each file. In a subroutine or function, you don't have to worry about how the code in the subroutine or function works, because you have defined a set of parameters that should be passed to it. In addition, as long as the name of the sub/fn stays the same, you won't have to change any calls to the file.

In short, don't do your includes this way. It eliminates some of the benefits of using include files and makes your code a real mess for future programmers to work on.

Here's a partial example of an include file I frequently use:

```
<%
Option Explicit
Const DQ = """"
Const SQ = "'"

Function OpenDB()
    Dim cnDB          ' As ADODB.Connection
    Set cnDB = Server.CreateObject("ADODB.Connection")
    cnDB.ConnectionString = _
       "Provider=SQLOLEDB;" _
         & "Data Source=VOYAGER;" _
         & "Initial Catalog=Northwind;" _
         & "User ID=sa;" _
         & "Password=;"
    cnDB.Open
    Set OpenDB = cnDB
End Function
... more code ...
%>
```

This file is included at the top of each file in my application. The Option Explicit is automatically added to every file, preventing those errors. I've also defined some constants in this page that will be used in every file that uses this include file. Finally, I start adding my functions and subroutines, one after the other. Note that I've included my ASP delimiters at the beginning and end of this file. This eliminates any problems if the file that includes this file doesn't have these delimiters immediately before or after the call to this page.

You'll be using include files throughout the book to save on coding effort: once you've got a useful function, there's no reason to copy it from one file to the next. The functions covered earlier would be good candidates to be moved into your own include file.

Done!

REVIEW

This chapter was designed to teach you how to use good programming practices with Active Server Pages. Just because you can write quick and dirty code with ASP doesn't mean that it's a good idea. Using modular programming, include files, and some good coding conventions will make your code much easier to maintain and expand in the future.

QUIZ YOURSELF

1. Define black-box programming. (See "Creating Modular Code")
2. What VBScript structure allows us to create reusable blocks of code? (See "Creating Modular Code")
3. Why should you comment your code? (See "ASP Development Tips")
4. What two attributes are available to the #include directive? (See 'Server-Side Includes")
5. How can you print a double quote character using a Response.Write statement? (See "Don't Embed HTML")

Getting Other User Information

Session Checklist

✔ Learn about cookies and what you can use them for

✔ Create, update, and remove cookies with the Response object

✔ View information provided by and available to the Web server

**30 Min.
To Go**

S o far, you've been getting data from forms the user has filled out and read information from the URL via the QueryString collection. There are several other sources of key information that you have available to you in ASP, and this chapter covers how to use these sources.

Using Cookies

Each time you request a page from a Web server, regardless of how many other pages you've requested, it's like you're starting a new conversation. The server doesn't actively maintain any information about what pages you've gotten so far. Doing that for every user would quickly overwhelm any Web server, especially a very busy one.

However, without some method of maintaining state, the types of applications you can build are quite limited. For instance, if the server doesn't know who you are, it can't remember that you added three items to a shopping cart. It won't know that you logged in successfully and want to automatically log into the site on each successive visit. The list goes on and on.

For this reason, one of the early additions to Web browsers and servers was the ability to manage persistent pieces of data between pages and Web browsing sessions. These pieces of data are called *cookies*. Why the name cookies? A *magic cookie* is a term that has been used in a number of different computing systems to represent a piece of data that has a special purpose. The name just stuck and is now used primarily when discussing Web browsers and servers.

Cookie concepts

Before we talk about using cookies, you should think about what you should use them for. There are two types of cookies, temporary and permanent. A temporary cookie exists as long as the browser window stays open. As soon as the browser window closes, any temporary cookies are removed. Temporary cookies are kept in the browser's memory, but work just like permanent ones.

Permanent cookies are written to your computer's hard disk. Depending on the browser you're using, each site's cookies may be in a separate file or in a single database. Internet Explorer stores cookies as individual files. The format of the file isn't really important, since you don't have to worry about how the browser manages the cookies. You can use cookies in a number of different applications to help create a better experience for the user. One example is common at many Web sites that feature user IDs and passwords. The first time you visit the site, you pick a user ID and password. To make it easier for you to visit the next time, the server gives you a cookie that indicates what your user ID and password are. The next time you visit the site, the cookie is automatically returned to the Web server. The Web server looks at the value, determines that you logged in correctly, and lets you into the password-protected part of the site.

A similar example is a shopping cart. When you visit a site with a store, once you select an item, it's put in an imaginary shopping cart. The store's server gives you a cookie that links your browser with your shopping cart. Some stores allow you to maintain a shopping cart between Web visits. In this case, a permanent cookie is stored on your machine with the unique ID of the shopping cart.

The shopping cart concept has also led to the "wish lists" provided by many of the major e-commerce sites. Wish lists are basically implemented like permanent shopping carts. You add an item to a wish list and the server generates a unique ID for your list and stores it on your machine as a cookie.

Cookies are also used in advertising. On my Techniques sites (VB Techniques, ASP Techniques), each time you see an ad, I generate a temporary cookie with the unique ID of that impression — impression being defined as a user seeing a particular ad. To keep track of the impressions, I store the visit in a database. If you click the ad, the unique ID of the impression is given back to the server so that it can record the fact that your impression turned into a *clickthrough* (meaning that you responded to the ad by visiting the site being advertised).

Other ad providers, such as DoubleClick, use cookies in a different way. DoubleClick provides ads for many different Web sites. The first time you see a DoubleClick ad, a cookie is written to your browser from DoubleClick's server. While the server doesn't know who you are specifically, the cookie lets the server track what sites your browser is visiting. For instance, if you're into stock picking and trading, you will visit a related group of sites. As you visit more and more sites, DoubleClick is able to create a profile of your viewing habits. With a detailed profile, it is able to send you an ad related to what you have visited in the past. If it sends you a relevant ad, you're more likely to click on it. In addition, DoubleClick can tell its advertisers that it can target ads to a particular group of users. That makes the ads more valuable to the advertisers, and, in turn, DoubleClick gets more money for the ads.

There are many other applications that make use of cookies. You'll probably come up with a few of your own. However, the basic idea is to give the browser some piece of data that is passed back later when the user visits your site again.

Best practices

There are a few rules you should follow when using cookies. These rules will make the experience for your user better and not cause any confusion about privacy issues or make the user worry about what you're doing with the cookies.

**20 Min.
To Go**

Keep them short

Since cookie data have to be passed back and forth on every single request to a server, you need to keep the amount of cookie data you're using short. Cookies can be big, but generally there's no need for them to be. Don't, for instance, store a user's shopping cart in a cookie. Store it in a database and give the user a reference to the cart's database record.

Don't Put Sensitive Information In Cookies

Cookie text is sent across the Internet unencrypted, which means that someone "tapping" the connection can potentially intercept it. In addition, permanent cookies stored on disk are stored unencrypted. This means that anyone looking at your machine's files can see the cookie files and read them in any text editor. When Web sites first started using cookies a number of years ago, well-intentioned commerce sites would store credit-card numbers as cookies on user's browsers. Users were alarmed to discover that their credit card information was being passed back and forth, and the commerce sites began storing only customer numbers as cookies. Credit-card numbers are now stored in secure databases. This minor mistake did give cookies a bad name and made a lot of people paranoid about what can make it into cookie files.

Explain your use of cookies to your users

Most commercial Web sites now post their privacy policies. Yahoo!, for instance, asks you if you want a permanent cookie stored on your machine. At the same time, it explains what this entails. The document is well written and explains in clear terms what the cookie does. As long as you're explaining what you're doing, most users will be fine with it.

Use permanent cookies sparingly

There are very few cases in which permanent cookies are required. Since cookies can be removed by the user, using permanent cookies everywhere might cause problems if the user decides to remove cookies from his or her machine. Unless you need to maintain a value for a long time between visits user, use a temporary cookie.

Remove cookies

If the user has chosen to log out of your application, be sure to remove any cookies you've created. Yahoo! has a Sign Off link that will actually remove the cookie from your machine. Since the cookie logs you in automatically, you'll be prompted to log in on your next visit. While users can remove the cookies themselves, it's better if you do it for them when you're all done with the cookies.

Creating and updating cookies

Creating a cookie is easy to do: you can create temporary and permanent cookies with the addition (or deletion) of a single line of code. Here's how you do it:

```
Response.Cookies("cookiename") = "cookievalue"
```

Using the Response object, specify a name for the cookie and its value. The value of the cookie can be any data type, but will be returned later as text. The cookie name can be any name, including ones with spaces. The value can also be whatever you want it to be. In this section, we'll be generalizing the name with *cookiename* and the value with *cookievalue*.

If the cookie doesn't exist, this line will create it. If the cookie already exists, this line will modify the cookie's value. To make a cookie permanent, you have to provide an expiration date and time. Once you've created or updated the cookie value, add this line:

```
Response.Cookies("cookiename").Expires = DateAdd("d", 30, date)
```

The value following the Expires property can be any date value. This particular example determines the date 30 days from now and uses it as the expiration date. You can also use a constant for your date value:

```
Response.Cookies("cookiename").Expires = #12/31/2049#
```

This sets the cookie to expire on December 31, 2049. Hopefully we'll have something better than cookies by then.

You can set your cookie to expire 30 days from its creation, but update the expiration every time the cookie is read or updated with other values. This way allows the cookie to expire if it isn't being used.

Viewing cookies

Once you've created a cookie, you can view it through the Request.Cookies collection, even if you created the cookie on the same page on which you're attempting to read it. Note that if you attempt to read the Response.Cookies collection, you'll get an error. You have to read the Request.Cookies collection to get the value back.

As I mentioned earlier, any value returned from the Cookies collection will come back as text, so if you're going to do calculations on it, be sure to use one of the C-functions (CInt, CLng, and so on) to convert it to a number within the variable.

Removing cookies

To remove a cookie, simply set its value to an empty string, as shown here:

```
Response.Cookies("cookiename") = ""
```

If the cookie was permanent, this will remove it from the disk. If it was temporary, this will remove it from memory. The cookie will be removed regardless of what the expiration date is. In Internet Explorer, removing a permanent cookie that is the only cookie value being kept will remove the cookie file.

Usage notes

There are a few rules you have to follow when creating, modifying, and deleting cookies. Any calls to Response.Cookies should be made before the HTML is sent to the user. This is because the cookies are sent as part of the page header. If you don't follow this rule, you'll get this error message:

```
Header Error

/class/CreateCookie.asp, line 3

The HTTP headers are already written to the client browser. Any
HTTP header modifications must be made before writing page
content.
```

Once you understand that the cookies have to be written first, this message makes more sense. Otherwise, it can be quite confusing.

The exception to this rule is when page buffering is turned on. Buffering is turned on by default in Windows 2000. In this case, no output is sent to the browser until the page is complete. This allows the header to be written with all the required changes. You can control buffering by setting the Response.Buffer property to True or False. Note that under Windows NT 4, buffering was turned off by default. If your pages rely on buffering being turned off, you may have some errors under Windows 2000's Web services. Refer to the IIS documentation on how to change buffering for the entire Web server or Web site.

Wrapping up

You're going to be using cookies later in the book to help personalize some Web pages, so you'll get some more practice with them later. There's nothing more to them than what you've seen in this section. What you do with cookies is where their power comes into play.

**10 Min.
To Go**

Using Server Variables

As I mentioned in the introduction, each time someone requests data from your server, a number of key pieces of information are provided by the user's browser about that user's environment. Things like the person's hostname and/or IP address, browser type, operating system, and more are stored for possible use by your Web pages. These pieces of information are known as *server environment variables* and are exposed for use through the ServerVariables collection of the Request object. This section will show you what these variables hold and how you can use them.

Table 16-1 shows you all the variables available for use in Active Server Pages.

Table 16-1
HTTP Environment Variables

Variable	Description
ALL_HTTP	All HTTP headers not already parsed into one of the other variables described in this table. These variables are of the form HTTP_*header field name*. The headers consist of a null-terminated string with the individual headers separated by line feeds.
AUTH_TYPE	The type of authentication used. For example, the string will be "Basic" if Basic authentication is used, "Integrated Windows NT Authentication" if integrated authentication is used, and so on. Other authentication schemes will have other strings. Since new authentication types can be added to the Web server, it is not possible to list all the string possibilities. If the string is empty, no authentication is used.
AUTH_PASSWORD	The value entered in the client's authentication dialog box. This variable is only available if Basic authentication is used.
AUTH_USER	The value entered in the client's authentication dialog box.
CONTENT_LENGTH	The number of bytes the script can expect to receive from the client.
CONTENT_TYPE	The content type of the information supplied in the body of a POST request.
DOCUMENT_NAME	The current filename.
DOCUMENT_URI	The virtual path to the current document.

Continued

Table 16-1   *Continued*

Variable	Description
DATE_GMT	The current date in Greenwich Mean Time (GMT).
DATE_LOCAL	The current date in the local time zone.
GATEWAY_INTERFACE	The revision of the CGI specification used by the Web server.
LAST_MODIFIED	The date that the current document was last modified. The date will be displayed in the format specified by the #config directive, if applicable.
PATH_INFO	Additional path information, as given by the client. This consists of the trailing part of the URL after the script name and before the query string, if any.
PATH_TRANSLATED	The value of PATH_INFO, but with any virtual path expanded into a directory specification.
QUERY_STRING	The information that follows the question mark (?) in the URL that referenced this script.
QUERY_STRING_UNESCAPED	Unescaped version of the query string; that is, a version that is not URL-encoded.
REMOTE_ADDR	The IP address of the client or agent of the client (for example, gateway or firewall) that sent the request.
REMOTE_HOST	The host name of the client or agent of the client (for example, gateway or firewall) that sent the request.
REMOTE_USER	The user name supplied by the client and authenticated by the server. This name comes back as an empty string when the user is anonymous (but authenticated).
REQUEST_METHOD	The HTTP request method (GET and POST are most common).
SCRIPT_NAME	The name of the script program being executed. For ASP pages, this will be the pathname to the ASP file.

Variable	Description
SERVER_NAME	The server's host name or IP address.
SERVER_PORT	The TCP/IP port on which the request was received. By default, the port is 80.
SERVER_PORT_SECURE	A string of either 0 or 1. If the request is being handled on a secured connection, this will be 1; otherwise it will be 0.
SERVER_PROTOCOL	The name and version of the information retrieval protocol relating to this request. This is usually HTTP/1.0.
SERVER_SOFTWARE	The name and version of the Web server answering the request. This will vary, but IIS for Windows 2000 returns "Microsoft-IIS/5.0."
URL	The base portion of the URL. Parameter values will not be included. The value is determined when the Web server parses the URL from the header.

To see the values of all of these variables you can create a simple variable dump page, as shown in Listing 16-1.

Listing 16-1
Page to dump out all environment variables

```
<%
Option Explicit
Dim item              ' As Variant

For Each item in Request.ServerVariables
   Response.Write item & ": " _
      & Request.ServerVariables(item) _
      & "<br>" & vbCrLF
Next ' item

%>
```

The For Each/Next structure iterates through all the items in a collection. The variable item goes through all the values in the ServerVariables collection. The code within the loop prints out the name of the ServerVariable as well as the values. Here is an example from my own Windows 2000 Server:

```
ALL_HTTP: HTTP_ACCEPT:image/gif, image/x-xbitmap, image/jpeg,
image/pjpeg, application/vnd.ms-powerpoint, application/vnd.ms-
excel, application/msword, */* HTTP_ACCEPT_LANGUAGE:en-us
HTTP_CONNECTION:Keep-Alive HTTP_HOST:localhost
HTTP_REFERER:http://localhost/cc/ HTTP_USER_AGENT:Mozilla/4.0
(compatible; MSIE 5.01; Windows NT 5.0) HTTP_ACCEPT_ENCODING:gzip,
deflate
ALL_RAW: Accept: image/gif, image/x-xbitmap, image/jpeg,
image/pjpeg, application/vnd.ms-powerpoint, application/vnd.ms-
excel, application/msword, */* Accept-Language: en-us Connection:
Keep-Alive Host: localhost Referer: http://localhost/cc/ User-
Agent: Mozilla/4.0 (compatible; MSIE 5.01; Windows NT 5.0) Accept-
Encoding: gzip, deflate
APPL_MD_PATH: /LM/W3SVC/1/Root/cc
APPL_PHYSICAL_PATH: D:\Web\ASP Crash Course\
AUTH_PASSWORD:
AUTH_TYPE:
AUTH_USER:
CERT_COOKIE:
CERT_FLAGS:
CERT_ISSUER:
CERT_KEYSIZE:
CERT_SECRETKEYSIZE:
CERT_SERIALNUMBER:
CERT_SERVER_ISSUER:
CERT_SERVER_SUBJECT:
CERT_SUBJECT:
CONTENT_LENGTH: 0
CONTENT_TYPE:
GATEWAY_INTERFACE: CGI/1.1
HTTPS: off
HTTPS_KEYSIZE:
HTTPS_SECRETKEYSIZE:
HTTPS_SERVER_ISSUER:
HTTPS_SERVER_SUBJECT:
INSTANCE_ID: 1
INSTANCE_META_PATH: /LM/W3SVC/1
```

```
LOCAL_ADDR: 127.0.0.1
LOGON_USER:
PATH_INFO: /cc/ch16_listing1.asp
PATH_TRANSLATED: D:\Web\ASP Crash Course\ch16_listing1.asp
QUERY_STRING:
REMOTE_ADDR: 127.0.0.1
REMOTE_HOST: 127.0.0.1
REMOTE_USER:
REQUEST_METHOD: GET
SCRIPT_NAME: /cc/ch16_listing1.asp
SERVER_NAME: localhost
SERVER_PORT: 80
SERVER_PORT_SECURE: 0
SERVER_PROTOCOL: HTTP/1.1
SERVER_SOFTWARE: Microsoft-IIS/5.0
URL: /cc/ch16_listing1.asp
HTTP_ACCEPT: image/gif, image/x-xbitmap, image/jpeg, image/pjpeg,
application/vnd.ms-powerpoint, application/vnd.ms-excel,
application/msword, */*
HTTP_ACCEPT_LANGUAGE: en-us
HTTP_CONNECTION: Keep-Alive
HTTP_HOST: localhost
HTTP_REFERER: http://localhost/cc/
HTTP_USER_AGENT: Mozilla/4.0 (compatible; MSIE 5.01; Windows NT
5.0)
HTTP_ACCEPT_ENCODING: gzip, deflate
```

Done!

Depending on the browser and your server, your values will vary. Use the explanations in the earlier table to use these values. You'll be using them throughout the rest of the book as well.

REVIEW

In this chapter you learned how to read and use additional information provided to your Web page. You learned that using cookies can provide personalization and some automatic operations for your users. You can use the server variables provided in the ServerVariables collection to provide information about the user and/or the server. You'll use some of these variables later in the book to make your code more reliable and easier to manage.

Part III—Saturday Afternoon
Session 16

QUIZ YOURSELF

1. What types of cookies can you create? (See "Using Cookies")
2. How can you update a cookie's value? (See "Updating Cookies")
3. Which collection do you use to read a cookie? To write a cookie? (See "Viewing Cookies")
4. Which server variable provides the name of the current ASP file? (See "Using Server Variables")
5. Which server variable provides the name of the user's browser? (See "Using Server Variables")

PART

III

Saturday Afternoon Part Review

Name all the data types that would be appropriate for the following data:

1. 54
2. 50000
3. 54.1
4. 11/20/2000
5. -250

Answer the following questions about arrays in VBScript:

6. What is the first index in an array?
7. What function can you use to determine the lower bound of an array? The upper bound?
8. How many dimensions can an array have? How would you declare a three-dimensional array (choose the number of indices yourself for each dimension)?

Answer the following questions about strings in VBScript:

9. How do you remove the spaces from the left-hand side of a string? The right-hand side? Both sides?
10. How do you generate a string with 25 spaces in it?
11. By default, are functions like InStr or Replace case-sensitive or case-insensitive?
12. Which statement causes random numbers to be truly random?

13. What is the difference between the Now and Time functions?
14. How can you determine the day you were born?
15. How can you determine what the date will be three months from now?

Answer these questions about creating loops:

16. Which type of loop do you use if you have a fixed beginning and end point?

17. How many times is this loop guaranteed to run, assuming that you do not know what the initial value of x is?

```
Do Until x > 10
   x = x + 1
Loop
```

Reverse the following conditions:

18. $x < 5$

19. $x > 5$ And $x <= 10$

20. $x > 10$ And $(x <> 15)$

PART

IV

Saturday Evening

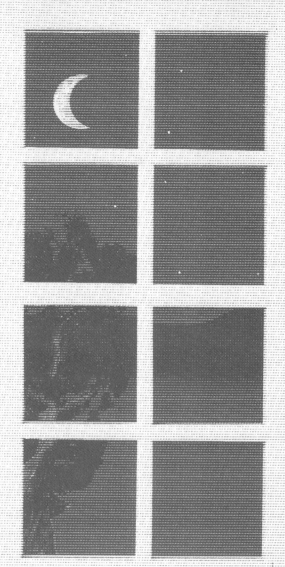

17

Creating a Database

Session Checklist

✔ Learn what a database is and how it's structured

✔ Build a database in Microsoft Access 2000 and Microsoft SQL Server 7

✔ Design a table and add data to the table

✔ Write queries to manipulate the data in the database

A key component of nearly every application is a permanent data storage system. This normally takes the form of a database. In this chapter, you'll learn to create databases in both Access 2000 and SQL Server 7.

30 Min.
To Go

Relational Databases

Most programs that you'll write will need a way to permanently store data. These data can deal with anything, from birth certificates to bank accounts. Large companies amass a great deal of data on a lot of things, and they need an organized way to store and manipulate those data. The solution is to create a database.

Early databases were nothing more than simple text-based files that could be loaded by a program and manipulated to generate some sort of result. However, things didn't stop there. Developers realized that in any set of data, relationships exist. For instance, a bank has customers. Each of those customers has one or more accounts, and each of those accounts has transactions. In addition, you can eliminate a lot of redundant data. For instance, without the relationship in place, you'd have to keep all of a customer's information on each bank-account record. You'd also have to keep all the account information, as well as the customer information, on each transaction. That simply isn't practical, as that amount of redundant data would quickly get out of hand.

This type of database is known as a *relational database*. Relational databases include Microsoft Access, Microsoft SQL Server, Oracle, IBM DB/2, Sybase, and many others. Most of these systems are also known as Relational Database Management Systems (RDBMS), since they can all (except for Access) maintain multiple databases within a single installation. Access is different from these systems in that while it is relational, it isn't designed to maintain more than one database in a file.

Using an RDBMS, a company might keep an inventory database, which includes all the data about its products, orders, and so on. It might keep a separate database of human resources information, which would include employee information, benefits, and so forth. The systems are related to different parts of the business and are often kept separate. However, there are cases in which databases overlap. In this particular case, the inventory database might keep track of which employees order products. Those employees might be stored in the human-resources databases.

For the purposes of this book, you'll be creating a single database within either Access 2000 or SQL Server 7. If you prefer to use a different database, that's fine too. As you'll learn in the next chapter, ASP can talk to nearly every database currently available through the use of several technologies available on Internet Information Server.

Tables

Now that you understand the concept of a database, let's drill down a bit further. Each database can hold lots of different types of data. For instance, a contact manager like ACT or Outlook holds data like this:

- Names and addresses
- Records of phone calls
- Upcoming events
- Task lists
- Notes

Each of these types of data requires different information to be valid. For instance, an upcoming event would need the start and end dates and times, while a name and address record wouldn't. For this reason, we store each type of data in a different part of the database, called a table. Each type of data gets its own table, and generally the table names match the data within the table.

Here are a few tips when naming your tables:

Keep the name short without being cryptic. For instance, you might want to give a table containing customer accounts the name CustAccts, but not CA. Table names can be quite long, depending on the database, but long names make for lots of extra typing.

Pick a prefix (such as tbl) to add to all your table names. That way it's easy for other programmers to immediately understand that you're selecting data from a table instead of from another source, such as a view or a query.

Some databases, like Access and SQL Server, allow you to put spaces in your table names. Don't do this. If you ever need to migrate your database to Oracle, those table names will have to change since Oracle doesn't allow spaces. In addition, you have to wrap each table name with square brackets when you use spaces. It makes for messier code and I try to avoid it.

Fields

Now that you've created a table, you have to create a way to store each piece of data. If you take a typical customer record, you might have this information in it:

- Name
- Company name
- Address
- Phone
- E-mail address
- And more...

Each piece of information is stored in a field in a table. A field is defined as part of the table, and it will generally have these attributes:

- A data type
- A minimum length
- A maximum length

Data type

A data type in a database is similar to a data type that you've used in VBScript and ASP. Each data type has a data value range. For instance, a *bit* in SQL Server can contain a 1 or a 0, much like a Boolean value that can be stored in a Variant within VBScript.

Minimum length

There are cases in which you have to require that certain pieces of data be provided. For instance, it doesn't make much sense to enter a customer's information without entering a name. In this case, the field has a minimum length. This is also known as a *not null* field, since the field can't be empty, or null. Fields that can be empty are also known as *nullable fields*. Every database enables you to mark a field as required or not. Based on your particular application, you'll have to decide which fields to require in every table.

Maximum length

Besides setting a minimum length, you can also set a maximum length. In some cases, there's no reason to have 50 characters in a field when you only need 10. For instance, a U.S. ZIP code can be in either of these formats:

- *nnnnn*
- *nnnnn-nnnn*

In this case, does it make sense to allow 40 characters in the field? Ten would be a better choice for a maximum length.

In other cases, such as in freeform text fields, you want to enable the user to type in an unlimited amount of text. There are special data types for just this purpose that can sort large amounts of text in the database efficiently.

Each numeric data type has a minimum and maximum value. For instance, the SQL Server int data type can handle numbers from approximately -2 billion to +2 billion, just like the Long data type in VBScript. Refer to your vendor's documentation for these lengths. If you try to put a value that isn't legal into a field, you'll generally get an error for your troubles.

Records and rows

Now that you've got the design for your data, you have to put data in. You can think of a table as a big grid, with the fields acting as columns. The rows in the grid represent a particular customer, for instance, with all the fields of data in the row helping to describe the customer. This is called a *record* or a *row*. In the ASP files you build later in the book, you'll be retrieving groups of rows from your tables and displaying them on your pages. You can use the terms record and row interchangeably and your fellow developers will understand what you're talking about.

**20 Min.
To Go**

Working with Microsoft Access

While I personally use and recommend SQL Server 7, not everyone has access to it or hardware that meets its requirements. In this case, Access will work fine as a database for the Web application you'll build later in the book. This section will show you how to create a database in Access 2000, design a table, and add data to it. Later in this chapter you'll learn how to query the database to return the answers to your requests.

All of the figures in this section were shot using Access 2000 running on Windows 2000 Server, so there may be minor graphical differences between what you see here and what you see on your computer.

Creating a database

The first thing you have to do is to create a database. In Access you work with a single database at a time, and that whole database is stored in a single MDB file. To get started, start Microsoft Access, and you'll be presented with the dialog shown in Figure 17-1.

Since you're going to create a brand-new database from scratch, pick Blank Access Database and click the OK button. The next dialog, shown in Figure 17-2, will prompt you for a location for your file. Find a place for your database and click the OK button when you're done.

At this point, Access will create your database file and show you the dialog shown in Figure 17-3.

Figure 17-1
Initial dialog in Microsoft Access

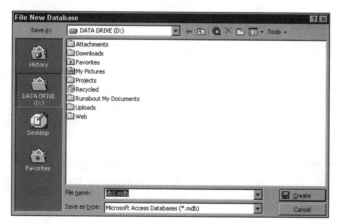

Figure 17-2
Select a filename and directory for your database in this dialog

This window gives you access to all the parts of your Access database file. You can add:

- Tables
- Queries that can be reused
- Forms that provide a user interface within Access
- Reports that can display well formatted data
- Web pages generated by Access
- Macros that can provide additional functions within your code
- Modules of additional code

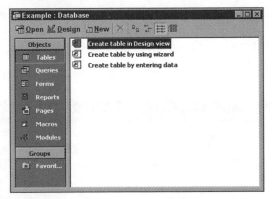

Figure 17-3
Primary database display window

We're only going to be focusing on the first two items in this book. If you are interested in learning more about Access, there are a number of excellent books on the market covering all the different versions of Access. If you get one, make sure it covers Microsoft Access 2000.

Creating a table

Now that the database is created, you can add a table to it. You'll need to decide what type of table you want to build for this example. I'll be building a contact manager that can hold names and addresses. Follow these steps to build your table:

1. Double-click the Create Table in Design View item in the dialog.

2. The next window you see, shown in Figure 17-4, is the table design window. In this window, you can add the fields to your table.

3. To add a field, you first have to pick a field name. Generally, the first field you create for your table is a unique value that will identify each row. This value is known as a primary key. I always prefix my primary keys with pk. Since this table will hold contacts, I will call the field pkContactID, since it is the primary key and will hold an identification value. Type the name of the field into the first box on the first row of this grid. Hit the Tab key when you're done entering the field name.

4. The second box displays the field's data type. Access has a special data type called an AutoNumber that will automatically assign a new value to every new record that I add to my table. That's the data type you should also use, so pick it from the dropdown list.

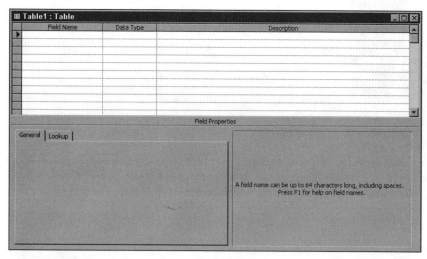

Figure 17-4
Table design window in Microsoft Access

5. The last thing to do for this field is to mark it as the primary key. While prefixing it with pk tells us that it's the primary key, we have to do a bit more work to tell the database that the field is the primary key. Click on the gray box next to the name of the field and the row will be highlighted. On the toolbar, click the key icon to mark the field as the primary key of the table. You'll see a little key icon show up in the gray area next to the field name. Put your cursor in the next row when you're done.

With the primary key identified and marked to Access, you can continue creating the other fields required for this table. Depending on the data you're storing, you'll have a different set of required fields. While you can create some now and add more later, remember that any new fields you add will have empty data for any existing records. Both SQL Server and Access allow for the easy modification of table structures, so be sure to keep this in mind.

Creating additional fields is the same as setting up the primary key field, except that you don't use the AutoNumber data type for any other field in the table. The other data fields that I'm going to add are shown in Table 17-1.

Table 17-1
Fields for Contact Table

Field Name	Access Data Type	Length
FirstName	Text	40
LastName	Text	40
Address	Text	120
City	Text	40
State	Text	2
ZIP	Text	10
Phone	Text	30
Fax	Text	30
Email	Text	80

Is this an exhaustive list of what you could put in your database? Of course not. You could add extra fields for birthdate, additional phone numbers, and so on. You might also want to support international addresses. In that case, you'd need to change your fields a bit. For instance, you might want to add on additional fields for extra lines of address. A client of mine in England has an address that takes up three lines, not including the company name. That doesn't include the city either. In addition, the English company's address obviously doesn't include a state that is two characters, and its postal code is in a different format. The phone and fax number format is also different. Be sure to keep this in mind when designing your databases.

10 Min. To Go

Working with Microsoft SQL Server

This section will show you how to create a table in SQL Server. Microsoft has really improved the tools in SQL 7 and the interface is now nearly identical to Access's. Unlike with other databases, with SQL 7 you don't have to write complicated scripts to create your tables. You do have the option to write database and table-creation scripts, but this is completely optional with SQL 7.

SQL Server, unlike Access, can manage multiple databases. However, to create another database, you may have to speak with your system administrator. Generally, database administrators don't give everyone the ability to create databases. However, we'll assume that you have permission. To create a database, follow these steps:

1. Start SQL Server Enterprise Manager. It is located on your Start menu in the Microsoft SQL Server 7.0 group, assuming you haven't changed it.

2. As shown in Figure 17-5, you'll see the SQL Server Group, which was added to the console by default. Click the plus sign next to Microsoft SQL Servers in the Tree pane, and then the plus sign next to SQL Server Group in the same pane, and you'll see the servers that are part of the group.

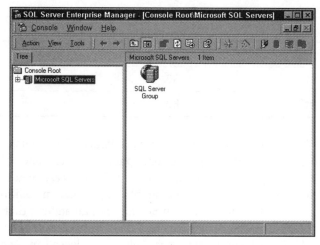

Figure 17-5
SQL Server Enterprise Manager

3. If the server you're using is not listed, you need to add it. Right-click SQL Server Group and select New SQL Server Registration, and the window shown in Figure 17-6 will appear.

4. If the server is running on your local machine and you haven't changed any passwords, you can put a period in the server-name box. That indicates that the server is local. In addition, you can leave the Use Windows NT Authentication option marked, since Enterprise Manager will then use the current user ID to check security on the database. The last option you should clear is the Show system databases and system objects option. By clearing this checkbox, you opt not to see all the internal databases and tables provided by SQL Server. You generally don't need them anyway. Once you've entered all the required information, click the OK button.

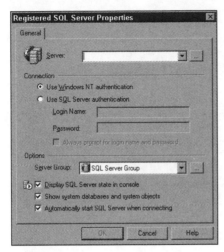

Figure 17-6
Server Registration dialog

If you are using another SQL Server installation or require additional assistance, please talk to your system or database administrator. There are many different options for connecting to SQL Server that we just don't have space to cover. Your DBA or SA is the best person to provide you with the correct information to connect to your server properly.

5. Once you've got the server registered you can click the plus sign next to the server name and you'll see the dialog shown in Figure 17-7. Click the plus sign next to Databases for the next step.

6. If your DBA has already created a database for you to use you can click the plus sign next to it and skip this step. If you have to create a new database, right-click Databases and select New Database from the popup menu that appears. The dialog shown in Figure 17-8 enables you to create a new database, assuming you have the appropriate privileges. Type in a name for the database and leave the rest of the options as they are. SQL Server will automatically specify the filenames for you and allow the database to automatically grow, as necessary. When you're done, click the OK button and SQL Server will create the database for you. You'll see it in the list below the server. Click the database name and continue to the next step.

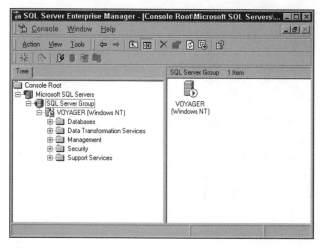

Figure 17-7
Server registration was successful: now you can see all the parts of the server

Figure 17-8
Create Database dialog

7. In the dialog shown in Figure 17-9 you can see all the parts of your database. On the left you see entries for all the types of objects, and on the right you see a summary and a list of the most common tasks. You can access a full list of tasks by right-clicking the database name and selecting All Tasks.

8. To create a new table right-click the Tables entry on the left-hand side of the window and select New Table from the popup menu. You'll be prompted for a table name, which should follow the same rules that you have established for Access table names. I would suggest a prefix of tbl for your tables, as before. Since this is a contact table, the name tblContacts is a good one to use. Once you enter the table name, you'll see the window shown in Figure 17-9.

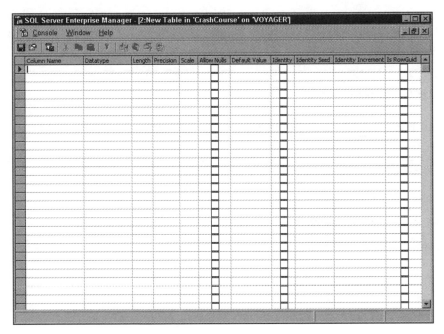

Figure 17-9
Database table design window

9. The first column, as in Access, is where you specify the field name. The first field you create should be the primary key. I always prefix my primary key fields with pk to help identify them more easily.

10. The second column is the data type. For a numeric primary key you can use the integer data type. It has a range of approximately -2 billion to +2 billion, much like the Long data type in VBScript. There are other numeric data types, so feel free to choose the one you think is best suited to the range you'll need.

11. For integers the length and precision fields will fill in automatically. Since the primary key is always required, clear the checkbox in the Allow Nulls column.

12. Finally, to tell SQL Server to generate a new value for each record, mark the Identity checkbox and SQL Server will fill in the starting and increment values for you (they both default to 1). You should also highlight the row and click the key icon on the toolbar to mark the field as the primary key.

Congratulations, you just created a SQL Server table. The rest of your task is to create the other fields for the table. If you're creating the contacts table as you did in Access, Table 17-2 shows a list of the fields to use.

Table 17-2
Fields for Contacts Table

Field Name	Access Data Type	Length
FirstName	varchar	40
LastName	varchar	40
Address	varchar	120
City	varchar	40
State	varchar	2
ZIP	varchar	10
Phone	varchar	30
Fax	varchar	30
Email	varchar	80

varchar stands for *variable character length*. If a field only needs 10 characters, the database will only use that many characters (plus a little bit of overhead). In addition, the database won't store extra spaces in the field. You can also use the char data type if you know that a field will always be the same number of characters. The char data type stores all the characters and right-pads whatever is in the field with spaces, if necessary.

Database Development Tips

Now that you've gotten some experience in creating databases in Access and/or SQL Server, there are a few simple tips you should keep in mine when you're building databases. These tips will make it easier for you to build and deploy your databases, and will save you rework in case of disaster.

Back up your database

You should make a backup copy of your database before starting to add data to it. This is because once you start adding data to tables with AutoNumber or identity fields, you can't reuse numbers. If you are deploying the database for a client, for instance, the client might wonder why the first value is 103 instead of just 1. By keeping a backup of an empty database, you can always start over if you need to.

With Access, backup is as simple as making a copy of the database before adding data to it. If you're using SQL Server, the best way to back up the database structure is to tell SQL Server to generate SQL scripts for the database. If you need to rebuild the database, the SQL script contains all the information that SQL Server needs to rebuild a new copy of the database.

Adding test data

Once you've gotten your table created you can start entering data. If you select View ⇨ Datasheet View, you'll see a large grid with a column for each field in your table. The only field you shouldn't try to enter data into is the primary key, if you're using an AutoNumber field for your primary key. Access will automatically add the value when you have entered all the fields or when you move to a new row. To make it easier to learn how to write queries against your database, be sure to add at least 10 to 15 rows into the table you just created.

You can also enter data directly into SQL Server by right-clicking the table name and then selecting Open Table ⇨ Return All Rows from the popup menu. You can enter data into most of the fields this way, as long as the field is not a binary or large text field (text or ntext data types).

Test data lets you make sure that your queries and searches work properly. Without test data to use, you can't make sure things are working right. We'll be creating queries in the next chapter.

Add more tables

Very few databases will have just a single table. Once you've created one table you can create the others that are required. In the third part of the book, you'll be building a database that has quite a few tables in it. You'll also learn how to make relationships between tables. The whole point of creating a relational database is to define relationships between tables.

Done!

One important thing to remember is that good database design is as important, if not more important, than application design. If the database is designed poorly, it's going to cause performance problems in your application. It can also make the application difficult or impossible to expand with new features.

REVIEW

Database design and development is a topic that requires a book of its own. However, you should be familiar with the tools you use to create databases and tables in both Access and SQL Server 7. The graphical interfaces for both of these databases make these once-cumbersome tasks a piece of cake. You'll be creating tables throughout the rest of the book so be sure to get some practice time in with your own databases.

QUIZ YOURSELF

1. What's the definition of RDBMS? (See "Relational Databases")
2. What's the name of the field that uniquely identifies a record in a table? (See "Working with Microsoft Access")
3. What is the difference between the SQL Server char and varchar data types? (See "Working with Microsoft SQL Server")
4. What SQL Server data type would be the best selection for these values: (See "Working with Microsoft SQL Server")
   - 32000
   - 32.15
   - 12-Nov-2000

Introduction to SQL

Session Checklist

✔ Learn to create data selection queries

✔ Sort result sets

✔ Filter data by your own criteria

✔ Combine multiple tables to create a single result set

✔ Learn to create new records in your database tables

✔ Update existing rows of tables

✔ Delete records from your database tables

**30 Min.
To Go**

I n the previous chapter, you learned to create databases in both Access and
SQL Server. In this chapter, you'll learn to get data from your database using
Structured Query Language (SQL). SQL is a language used in nearly every relational database on the market. These databases allow you to use ANSI SQL, which
is a standardized version of SQL. The SQL covered in this chapter covers basic features available in most relational databases.

Retrieving Data with SQL

Now that you've learned to create a database, you have to learn how to select data from it. This chapter will teach you how to use Structured Query Language (SQL) to accomplish this task. SQL is the standard language used by nearly every relational database currently available. While each database vendor adds some of its own commands to its version of SQL, in this chapter you'll be learning ANSI SQL, a base-level version of the language that nearly every database vendor supports, at a minimum. SQL is really powerful and easy to learn.

For the exercises in this chapter, you'll be using the Northwind Traders database included with both Microsoft Access and SQL Server 7. In Access 2000 the file is called Northwind.mdb and is located in the SAMPLES directory in your Microsoft Office installation directory. For SQL Server, assuming you installed the samples, there will be a database called Northwind. There are some extra tables in the SQL Server version that aren't included in the Access version, but we won't be focusing on those tables. The sample tables all include a good selection of data that makes it easier to learn how to perform the various SQL tasks you're going to learn to perform in this chapter.

Each query you write will return a result set. You may be returning all the rows in a table (or multiple tables), none of the rows, or something in between. You'll learn to control the fields returned from your queries, as well. You can return all the fields, but if you have a very large result set, the fewer fields you bring back, the quicker the data will be available to your program.

You can test your queries in several tools, depending on what database you're using. Within Access, you can create new queries from the main database window that appears when you open your database. Access includes several tools that enable you to "draw" your query. However, this chapter will teach you how to write the SQL you need to perform the work. Once you understand the SQL behind the scenes, you can better use the available tools, both in Access and SQL Server. The main reason to learn SQL is so that you can look at other people's code without the aid of tools like Access, which aren't always available to you. In addition, there are many cases in which you'll need to modify existing code.

Within SQL Server, you'll typically test queries in the Query Analyzer, which is another tool that is installed when you install Enterprise Manager. It's also located in the SQL Server 7.0 program group. It's designed to connect to any SQL Server database and enables you to enter in queries as plain text.

Now, with the introduction out of the way, let's write some queries.

Selecting Data

A lot of what you'll be doing with databases is selecting data. You may use these data to show a page to a user, fill up a dropdown list box, or do something else. You'll be learning a number of additional selection options later in the chapter, but for now let's do something simple.

In the Northwind Traders database (both Access and SQL), you have the following tables:

- Categories
- Customers
- Employees
- Order details
- Orders
- Products
- Shippers
- Suppliers

To create a data selection query you have to at least know the table name. The simplest query is known as a Select query, since that's the keyword you use to build the query. Here's the code for it:

```
SELECT * FROM Customers
```

This query will use the Customers table to build a result set. The asterisk (*) indicates that all fields in the Customers table should be returned. This particular query should return about 90 rows, assuming you haven't added or removed other rows to that table.

Once you've figured out the fields you want, you can specify those fields in your query. Here's an example that returns just the customer's name:

```
SELECT CompanyName FROM Customers
```

You can also include multiple fields by separating them by commas, as shown here:

```
SELECT CompanyName, Phone, Fax FROM Customers
```

This returns the company name, phone, and fax numbers from all the rows in the table. The columns are returned in the order specified in the query. The order in which you list the columns generally isn't important, unless you want the data to look a particular way in a query that you're creating for someone to use without some other sort of interface. In addition, field names and keywords don't have to match case exactly. SQL will generally be able to figure out which field you mean, even if you have uppercase letters in the wrong places. I generally use uppercase for the SQL keywords and mixed case for the table and field names. It makes it a bit easier to see which keywords are which.

Another thing you can do is give each column a new name, if you like. For instance, you can rename the CompanyName field Company Name to make it look more normal in reports. The AS keyword renames, or *aliases*, a column. Here's an example:

```
SELECT CompanyName AS 'Company Name', Phone, Fax FROM Customers
```

When you select data using this query, the column alias will be listed at the top, as shown in Figure 18-1.

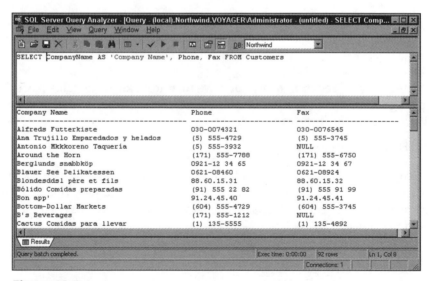

Figure 18-1
Column aliases are used at the top of each column's data

You'll be using column aliases again when you combine database tables that have the same field names. SQL requires that each field have a unique name. Aliases enable you to rename duplicate columns.

Sorting Data

One of the things that the database does well is sorting data. The database server knows all sorts of "tricks" to sort the data more quickly. Remember the primary key that you added to the table? That's one of the tools that the database uses to sort data. The database creates an index on that particular field. Just as the index in the back of a book lets you quickly find information, an index in a database helps sort and find data. If you're frequently sorting data by company name, you can create an index on that field. That's a topic for another book; for now, we'll focus on using the database to sort your data.

The simplest way to sort data is to add an ORDER BY clause to your SELECT statement. For instance, if you wanted to sort the Customers table by company name, here's the statement you'd need:

```
SELECT * FROM Customers ORDER BY CompanyName
```

One important point is that you can sort the data by a field that you haven't selected. Here's an example of that:

```
SELECT CompanyName FROM Customers ORDER BY Country
```

By default, the sorting will be done alphabetically in ascending order. You can control the order by adding on an extra keyword after the field name: DESC. This will change the order to descending order. Here's the new query:

```
SELECT CompanyName FROM Customers ORDER BY Country DESC
```

This will return all the company names in reverse alphabetical order by their country.

You also have the option to sort by several fields. For instance, if you wanted a list of companies, sorted first by country and then by company name, you can specify the sort fields separated by commas. Here's that particular query:

```
SELECT CompanyName, Country
FROM Customers
ORDER BY Country, CompanyName
```

This query will return the results shown in Figure 18-2.

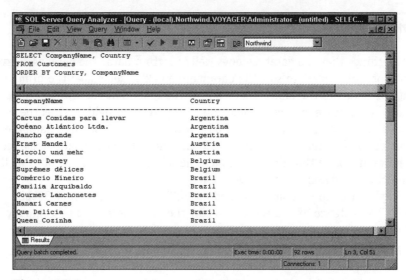

Figure 18-2

Customers sorted by country and then by company name

Note that this query is broken onto multiple lines. SQL doesn't care how you format the query as long as all the keywords are used properly. You can also mix and match the sorting direction in this query, as shown here:

```
SELECT CompanyName, Country
FROM Customers
ORDER BY Country DESC, CompanyName
```

This query will return the results shown in Figure 18-3.

You can also specify the sorted fields by number. For instance, this query:

```
SELECT CompanyName, Country
FROM Customers
ORDER BY Country, CompanyName
```

can be rewritten like so:

```
SELECT CompanyName, Country
FROM Customers
ORDER BY 2, 1
```

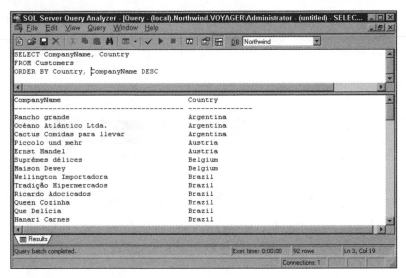

Figure 18-3
Customers reverse-sorted by country and then by company name

The numbers (starting with one) map to the fields in the order in which you list them. This is especially helpful if you are using formulas in your SELECT statement. By specifying the column number for sorting, you eliminate the need to duplicate your work in both the SELECT clause and the ORDER BY clause.

Depending on the database, you can also usually sort by column aliases. Some databases support this feature and others don't. Remember that if you can't sort by a column alias, you generally can sort by a column number.

Filtering Data

**20 Min.
To Go**

Being able to return all the rows in a table is helpful, but if you've got a million rows, you're generally not going to want to return all of them. Generally, you're going to want to return rows that match a particular set of criteria. In the SQL language, you add a WHERE clause to specify records to select from a table or a set of tables.

The WHERE clause is easy to set up. In general, the criteria are in this format:

```
Field = Value
```

You can combine these pairs with joining words, such as AND or OR. The criteria can be grouped using parentheses, as well. Let's start with an easy one that returns the complete product record for the product whose product ID is 5. Here's the query you would use:

```
SELECT * FROM Products WHERE ProductID = 5
```

This query returns the result shown in Figure 18-4.

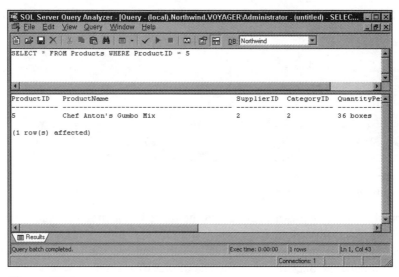

Figure 18-4
Chef Anton's Gumbo Mix is product #5

If you're checking string data, be sure to wrap the criteria in single quotes, as shown here:

```
SELECT * FROM Customers WHERE CustomerID = 'ALFKI'
```

Numeric data, such as the previous query, doesn't require you to put single quotes around the data. If you're working with date values, you'll have to check your database documentation. SQL Server requires single quotes around date data, but Access uses pound signs (#) in certain cases.

Regardless of what you put in the WHERE clause, all the other rules you've already learned for constructing SQL statements still apply. For instance, if you just wanted the name of the product and the price, your SQL statement might look like this:

```
SELECT ProductName, UnitPrice
FROM Products
WHERE ProductID = 5
```

This query returns the result shown in Figure 18-5. You should note that even though the field is named UnitPrice, no currency symbols are added to the result. You can add them after the fact with some of the built-in functions or within your ASP code.

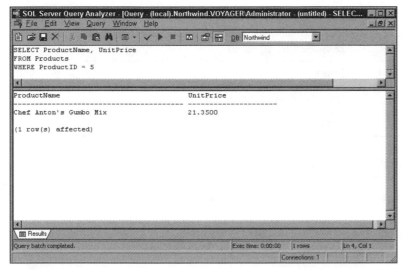

Figure 18-5
Query result

Using comparison operators

Besides using simple equality tests, you can use any of the comparison operators shown in Table 18-1.

These operators give you more flexibility in the data you can return. For instance, if you wanted to find all the products whose unit price was over twenty dollars, you could create this query:

```
SELECT ProductName, UnitPrice
FROM Products
WHERE UnitPrice >= 20
ORDER BY UnitPrice, ProductName
```

Table 18-1
SQL Comparison Operators

Operator	Meaning
=	Equal to
<>	Not equal to
<=	Less than or equal to
<	Less than
>=	Greater than or equal to
>	Greater than

The result of this query is a list of all the products whose price is greater than or equal to 20 dollars, and the results are sorted first by unit price and then by product name. A sample of the output is shown in Figure 18-6.

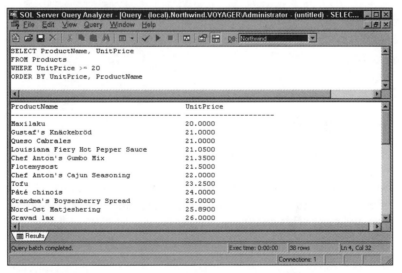

Figure 18-6
Results of product pricing query

Creating compound conditions

Using these operators and the joining words AND and OR, you can create a range of values for rows to match. For instance, you can modify the previous example to show products whose price is between 20 and 40 dollars, inclusive. Here's the new code:

```
SELECT ProductName, UnitPrice
FROM Products
WHERE UnitPrice >= 20 AND UnitPrice <= 40
ORDER BY UnitPrice, ProductName
```

By requiring that the price be greater than 20 and less than 40, you've set up this condition:

```
20 <= UnitPrice <= 40
```

You unfortunately can't write the condition this way, so you have to break it into two conditions. However, some databases (including SQL Server) enable you to specify that a value be between two others, as shown in this rewrite of the previous example:

```
SELECT ProductName, UnitPrice
FROM Products
WHERE UnitPrice BETWEEN 20 AND 40
ORDER BY UnitPrice, ProductName
```

The BETWEEN keyword indicates that the field specified should have a value between the two values following the keyword. This keyword implies that the end points are valid values, as well.

Using the LIKE keyword

There are also cases in which you'll want to search your database for substrings within your fields. For instance, let's say you wanted to find any products with the word "sauce" in their name. You can't simply use this query:

```
SELECT * FROM Products WHERE ProductName = 'sauce'
```

You can't use this query because none of the products have a product name that's just the word "sauce." They all include other words In this case, you need to use the LIKE keyword instead of the equals sign. Here's the correct query:

```
SELECT * FROM Products WHERE ProductName LIKE '%sauce%'
```

The results of this query are shown in Figure 18-7 and include the two products in the database that have the word "sauce" in their names.

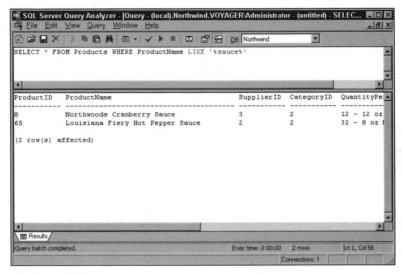

Figure 18-7
Results of LIKE keyword query

By specifying the LIKE keyword, you tell SQL that you want to find a string matching the one you've specified. However, you also have to use the percent characters on either side of the keyword you're looking for. The percent sign acts as a wildcard character: that is, it will match any number of characters wherever it finds a percent sign. In this case, the database will match any number of characters on either side of the word "sauce." If you only wanted to match characters before the word "sauce," you would use this version of the query:

```
SELECT * FROM Products WHERE ProductName LIKE '%sauce'
```

This would match any product name where the last word is "sauce."

If you're using Access directly, you have to use an asterisk instead of a percent sign when you're writing these queries. However, when you use ADO to run your query, you still use a percent sign, even with Access as the database.

Joining Tables

One of the features of a relational database is the ability to let you create relationships between tables. This feature enables you to eliminate redundant data in tables. However, when you are retrieving data, you have to combine the tables to retrieve all the relevant data from all the different tables. This is called a *join*. Joining tables is an important skill to learn, since it's a task you'll often perform when working with a relational database.

There are two important steps in making a join between two tables. The first step is to make sure, through the use of primary and foreign keys, that tables are related to each other. A primary key is the value that uniquely identifies each record in a table. If you want to relate one table to another, you put a copy of the other table's primary key into your table. This key is known as a foreign key, since the value is a key in another table.

The Northwind Traders database includes a number of relationships that you can join. For instance, the Products table includes relationships to the Categories and Suppliers tables. The CategoryID value on the Products table helps identify that a product is in a particular category. If you wanted to create a list of products and their category names, you could create this query:

```
SELECT P.ProductName, C.CategoryName
FROM Products P, Categories C
WHERE P.CategoryID = C.CategoryID
```

You've added a few new features to your query to make it work. First of all, you've added aliases to each table name. The values P and C are aliases for the names of the tables that make up your query. You have to do this because the field CategoryID is in both the Products table and the Categories table. You have to specify which is which when you do your join. You also specify that the ProductName field should come from the Products table and the CategoryName field should come from the Categories table. In this particular case, you could omit the table prefixes since the ProductName and CategoryName fields are not duplicated. However, I generally specify which table provides each field. The result of this query is shown in Figure 18-8.

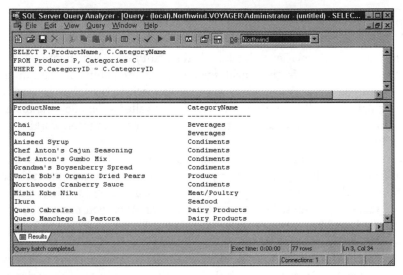

Figure 18-8
Products and categories together

You can also specify that the data be sorted in a particular order, even when you're combining data. For instance, if you want to sort the products by category and then by product name, the query becomes:

```
SELECT P.ProductName, C.CategoryName
FROM Products P, Categories C
WHERE P.CategoryID = C.CategoryID
ORDER BY 2, 1
```

As with sorting, you don't have to specify fields in a particular order for the join to work properly. The following query would produce the same result:

```
SELECT C.CategoryName, P.ProductName
FROM Products P, Categories C
WHERE P.CategoryID = C.CategoryID
```

This particular query is called a *two-table join*. You can create any number of joins as your database and data structure requires. For instance, with the Products table, you can easily create a three-table join with an additional field selection and WHERE clause. Here's a new query that just does that:

```
SELECT C.CategoryName, P.ProductName, S.CompanyName
FROM Products P, Categories C, Suppliers S
```

```
WHERE P.CategoryID = C.CategoryID
AND P.SupplierID = S.SupplierID
ORDER BY 1, 2, 3
```

The result of this query is shown in Figure 18-9.

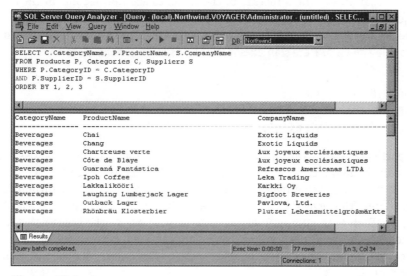

Figure 18-9
Results of a three-table join

While you can continue to join tables, remember that each additional join will cause the query to run longer. Joining on foreign and primary keys that are all the same data type speeds things up, as does making the query a stored procedure (SQL Server) or saved query (Access).

In the database you'll create later in the book, you'll be prefixing the foreign keys with fk and the primary keys with pk. This makes it easier to create the joins because you don't have to worry about getting confused with duplicate fields. It also helps document the tables and makes it easier to understand how the joins work just by looking at the code.

Adding Database Records

In the previous chapter, you learned to select data from your database. Selecting data, however, is only part of your job as an application programmer. You also have to provide mechanisms for adding new records. In this section you'll learn to create new records in your database tables. You'll be doing this using either Access or SQL Server, depending on what you've got installed.

To start with, create a single database record in the Shippers table, since it's relatively short. The statement you'll be using is known as an INSERT statement. It is used, regardless of the structure of the table, to add new records in the SQL language.

To create a new record, specify the fields into which you're putting data and then provide the data. Here's an example of the syntax for the statement:

```
INSERT INTO Shippers
(CompanyName, Phone)
VALUES
('Crash Course Shipping', '(703) 555-1212')
```

This particular statement is broken into four parts. The first line specifies the table to add the new record to. The next line specifies the fields into which you'll be putting data. Each table field should be separated by commas and surrounded by parentheses. The keyword VALUES separates the list of fields from the list of data values. Each of the data values needs to match up with the fields listed, and the values need to be in the same order. In this particular case, `Crash Course Shipping` will go into the CompanyName field, and the phone number will go into the Phone field.

Note that you didn't supply a value for the ShipperID field. That's because the database will automatically supply a value for that field when a new record is created. If you are adding data to a table without an identity or AutoNumber field in it, you'll need to supply the value for the field.

As far as which fields to provide values for, the only requirement is that you provide values for all database fields that are marked as required. If there are fields that aren't required, you can either supply a value or omit it.

If you're providing all the values for each field in the table, you can omit the first list of fields. By default, SQL will assign each value listed to the fields in order. However, this is generally not a good idea, especially since tables can change. If you add an extra field and don't have the fields listed, your INSERT statements will fail. In addition, if you supply the field names, you don't necessarily have to list the fields in the same order in which they appear in the table. This gives you a little bit of flexibility in writing your SQL code.

One of the best things about INSERT statements is that they're really simple to write. There are several other options for inserting rows into a table, but we're going to skip them for now. These other options enable you to insert a batch of rows from one table into another. For what you'll be doing later in the book, you won't need these features at all. However, be aware that the features are available in most databases. They're handy when you need to move data from one database table to another, for instance.

**10 Min.
To Go**

Modifying Database Records

Once you've got records in your database, you have to have a way to modify them. Depending on how you write the statement you'll modify either zero, one, or many records in a table. As with the INSERT statement, you'll only be working with a single database table at a time.

The statement you'll be using to do this work is the UPDATE statement. This statement is similar to the INSERT statement with a few important differences. Here's a simple example that changes the name of a customer in the Customers table:

```
UPDATE Customers
SET CompanyName = 'Northstar Deli'
WHERE CustomerID = 'ALFKI'
```

The first part of the statement specifies the table to update — in this case, the Customers table in the Northwind Traders database. The next line specifies what to change. The SET keyword is used once, and then the field and value pairs follow, separated by commas. In this case you're only changing one value, so you only have one name/value pair. The last part of the statement is probably the most important part. The WHERE clause restricts the records you want to change. If you forget to specify the WHERE clause or specify it incorrectly, you may end up modifying more records than you should. The rules for the WHERE clause are exactly the same rules you learned in the last chapter.

In this particular statement, the only field that will be modified is the CompanyName field. If you want to change more than one field at a time, you can use a statement like this:

```
UPDATE Customers
SET CompanyName = 'Northstar Deli', ContactName = 'Eric Smith'
WHERE CustomerID = 'ALFKI'
```

As with everything else in SQL, you can change the spacing and indenting on your statement without any fear of it not operating correctly.

One problem that you could have here, as with the INSERT statement, is with single quotes. For instance, let's say that the new name for my company is Eric's Deli. The statement to change the record would be as follows:

```
UPDATE Customers
SET CompanyName = 'Eric's Deli'
WHERE CustomerID = 'ALFKI'
```

If you count up the single quotes, you end up with five total. A simple rule to follow is that you always have to have an even number of single quotes in your statement. In this case, the single quote in the company name will cause an error in the SQL statement. The simple fix is to change all the single quotes in the company name itself into two single quotes. Here's the corrected version:

```
UPDATE Customers
SET CompanyName = 'Eric''s Deli'
WHERE CustomerID = 'ALFKI'
```

Note that I don't change all the single quotes to two single quotes; only the ones that are actually values I'm putting into the database.

While you generally need to supply a WHERE clause for every UPDATE statement you write, there are cases in which you'll want to update all the records in your database. For instance, let's say that Eric's Deli decided that it had to increase prices to help cover the rent, and that all prices need to increase by 5%. Raising prices is easy to do with an UPDATE statement:

```
UPDATE Products
SET UnitPrice = UnitPrice * 1.05
```

In this case, since I want to update all the products, I leave off the WHERE clause. Just as leaving the WHERE clause off a SELECT statement brings back all the records, leaving it off an UPDATE statement updates all the records.

Deleting Records

The last method you have for modifying database data is deleting records. While the actual statement is easy to write, deleting records is not an easy topic to cover. Let's take care of the syntax first, though.

Here's a simple example of a DELETE statement:

```
DELETE FROM Customers
WHERE CustomerID = 'ALFKI'
```

The DELETE statement, like the others covered in this chapter, works on a single table at a time. The table name follows the DELETE FROM keywords, and after that you specify a WHERE clause. The WHERE clause is constructed like the UPDATE and SELECT statements. In this case, you wrote a statement to delete the customer whose customer ID is ALFKI.

As with the UPDATE statement, you can leave off the WHERE clause from the DELETE statement. However, this has the nasty side effect of wiping out your table contents. Any time I am deleting data, I always check to see how many records I would be deleting by changing the DELETE statement into a SELECT statement. For instance, I would change the previous DELETE statement into this before running it:

```
SELECT * FROM Customers
WHERE CustomerID = 'ALFKI'
```

This is important when you're coding your applications, especially when you're first learning SQL. It's very easy to write the wrong WHERE condition and get a somewhat unpleasant result.

Now that we've covered the syntax, let's talk about the downside of deleting data. The first problem is that once a record is deleted, it's gone for good. There are some advanced methods for rolling back a transaction, but generally they are used for errors only. Let's say that you are writing a system for the IRS. Do you think it would be a good idea to allow a taxpayer's record to be deleted once he or she is dead, for instance? Once the record is deleted, it's as if the record never existed. This means that the system can't provide a historical or archived copy of the data.

The second problem is that any tables related to the taxpayer table, such as the table that records how much Uncle Sam took from your paycheck each month, won't work properly. This is because tables are interlinked with foreign keys. If you delete the record whose primary key matches my foreign key value, my foreign key value is no longer valid.

In general, most systems don't allow deletions of data, except in a few cases. You might be able to delete notes about a person, or delete a person if there is absolutely no other related data about the person in the system. In most cases, the solution is to mark the person as inactive, as unavailable, or with some other flag indicating that the data are no longer current. This preserves the relationships among your tables but at the same time shows that the record you wanted to delete has changed status in some way.

While you won't need to deal with this issue in your application, keep it in mind as you build other applications. You need to be extremely careful when deleting data.

Done!

REVIEW

Using relational databases is an important skill that every developer should have on his or her resume. Relational databases are found in nearly every system available today and are incredibly easy to create and maintain. While good database design does take practice, following a few simple rules makes it easy to create the types of queries you created in this chapter.

You also learned the basic methods for changing data in your database. You can add records with the INSERT statement, modify data with the UPDATE statement, and delete data with the DELETE statement. These statements are easy to understand but some of them have nasty side effects when not used properly. Be sure you know what you're aiming at before firing off these statements.

QUIZ YOURSELF

1. What type of key lets us create joins between tables? (See "Joining Tables")
2. What clause do you add to a SELECT statement to sort data? (See "Sorting Data")
3. What occurs if you omit the WHERE clause from an UPDATE statement? (See "Modifying Database Records")
4. What two ways can you list fields to be sorted in a SELECT statement? (See "Sorting Data")
5. How do you alias a table for use in a join query? (See "Joining Tables")

SESSION

19

Introduction to ADO

Session Checklist

✔ Learn the differences among ADO, OLE DB, and ODBC

✔ Learn how to make a connection to a database with ADO

✔ Learn how to retrieve data from a database with ADO

**30 Min.
To Go**

Active Data Objects is a fast, easy way to access data from databases. More efficient than older technologies in tools like Visual Basic, ADO is also where Microsoft is putting all their database access development efforts, so you can be sure that the technology will be supported in the future.

Microsoft's Universal Data Access Strategy

One of the major complaints that developers using Microsoft products have had is that the array of choices for getting to databases is confusing. Early on, you could only use the Open Database Connectivity (ODBC) Application Programming Interface (API), which was not particularly easy to implement, especially in the VB environment. API programming is tricky to do and most programmers avoid doing it except when absolutely necessary. Visual Basic started including a variety of objects to connect to databases, including Data Access Objects (DAO), which was designed for the Microsoft Access database; and Remote Data Objects (RDO), which was designed for enterprise databases like Oracle and SQL Server.

While both technologies worked fine, you couldn't take your understanding of one and work with the other. The object models were different enough to require you to relearn what you had learned in one model. There was also the ongoing confusion about when to use one instead of the other. In addition, some of the older methods, such as talking directly to the ODBC API, were still available, as were some variations like ODBCDirect.

Something had to change to simplify the whole landscape, and that change was the introduction of Active Data Objects. ADO is a key component of Microsoft's Universal Data Access (UDA) strategy. The idea is to give programmers a single set of objects that can be used in any Microsoft environment and for any platform. If you are using VB with SQL Server, you can use ADO. If you are using VB with Oracle, you can use ADO. If you're using Windows CE or ASP, you can use ADO. See the point?

This section introduces several important components of the UDA strategy:

- OLE DB
- ODBC
- Active Data Objects

OLE DB

OLE DB is a technology designed by Microsoft to make it easier to access all types of data through a single set of interfaces. Most programmers know how to access some type of database, whether Access, Oracle, SQL Server, or dBase; however, each one of these databases has a slightly different query language. Some are similar to standard SQL, but dBase has a different language that is not like SQL at all.

Besides traditional databases, there are other sources of data that might be of interest to your users. If you're working on a Web server, you may wish to access data that Microsoft Index Server has produced from your Web site. Index Server is designed to make searchable indexes of your Web data. You may also want to access information in plain text files or in other known document types, like Microsoft Word or Adobe Acrobat. You may also have a need to do some data mining using Online Analytical Processing (OLAP) tools.

All of these sources of data are now accessible through OLE DB. OLE DB uses a driver called a provider. A provider knows how a particular type of data is arranged, regardless of the type of data. The provider translates the request given to it into a request it can process against its particular type of data. The programmer only has to worry about submitting a request that resembles standard SQL language, and the provider takes care of the rest.

OLE DB emphasizes the break between the components involved in an application. The application submits a request to the provider, which then translates the request to the data source so that the data can be sent to the application. If the data source driver changes, it won't necessarily affect the application's functionality. This helps to protect your applications from the whims of your product vendors, who tend to change their interfaces just as you've gotten used to them.

ODBC

Open Database Connectivity (ODBC) is a specification for a database API. The API is an independent standard supported by a variety of product vendors, including Oracle, Informix, Sybase, and Microsoft. Drivers for these databases are provided by both the vendors and third-party companies such as Intersolv.

While OLE DB is able to talk directly to several different types of databases, there are some databases that do not yet have OLE DB providers available. In these cases, you can use the ODBC driver for the database in conjunction with the OLE DB provider for ODBC. Using this method creates an extra layer of interface between your code and the database — that is, ADO talks to OLE DB, which talks to ODBC, which talks to the database. This is a good method if you are planning to upgrade the application or the database at some point. Since more and more product vendors are releasing OLE DB providers, new applications should be built using ADO and OLE DB, even if that means using the extra layer of ODBC for the time being. This method will require the least code to change to OLE DB/ADO when your database releases an OLE DB provider.

Active Data Objects

Regardless of the driver combinations you are using, you will be using Active Data Objects to manipulate the data. ADO provides a number of objects that are used to traverse all types of data. If you're familiar with DAO or RDO, using ADO should be pretty easy for you. There are a few differences, as you'll see in the next section of this chapter. ADO defines seven objects:

- Connection
- Command
- Recordset
- Parameter
- Field

- Property
- Error

In addition, there are four collections used in ADO:

- Fields
- Parameters
- Properties
- Errors

We're not going to be covering all of these objects, but we'll cover the important ones in this chapter. You'll learn about several more of them in Chapter 30. If you'd like more information about what you can do with these objects, you can refer to the MSDN Library available online at http://msdn.microsoft.com/library.

20 Min. To Go

The Connection Object

A Connection object represents a single session with a data source. In ADO, you can have multiple Connection objects with each one pointing to a different data source. This can be helpful if you are accessing multiple data sources and combining the results on a Web page of some sort. In the case of a client/server database system, it may be equivalent to an actual network connection to the server. Depending on the functionality supported by the OLE DB provider, some collections, methods, or properties of a Connection object may not be available. This section covers the use of the Connection object and how 'to use it to access data sources.

Making a connection

To get started with any other ADO object, you first have to have a Connection object. A Connection object is given information about how to connect to the data source, whatever that source is. Using the code shown in Listing 19-1 is one way you could connect to the BIBLIO database included with Visual Basic.

Listing 19-1
Connection code

```
Dim cnDB    ' As ADODB.Connection

Set cnDB = Server.CreateObject("ADODB.Connection")
```

```
cnDB.ConnectionString = _
   & "Provider=Microsoft.Jet.OLEDB.4.0;" _
   & "Data Source=C:\Visual Studio\VB98\Biblio.mdb"
cnDB.Open
```

 You can substitute any Access 2000 database following the Data Source parameter in the third line of code.

Using the Dim statement will help document your code by specifying what the variable is designed to hold. In this case, you are using the prefix dcn to specify a variable used to hold a Connection object. The next line uses the Server.Create Object method to instantiate a Connection object. However, the data connection is still not open. The third line specifies how to connect to the database. The Provider parameter specifies the OLE DB Provider to use; in this case, you are using the Jet 4.0 Provider, which corresponds to Access 2000. You also have to specify the pathname to the database in the Data Source parameter. Finally, the Open method activates the connection to the database.

The ConnectionString property will differ according to the data source you're using. Listing 19-2 shows a sample of code that can be used to connect to a SQL Server 7 database. Notice the extra parameters in the ConnectionString property.

Listing 19-2
Connection code for SQL Server 7 database

```
Dim cnDB    ' As ADODB.Connection

Set cnDB = Server.CreateObject("ADODB.Connection")
cnDB.ConnectionString = _
   & "Provider=SQLOLEDB;" _
   & "User ID=myuser;Password=mypassword;" _
   & "Initial Catalog=PUBS;" _
   & "Data Source=db.server.com"
cnDB.Open
```

To begin with, the Provider property is different for SQL Server. Next, SQL Server requires a user ID and password, so both of these parameters are provided in the ConnectionString property. You then need to specify both the database server and the database name you want to use. The Data Source can be a LAN server name, an Internet-style address as shown in the example, or a numerical IP address, such as 252.100.100.0.

Closing a connection

When you are at the end of your ASP page, you should always close any open data connections. This allows the data-source server to release the system resources associated with that connection. Too many connections left open will, over time, cause the system to run out of resources and grind to a halt. Closing a connection is quite easy. Simply use the Close method, as shown here: cnDB.Close

Before closing the connection, you should also make sure that any other objects using the connection have been closed. Otherwise you could possibly use an object that is no longer valid, which would cause an error.

10 Min. To Go

The Recordset and Field Objects

A recordset is just what its name says: a set of records. A record is a row from the result of a query. If the query accesses a single table, a record is one row out of the table. If the query joins more than one table, a record is a row from the result. The ADO Recordset object is fairly intelligent and knows how to manage the results to minimize the amount of delay. For instance, if you run a query that returns a large number of rows, the Recordset object knows to only bring back a small batch at a time. While this can cause problems when you are trying to determine the number of records you have, in most cases it will improve the performance of your application. This section covers the ways in which you can use the Recordset object to access your database.

Executing a query

The easiest way to create a recordset is to execute a query against your database. The results will be returned in a Recordset object. The code shown here will determine the number of customers in the Customers table in the Northwind Traders database, and return that value as a single row in a Recordset object. The code assumes that a data connection, stored in the cnDB variable, has already been defined and opened.

```
Dim rsCount    ' As ADODB.Recordset

Set rsCount = cnDB.Execute("SELECT COUNT(*) FROM Customers")
Response.Write "There are " & rsCount(0) & " customers."
```

Note that you don't use `Server.CreateObject` to instantiate the `Recordset` object before using it; rather, you let the `Execute` method do its thing and return a `Recordset` object for you. When you are printing the number of records, using a zero subscript in the rsCount variable will return the first field of the first record. In this case, the count of records will be there.

While you can use the `Execute` method to run SQL commands entered directly into your ASP code, you can also use it to execute stored procedures (as they are known in Oracle and SQL Server) and predefined queries (as they are known in Access). In the following example, you want to run a stored procedure named spCountRecords. As you can see, the code is even shorter than the previous example.

```
Dim rsCount     ' As ADODB.Recordset

Set rsCount = cnDB.Execute("spCountRecords")
Response.Write "There are " & rsCount(0) & " customers."
```

 The method by which you create a stored procedure or query will vary with the database that you are using. Refer to your database documentation for help with creating queries and stored procedures.

Using the `Execute` method is the method that uses the least code to retrieve a read-only recordset for use in ASP.

Besides creating recordsets, the `Execute` method can execute all the other types of queries, such as updates and deletes. Since these queries don't return recordsets, you can call the `Execute` method like this:

```
cnDB.Execute "DELETE FROM Customers " _
    & "WHERE CustomerID = 'ALFKI'"
```

For updates, you may want to look a little bit further in the chapter to see how to edit records in a recordset. It's a lot less complicated than building an update query in SQL.

Opening a recordset

This method is much more flexible than using the `Execute` method of the `Connection` object and provides many more options for getting to data. It does require that you define and instantiate your Recordset object before using it, however. If you don't remember to do this, you'll end up with errors when you attempt to use the object the first time.

The code below opens a Recordset object using the same query you used in the Execute example. This code assumes that you have already opened a connection with the cnDB variable.

```
Dim rsQuery          ' As ADODB.Recordset

Set rsQuery = Server.CreateObject("ADODB.Recordset")
rsQuery.Open "SELECT * FROM Customers", cnDB
```

This will open a read-only, forward-only recordset of the Customers table. Forward-only is used for cases in which you are dumping data to a page, such as in a report or as part of a data entry form. This type of recordset is more efficient than the static recordset since it doesn't need to store as much navigation information, and once you've passed a record, it can get rid of the record, thus saving your system resources. This can be especially important on heavily-loaded systems that need to get every bit of performance out of every piece of code.

The previous code takes advantage of the default parameter values used in the Open method. The following code lists all of the arguments with their proper values. For this code to work, the constants prefixed with ad must be available to your page. You can do this either by including the adovbs.inc file that is located on your server or by using a METADATA tag, which is covered in Chapter 23. Otherwise, the constants being used here (prefixed with ad) won't resolve.

```
Dim rsQuery          ' As ADODB.Recordset

Set rsQuery = Server.CreateObject("ADODB.Recordset")
rsQuery.Open "SELECT * FROM Customers", cnDB, _
    adOpenForwardOnly, adLockReadOnly
```

The adOpenForwardOnly constant, which is the default value, specifies the cursor type. In this context, a cursor is a pointer into a recordset, and not the icon that marks where you type. The valid values for this parameter are shown in Table 19-1.

Table 19-1
CursorType Parameter Values

Constant	Value	Description
adOpenForwardOnly	0	Creates a read-only recordset that can only scroll forward

Constant	Value	Description
adOpenKeyset	1	Cursor enables you to add, modify, and delete records, but you won't see changes made by other users while your recordset is open
adOpenDynamic	2	Cursor enables you to add, modify, and delete records, and you will see any changes made by other users
adOpenStatic	3	Creates a read-only recordset that has all capabilities for positioning and bookmarking

The adLockReadOnly constant, which is also the default value, specifies the method by which the records should be locked. In this case you don't want to change the records, so the read-only constant is the appropriate choice. The other available values are shown in Table 19-2.

Table 19-2
LockType Parameter Values

Constant	Value	Description
adLockReadOnly	1	Records are read-only and cannot be changed
adLockPessimistic	2	Records are locked when you start editing them
adLockOptimistic	3	Records are locked when you call the Update method to commit your changes
adLockBatchOptimistic	4	Required if you are performing batch updates to a set of records

As you have probably figured out already, some of the constant combinations you could make don't really make sense. For instance, using any type of lock with a static recordset will be ineffective, since you can't edit the records anyway. When you are editing records, however, having these options available will make your programming easier to predict. If you are in a high-traffic environment, pessimistic locking of records will prevent two users from changing the same record simultaneously. In a lighter-traffic environment, optimistic locking may be more appropriate since it only locks the records for the occasional update you may need to make.

Navigating in a recordset

Once the recordset is open, you need to be able to navigate through the records. You can display them or process them as you loop. You can use the following code for any type of recordset to loop through the records.

```
Dim rsQuery          ' As ADODB.Recordset

Set rsQuery = Server.CreateObject("ADODB.Recordset")
rsQuery.Open "SELECT * FROM Customers", cnDB

Do While Not rsQuery.EOF
   Response.Write rsQuery("CustomerName")
   rsQuery.MoveNext
Loop

rsQuery.Close
```

This code makes the assumption that the Customers table has a field called CustomerName. Obviously, if you don't have that field in your table, use the correct field name. After you open the recordset as a read-only, forward-only recordset (remember the default values), a Do loop works through the records until the end of file (EOF) flag is True. The EOF flag is True after the last record has been passed by the cursor. This means that you can look at the last record and do another MoveNext, and the EOF flag will be True. After the loop exits, close the Recordset using the Close method. As with the Connection object, you should close all your Recordset objects when you are done with them. This helps conserve system resources.

All of these methods are available for navigating in a recordset, unless it's a forward-only recordset, in which case only MoveNext and MoveFirst are available from this list.

- MoveFirst
- MoveLast
- MoveNext
- MovePrevious

Remember to check for EOF before performing a MoveNext, and check for beginning of file (BOF) before performing a MovePrevious while moving backwards. This will prevent errors from occurring.

Editing records in a recordset

Once you've opened the Recordset properly, you can edit the records in that Recordset. As an example, the code in Listing 19-3 will update the name of a customer (stored in the ContactName field) in the Customers table of the Northwind Traders database. This code includes the code to make a connection, since this is code you'll be using frequently.

Listing 19-3
Editing a Record

```
Dim cnDB          ' As ADODB.Connection
Dim rsQuery       ' As ADODB.Recordset

Set cnDB = Server.CreateObject("ADODB.Connection")
cnDB.ConnectionString = "Provider=Microsoft.Jet.OLEDB.4.0;" _
    & "Data Source=c:\db\nwind.mdb"
cnDB.Open

Set rsQuery = Server.CreateObject("ADODB.Recordset")
rsQuery.Open "SELECT * FROM Customers " _
    & "WHERE CustomerID = 'ALFKI'", _
    cnDB, adOpenKeyset, adLockOptimistic

rsQuery("ContactName") = "The New Name Goes Here"
rsQuery.Update
rsQuery.Close
cnDB.Close
```

Be sure to point the database path to your own database, or you'll get an error. In this example, you select the record you wish to edit by using a simple SELECT query. The recordset is created as a keyset with optimistic updates. The assumption being made here is that you don't need to see other people's changes to this one record in this recordset, which you will close after making the update. Optimistic locking doesn't make the record lock until the Update method has been called. Note that, unlike with DAO, you don't have to call an Edit method explicitly. As soon as you make a change to a field, as you do to the ContactName field, the record is considered "edited." You still need the Update method to commit the changes at the end.

One advantage of this method is that you don't have to worry whether the values you are storing into the fields contain single quotes. Single quotes, if placed into a SQL Update statement, will cause errors unless each single quote is replaced with two single quotes. If you are putting data into a field this way, you can include all the single quotes you want and no errors will occur.

Adding new records to a table

Adding records is similar to editing, except for a few small details. The code shown in Listing 19-4 will add a new record to the Shippers table in the Northwind Traders database. Remember to change the pathname to your database so the code will work properly.

Listing 19-4
Adding a record via ADO

```
Dim cnDB          ' As ADODB.Connection
Dim rsQuery       ' As ADODB.Recordset

Set cnDB = Server.CreateObject("ADODB.Connection")
cnDB.ConnectionString = "Provider=Microsoft.Jet.OLEDB.4.0;" _
    & "Data Source=c:\nwind.mdb"
cnDB.Open

Set rsQuery = Server.CreateObject("ADODB.Recordset")
rsQuery.Open "SELECT * FROM Shippers", _
    cnDB, adOpenKeyset, adLockOptimistic

rsQuery.AddNew
rsQuery("CompanyName") = "Joe and Larry's Shipping Company"
rsQuery("Phone") = "800-BREAK-IT"
rsQuery.Update
rsQuery.Close
cnDB.Close
```

Adding the new record starts with the AddNew method. After that, you supply each of the required fields with a value, and the Update method finishes the job. If you wish, you can check the Shippers table in the database to see the new record.

Also, if you look at the table design for this table, you should notice that there are actually three fields in the table. The one not specified here is an AutoNumber field that automatically supplies a unique ID for the shippers you add. Since the table has a default value, you don't need to even specify it when you add the record.

Done!

REVIEW

This chapter was designed to teach you the essentials of Active Data Objects as they are used in ASP applications. The `Connection` object represents a single session of communication with the database. The Recordset represents the results of a query against the database and can be used in both read-only and read-write modes. You'll be using these objects later in the book to build the eOrganizer application, which is database-driven.

QUIZ YOURSELF

1. Which object do you need to perform any actions with a database? (See "Making a Connection")

2. What type of Recordset object is the most efficient? (See "Opening a Recordset")

3. What property indicates that you have read all the records in a Recordset object? (See "Navigating in a Recordset")

4. What methods do you have for navigating a Recordset object? Which of them are available regardless of the Recordset type? (See "Navigating in a Recordset")

5. What type of Recordset object is required to add or update records? (See "Editing Records")

6. Which method is used before you start editing a record? (See "Editing Records")

7. Which method is used before you start adding a new record? (See "Adding Records")

Debugging and Error Handling

Session Checklist

✔ Learn some tips and techniques for debugging your ASP files

✔ Learn to handle errors cleanly with the built-in features of VBScript

✔ Create a heavy-duty error-logging routine that you can use in multiple applications

30 Min. To Go

As with any other language, debugging and error handling is a key part of ASP development; nevertheless it's one of the least used features. Many programmers are content to let errors occur without any follow-up to the user. In this chapter, you'll learn about the capabilities of ASP to provide information about errors and handle them in a graceful way instead of just showing an unresolved server error to the user.

Debugging ASP Scripts

One of the most difficult things about writing ASP is that the development environment is not the best. There are some additional capabilities currently available through Visual InterDev; however, you may not always have these features available to you, because that software must be installed on your server for the few debugging features to work properly. In this section you'll learn to debug your code without having to use those features. Most of the tips and techniques covered in this section can be used in other languages.

Keep it simple

One of the biggest problems that I see in code that people want me to debug is that they haven't narrowed the problem down at all. They give me a file with 500 lines of code in it and ask me to find the problem they're having. The idea is to start with the simplest piece of code you can and build up from there. Let's take a typical page that opens a database connection, gets some data, and shows it on the page. The developer is not seeing the data come out properly and is getting some error that doesn't make sense. Here's how I would recommend you go about finding the problem:

1. Create a new page that only makes a database connection using the same code as the page in question.
2. Make sure the database connection works properly by requesting all records from a table using the `Execute` method of the Connection object.
3. Try looping through the records and dumping them out. See if there are data in the fields that are problematic for your display routine. One common problem is that if you're trying to manipulate a field that has a Null value in it, you'll get an error when you try to use it. Try combining an empty string with your database field before manipulating the variable.

At some point, with this method, you'll probably recreate the error you're having. The idea is that if you can narrow down the problem, it's much easier to find the actual cause.

Use modular code

One easy way to write more reliable code is to use subroutines and functions. The idea is that if you can make sure a simple block of code works properly, you can reuse it again without having to retest it. By combining the small blocks of code, you can create more reliable code without having to retest every time.

In addition, using subroutines and functions enables you to do "black-box programming." As long as the input and output arguments stay the same, you can change the implementation of a function or subroutine at will. Being able to test these blocks of code means that when a problem occurs, you can generally skip retesting these sections of code.

Print everything out

When you're trying to debug code, don't assume that variables will always hold what you think they do. When I'm checking my code, I print out all the data values all the way through a routine. That way I know exactly what's going on.

The problem is that you can't always just print the data to the Web page, since that can cause the page to incorrectly appear in the browser. Instead, if I'm generating debugging messages, I print them as HTML comments to the Web page. That way they are in the source but don't destroy the HTML tables or any of the graphical layouts that I might have set up.

Here's a routine that I created to automatically create HTML comments for me:

```
Sub WriteComment(strText)
    Response.Write "<!-- " & strText & " -->" & vbCrLf
End Sub
```

If you use this routine throughout your pages to print out the debugging values, you can easily turn it off by commenting out the `Response.Write` statement. That enables you to leave the debugging code in your pages but only make it visible when you're working with the code.

Use constants

A common problem is that in page-to-page communications, you expect one value and in fact you get another. Your code operates incorrectly because the value or code you were expecting doesn't make it over from the previous page. A simple way to eliminate this problem is to always use constants. You can place these constants in a common include file that you put in all your files. As long as all the pages use and look for the same set of constants, you won't have this problem.

Constants are also an easy way to make it easier to change data in your applications. For instance, let's say that you have a sales-tax rate in your application. As long as you use the constant when you're doing your calculations, you can easily change it when your local government decides to crank up the tax rate a bit.

Create trace messages

Besides printing out the data values, you can also print comments out to indicate where in your program you are. For instance, you might put a comment before a problematic line and a comment after it. If one comment prints and the other doesn't, you have a problem on that line. If both comments print out, you'll have to look elsewhere for the application.

Turn buffering off

One of the things I do frequently while I'm programming is dump values out to indicate where I am as the page executes. However, if an error occurs, you may or may not see the lines you created with `Response.Write`. The property that controls how data is sent to the browser is the `Response.Buffer` property. If buffering is turned on (which it is by default in Windows 2000), you will see the error message but no other text. If buffering is turned off (as in Windows NT 4), you'll see any text generated up to the point at which the error occurred. If you're building your pages and anticipate errors, just turn buffering off, either at a site-wide level or on a per-page basis with this code:

```
Response.Buffer = False
```

Check your quotes

Another common problem when writing ASP code is to not have your single and double quotes written properly. In the last chapter, you learned that single quotes in SQL statements have to be changed to two single quotes if they are to go into the database properly. The same is true with double quotes. If you're printing out a line of HTML that has double-quote characters in it, you have to print two double-quote characters next to each other to get the one character to print properly.

A trick I use is to create constants called SQ (for single quote) and DQ (for double quote) and concatenate them with my text. Here's an example of how you might print out a link in your ASP code:

```
Response.Write "<a href=" & DQ & strSite & DQ & ">My Site</a>"
```

The somewhat ugly equivalent of this code would be:

```
Response.Write "<a href=""" & strSite & """>My Site</a>"
```

All these double-quote characters are a common source of errors. Using the constant makes it easier to see when you're printing out double-quote characters and when you're using them to mark the beginning and ending of strings.

Error Handling

**20 Min.
To Go**

Error handling in VBScript is one of the weakest features in the language. While tools like Visual Basic and Visual C++ have extensive capabilities for managing errors, VBScript has one. This section will show you how to perform error handling in spite of this limitation.

The basics

VBScript provides you with two options for error handling. The first is not to do it, which isn't a particularly good choice. The second is On Error Resume Next. If you're familiar with it from Visual Basic, it does the same thing here. In case of error, control passes to the next line following the error. The result of this is that you have to check for an error everywhere you think one might occur. This is a major pain, and because it's such a pain, many programmers fail to perform error handling at all. Look at the code below, which is an excerpt from a fictional page.

```
Dim intNumber, intDivisor

On Error Resume Next
intNumber = 15
intDivisor = 0

Response.Write intNumber / intDivisor
If Err.Number <> 0 Then
    Response.Write "Error #" & Err.Number _
        & ", " _
        & Err.Description & ", occurred."
End If

' more code would follow
```

In this small example, you see how error handling is done in VBScript. You first initiate error handling with the On Error Resume Next line. You then write your code as usual. Anywhere you think an error might occur — in this case, after a divide by zero line — you add error handling. Checking the `Err` object's `Number` property will tell you if an error occurred. If so, you have to deal with the error and either bail out or continue, depending on the error.

Once you've detected an error, you have to figure out what to do with it. The error itself will, in most cases, determine what you can do next. Syntax-related errors are pretty rare once you've gotten the page up and running, but they do happen occasionally. Run-time errors, such as invalid parameter values and illegal function calls, are more common. In many cases, you can avoid these errors with some extra data-checking. The best way to determine what to do in case of an error is to look at the possible errors and group them. Table 20-1 shows a list of the most common VBScript errors and their numbers. Note that this list doesn't include errors generated by other libraries, such as ADO or components you might create.

Table 20-1
VBScript Error Messages

Number	Message
5	Invalid procedure call or argument
6	Overflow
7	Out of memory
9	Subscript out of range
10	Array fixed or temporarily locked
11	Division by 0
13	Type mismatch
14	Out of string space
28	Out of stack space
35	Sub or Function not defined
48	Error in loading DLL
51	Internal error
53	File not found
57	Device I/O error
58	File already exists

Number	Message
61	Disk full
67	Too many files
70	Permission denied
75	Path/File access error
76	Path not found
91	Object variable or With block variable not set
92	For loop not initialized
94	Invalid use of Null
322	Can't create necessary temporary file
424	Object required
429	ActiveX component can't create object
430	Class doesn't support Automation
432	Filename or class name not found during Automation operation
438	Object doesn't support this property or method
440	Automation error
445	Object doesn't support this action
446	Object doesn't support named arguments
447	Object doesn't support current locale setting
448	Named argument not found
449	Argument not optional
450	Wrong number of arguments or invalid property assignment
451	Object not a collection
453	Specified DLL function not found
455	Code resource lock error
457	This key already associated with an element of this collection

Continued

Table 20-1 *Continued*

Number	Message
458	Variable uses an Automation type not supported in VBScript
500	Variable is undefined
501	Illegal assignment
502	Object not safe for scripting
503	Object not safe for initializing
1001	Out of memory
1002	Syntax error
1003	Expected ':'
1004	Expected ';'
1005	Expected '('
1006	Expected ')'
1007	Expected ']'
1008	Expected '{'
1009	Expected '}'
1010	Expected identifier
1011	Expected '='
1012	Expected 'If'
1013	Expected 'To'
1014	Expected 'End'
1015	Expected 'Function'
1016	Expected 'Sub'
1017	Expected 'Then'
1018	Expected 'Wend'
1019	Expected 'Loop'

Number	Message
1020	Expected 'Next'
1021	Expected 'Case'
1022	Expected 'Select'
1023	Expected expression
1024	Expected statement
1025	Expected end of statement
1026	Expected integer constant
1027	Expected 'While' or 'Until'
1028	Expected 'While', 'Until', or end of statement
1029	Too many locals or arguments
1030	Identifier too long
1031	Invalid number
1032	Invalid character
1033	Unterminated string constant
1034	Unterminated comment
1035	Nested comment
1037	Invalid use of 'Me' keyword
1038	'Loop' without 'Do'
1039	Invalid 'Exit' statement
1040	Invalid 'For' loop control variable
1041	Name redefined
1042	Must be first statement on the line
1043	Can't assign to non-ByVal argument
1044	Can't use parens when calling a Sub
1045	Expected literal constant

Continued

Table 20-1 *Continued*

Number	Message
1046	Expected 'In'
32766	True
32767	False
32811	Element not found

As you can tell from the error messages, many of these are syntax-related and will cause your application to fail. These errors should normally result in the page being exited immediately, since VBScript often won't let you continue with these errors.

10 Min.
To Go

Handling runtime errors

One of the worst things that a user can see on your site is an unhandled error, such as the one shown in Figure 20-1.

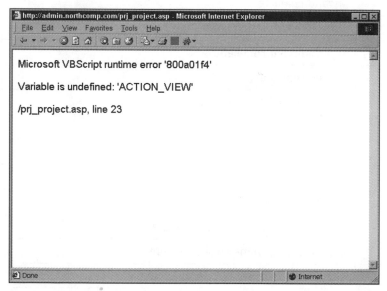

Figure 20-1
An unhandled error in the browser

It's much clearer to the user to see the message shown in Figure 20-2 instead.

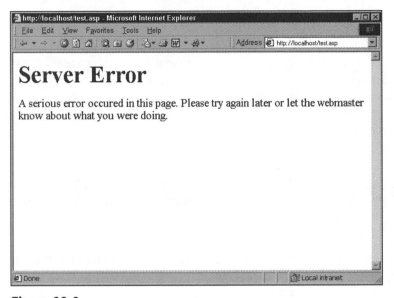

Figure 20-2
An appropriate message to show to the user

The user doesn't know what the error is or how to fix it, so why show him or her the actual message? It's easier to store the information for the developer and show the user a more generic message.

In the following code, the routine displays a simple message to the user but logs all the information in a text file on the server.

```
Sub LogError(strLocation)
    Dim objFSO      ' As Scripting.FileSystemObject
    Dim objStream   ' As Scripting.TextStream

    If Err.Number = 0 Then Exit Sub

    WriteLine "<p><font color=#FF0000><b>" _
        & "Server Error Occurred</b></font></p>"
    WriteLine "<p>An error occurred on the server " _
        & "and the page you requested cannot be executed.</p>"
```

```
Set objFSO = Server.CreateObject("Scripting.FileSystemObject")
Set objStream = objFSO.OpenTextFile("C:\weblog.txt", _
    ForAppending, True)
objStream.WriteLine Now() & ": [" & Request("SCRIPT_NAME") _
    & " - Err #" & Err.Number & "] " _
    & Err.description & " [Location: " & strLocation & "]"
objStream.Close
Set objStream = Nothing
Set objFSO = Nothing
Response.End
End Sub
```

Remember that the WriteLine routine was declared earlier in the chapter. Refer back to the previous listing to learn how to create it.

This routine, when it runs, will keep track of any errors in a text file out on the server. The developer can then look at the error log to determine what went wrong and what file it went wrong in.

Here's an example of how you would call this routine. Essentially, you check for an error after each call that could potentially cause an error. If an error is encountered, you display a message to the user, log the error, and exit.

```
<%
On Error Resume Next

Response.Write 5/0
LogError "After division call"

%>
```

The LogError routine would be elsewhere in this file or in an include file. The Web browser would display the simple message shown in Figure 20-3.

Behind the scenes, the developer would have access to all the information about the error. Figure 20-4 shows what the log would look like for a division by 0 error.

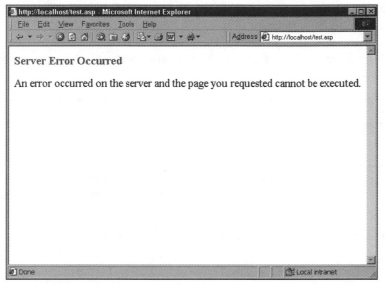

Figure 20-3
The user doesn't need all the details behind your error

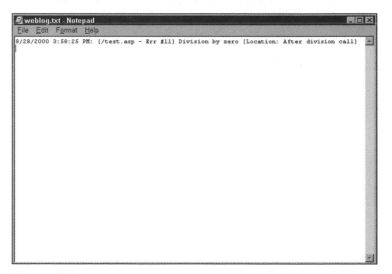

Figure 20-4
The error log would contain all the information about the error

This is just a sample of what you could create using the information in the Err object. You also have access to additional information through the ASP 3.0 ASPError object, which you get to by setting a variable equal to Server.GetLastError. Once you do that, you have access to all the properties of the ASPError object shown in Table 20-2.

Table 20-2
ASPError Properties

Name	Description
ASPCode	Returns the error number generated by Internet Information Server. Typically, this will be 500, which indicates a server error.
ASPDescription	Returns a more complete description of the error that occurred (if available) so you can provide more information to your users.
Description	Provides a short description of the error. It is typically a description that you might see in a Visual Basic error message. The ASPDescription property will sometimes hold a more complete description of the error.
FileName	Holds the name of the file that was being processed when the error occurred.
LineNumber	Holds the line number within the file where the error occurred. Remember that the actual error might not actually be on this line, especially if it is a case in which bad code earlier (such as missing tags or quotes) causes errors later.
Number	Holds the error number that occurred, as well as any COM error numbers.
Source	Returns a string indicating why the error occurred and whether it was an ASP error, a scripting error, or an error from a component.

Done!

You can mix and match these properties to generate the information you need into your error log.

REVIEW

The basic idea behind error handling in ASP is to minimize confusion on the user's part while storing information for the developer to use. Debugging is a matter of practice and is not overly difficult, once you know the basic techniques. We'll be covering some more debugging and error handling throughout the rest of the book as well.

QUIZ YOURSELF

1. What three key properties are part of the Err object that can be used in error handling? (See "Error Handling")

2. What does Option Explicit do and why is it helpful for debugging? (See "Debugging ASP Scripts")

3. What does buffering have to do with debugging ASP code? (See "Debugging ASP Scripts")

4. What technique can you use to display debugging output to the web page without destroying the look of an HTML page? (See "Debugging ASP Scripts")

IV

Saturday Evening
Part Review

1. What is the key difference between functions and subroutines?
2. Is there a subroutine that will run automatically when an ASP page is loaded?
3. How are parameters separated in a function or subroutine declaration?
4. What two methods can you use to include a file into another?
5. How do you create a temporary cookie? A permanent one?
6. How do you remove a cookie?
7. Which property do you specify to encrypt cookie text?

Define the following database terms:

8. Table
9. Field
10. Primary Key
11. Foreign Key
12. Index

Given a Customers table with the following fields:

- ContactName
- CompanyName
- Phone
- Fax

Answer the following questions:

13. Write a query to return all the fields in the table.

14. Sort the result set by the phone number.

15. Return all the companies whose phone numbers contain the value 703.

16. Add a new record to the table with these values:

   ■ ContactName: Joe Shmo
   ■ CompanyName: Joe Shmo Enterprises
   ■ Phone: (212) 555-1212
   ■ Fax: (212) 555-1213

17. Add a new record to the table with these values:

   ■ ContactName: Brian O'Leary
   ■ CompanyName: O'Leary's Foods
   ■ Phone: (202) 555-1212
   ■ Fax: (202) 555-1213

☑ **Friday**

☑ **Saturday**

☑ **Sunday**

P A R T

V

Sunday Morning

Introduction to the eOrganizer

Session Checklist

✔ Learning about the eOrganizer application

✔ Looking at eOrganizer's features

✔ How to get more information about eOrganizer online

30 Min. To Go

When I was in the Boy Scouts, their method of teaching was "learn by doing." The idea is that if you practice a skill, you'll retain the knowledge better. While you've been doing a little bit of code up until this point, the whole thrust of the last part of the book is to get you more comfortable with ASP technology by building a real application. While we'll keep the feature set simple, the application will provide you with a good base for building your own new features. Chapter 30 covers some of the enhancements you might want to make in your own application.

The eOrganizer Application

The application you're going to build is called *eOrganizer*. It is designed as a Web-based personal information manager. The features you'll be adding are common in applications such as Microsoft Outlook, Lotus Organizer, ACT!, and others. A number of Web-based information managers are also provided by several major companies, including Yahoo, Excite, and others.

As you'll see in the chapters that follow, building a large application is mostly a matter of putting in place a structure that is easy to follow and replicate. The other key part is to find commonly used functions and keep them in a common file that can be included easily.

The eOrganizer has five major functions:

- Contact Manager
- Event/Appointment Manager
- Task/To-Do Manager
- Note Manager
- Link Manager

In addition, the home page of the application contains a calendar that shows the current events and tasks due for a selected month. As you work through each of the successive chapters, you'll build each one of these features, as well as the common functions used in all the pages.

You'll also be building a database to store all the information that your pages let you create. We'll create the database for both Access and SQL Server, but you can use any database you like — you simply have to change how you're connecting to the database. The online sample application uses SQL Server 7, as does the code in this book. However, the SQL that is used is standard syntax and will work in most databases. A few of the functions used are specific to Access and SQL Server, however.

**20 Min.
To Go**

Touring the eOrganizer Application

Let's take a tour of the six functions available in the eOrganizer application. You'll be seeing more of these later, but it's helpful to know where you're going before you get started.

The eOrganizer Home Page

Figure 21-1 shows the home page for the application, a calendar showing all the events that are happening and the tasks that are due in a particular month.

This page is just an HTML table that you'll build in Chapter 29. You'll add in the data you create in the Event and Task Manager portions of the application. Navigation controls at the bottom of the calendar enable you to browse or jump to any month or year. In addition, icons are used to represent events and tasks that are occurring on the days during the month. Hovering over an icon lets you see all the information about that particular task or event.

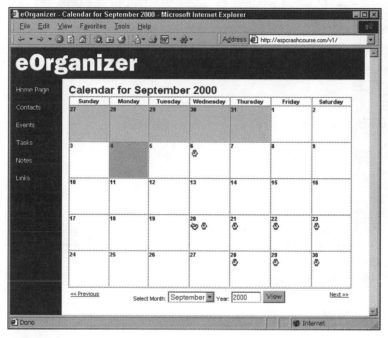

Figure 21-1
The eOrganizer home page

The Contact Manager

Figure 21-2 shows the Contact Manager portion of the application. This is used to keep track of names, addresses, phone numbers, and e-mail addresses of people or clients you might contact on a regular basis.

All of the contacts are shown on the quick reference page, along with links to retrieve, update, or delete the information (the R, U, and D links at the end of the line). This is a commonly used interface throughout the whole application. All of the formatting is done with the use of Cascading Style Sheet tags that you'll write and use throughout the application. This makes the application easy to change — if you don't like the colors, for instance. You make the change once and it's immediately changed throughout the application.

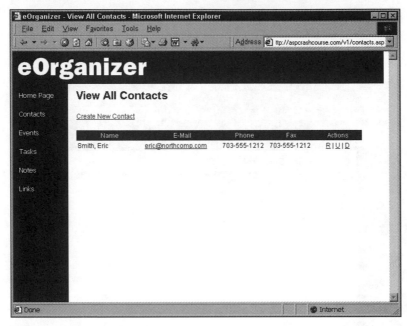

Figure 21-2
The Contact Manager page

The Event Manager

Events are appointments that can run for one day or many days during a month or into another month. The Event Manager page is shown in Figure 21-3. This is where you'll create and maintain events in the database.

While you can use this page to view upcoming events, the home page is a more convenient place to see this information. However, you need a place to enter the data, and that's done here.

The Task Manager

**10 Min.
To Go**

Everyone has things to do, and the Task Manager can help you keep an eye on what's due when so that you don't miss deadlines. The Task Manager page is used to enter and maintain the tasks on your schedule. Like events, task due dates are displayed on the eOrganizer home page calendar. However, this view, shown in Figure 21-4, is helpful if you need to see all the tasks on your plate.

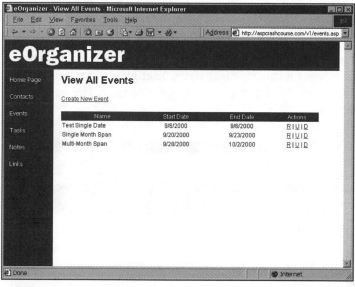

Figure 21-3
The Event Manager page

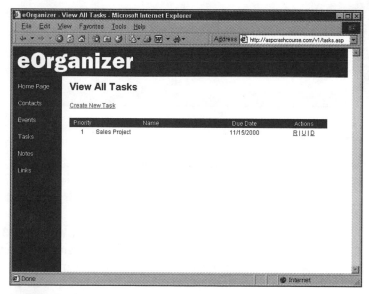

Figure 21-4
The Task Manager page

The Note Manager

You can think of the Note Manager as a place to put all those scraps of paper that you've got all over your office(s). You can use the Note Manager for whatever you want — frequent traveler numbers, client notes, user Ids and passwords for your favorite Web sites, or anything else you might want to track. The Note Manager is shown in Figure 21-5.

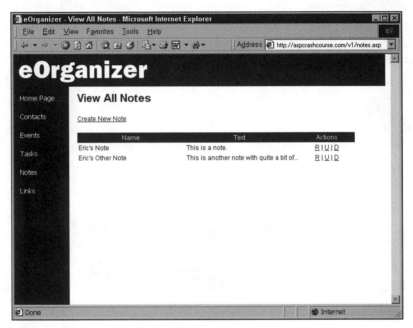

Figure 21-5
The Note Manager page

Each note enables you to enter a virtually unlimited amount of text.

The Link Manager

Ever get tired of having multiple sets of bookmarks or favorites for Web sites? I did too, so that's why I built the Link Manager. The Link Manager enables you to maintain a Web-based list of your favorite sites. This prevents you from losing favorites when you move to a different machine, or not having one available, such as when you create a favorite at work and don't have it at home.

The Link Manager window is shown in Figure 21-6.

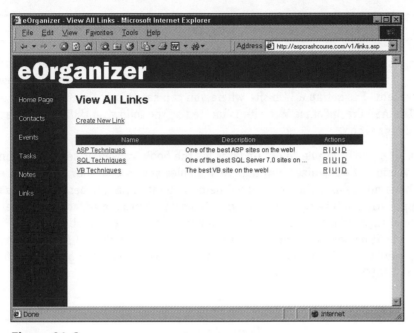

Figure 21-6
The Link Manager page

Common Features

Each one of these data managers includes functions to do the following:

- Create new records
- Update existing records
- Retrieve the details of a record
- Delete a record

Done!

The code for each is very similar. In fact, because all the programming you'll do in these chapters is modular, you only need to learn the basic structure once. After that, the only differences between the pages are in the actual data fields that you're manipulating. This makes it easy to add new types of data later.

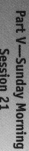

REVIEW

In this session, you were introduced to the eOrganizer and we began the steps to building an application. Because this application is meant as a base for your own development, I've set up a Web site where you can see this application evolve over time. The ASP Crash Course Web site is located at the following URL: `http://asp crashcourse.com`.

At this site, you'll be able to get updates for the book, as well as see a fully functional version of eOrganizer running. This enables you to test your own application's behavior against the one created here. In addition, a number of versions of this application will be posted over time. As new features are added, you'll see additional links added to this site for each new version of the application. Of course, you'll be able to download all the new code that is created for each one. Finally, you'll be able to access a list of other sites where you can get more information on ASP.

QUIZ YOURSELF

1. When dealing with any type of data, what logical functions do you generally need to provide for the user? (See "Common Features")

2. What technology lets us specify site wide fonts and change them by editing a single file? (See "Touring the eOrganizer Application")

3. How do we permanently store the information obtained using this application? (See "Touring the eOrganizer Application")

Creating the eOrganizer Database

Session Checklist

✔ Creating the database for the eOrganizer application

✔ Creating the five tables required for the application

I n the previous chapter, you were introduced to the eOrganizer. In this chapter, you're going to create the database for the eOrganizer application.

30 Min.
To Go

Creating the Database

We're going to create all five tables in this chapter:

- tblContacts
- tblEvents
- tblLinks
- tblNotes
- tblTasks

You can create the database in whatever database system you're using, whether it's Access, SQL Server, Oracle, or something else. All of the information provided in this chapter is targeted at SQL Server, but you can easily translate the data types listed into your own database format.

Creating the Contacts Table

The first — and longest — table you'll create is the Contacts table. I always prefix table names with tbl, so this table's name will be tblContacts in the sample database. The fields used for this table are shown in Table 22-1.

Table 22-1
tblContacts Fields

Field Name	Data Type	Description
pkContactID (required)	int	Primary key — identity value
FirstName	varchar(40)	First name
LastName	varchar(40)	Last name
Title	varchar(80)	Person's title
CompanyName	varchar(120)	Company name
Address1	varchar(120)	Space for address
Address2	varchar(120)	Space for address
City	varchar(40)	City
State	varchar(2)	State
ZIP	varchar(10)	Zip code (with space for zip code + 4)
Phone	varchar(40)	Phone number
Fax	varchar(40)	Fax number
EMail	varchar(120)	E-mail address

In this particular table, the only required field is the pkContactID field, which should also be marked as an identity (SQL Server), an AutoNumber (Access), or a sequence (Oracle). This will automatically generate a unique value for new contacts as they are entered into the system.

The field sizes used here are also used when we build the ASP file to enable data entry and modification. Each field will have a maximum length set so that we can't enter more text than the field allows. If you change the size of these fields, be sure to make the corresponding change in the ASP file.

In addition, if you need to store other information about a contact, feel free to add it. This is the list of fields we'll be working from when we build the Contact Manager page, but they all work the same way.

Creating the Events Table

20 Min. To Go

The next table to create is the Events table, or tblEvents. The fields are shown in Table 22-2.

Table 22-2
tblEvents Fields

Field Name	Data Type	Description
pkEventID	int	Primary key — identity value (required)
Name	varchar(80)	Short description of the event (required)
Description	text	Long description of the event
StartDate	datetime	Start date for the event (required)
EndDate	datetime	Date event is completed (required)

The ASP code you write will validate the input data to ensure that the required fields are supplied, but it's a good idea to mark them as required on the database table itself. This enforces data integrity in case you have other applications using this same table for other purposes.

You should also note that this table includes a field of type text. This type of field can store a very large amount of text. In Access, this is known as a Memo field. This field enables you to do free-form text entry and take as much space as your database allows.

Creating the Links Table

The next table you need to create will hold the Web site links that you save. The Links table fields are listed in Table 22-3.

Table 22-3
tblLinks Fields

Field Name	Data Type	Description
pkLinkID	int	Primary key — identity value (required)
Name	varchar(80)	Short description of the link (required)
URL	varchar(160)	Space for fairly long URLs (required)
Description	text	Long description of the link

The ASP file will take care of the validation of the fields, including ensuring that the URL entered at least conforms to the normal format: http://aspcrashcourse.com.

Creating the Notes Table

The Notes table is the next one to create, and its fields are listed in Table 22-4.

Table 22-4
tblNotes Fields

Field Name	Data Type	Description
pkNoteID	int	Primary key — identity value (required)
Name	varchar(80)	Short description of the note (required)
Description	text	Long text block for entering data

Creating the Tasks Table

The Tasks table is basically the same as the Events table, except for a renaming of one field and the addition of the Priority field. The fields are listed in Table 22-5.

Table 22-5
tblTasks Fields

Field Name	Data Type	Description
pkTaskID	int	Primary key — identity value (required)
Name	varchar(80)	Short description of the task (required)

Field Name	Data Type	Description
Description	text	Long description of the task
Priority	tinyint	Priority level of the task — currently 1 through 3 (required)
StartDate	datetime	Start date for the task (required)
DueDate	datetime	Date the task must be completed (required)

Database Tips

Here are a few tips before you start using your database:

- Make a backup of the database. Because your identity values can't be reused, you may want to keep a copy of the original database structure before you start loading data into it. With Access, you can just make a copy of the database file. In SQL Server, you can either make a backup of the database or have SQL Server generate a script with the database structure in it. Either way enables you to re-create the database later.

- Make sure you periodically back up your database once you start using it. Even though you're only using it for development, be sure to back it up every so often. This is especially important once you start using it more often and loading your own data into it. Your system administrator can help you set up a backup schedule for your SQL Server database; or, if you're using Access, you can just make a copy of the database periodically.

Done!

REVIEW

This chapter showed you the tables involved in the eOrganizer application. If you're not using Access or SQL Server, you can take the data types and field definitions and create the database in your own system. In Chapter 30, you'll see some additional ways you can expand the database with additional data types and features.

Part V—Sunday Morning
Session 22

QUIZ YOURSELF

1. What type of field in a table uniquely identifies the record?
    (See "Creating the Database")

2. Why should you make a backup of your database? (See "Database Tips")

3. What SQL Server type allows for a large block of text in a record?
    (See "Creating the Database")

Creating the eOrganizer Structure

Session Checklist

✔ Create the HTML toolbar and table structure that will be used for the application

✔ Build the common include file that will be used in all the ASP files

✔ Create the Cascading Style Sheet for the application

**30 Min.
To Go**

Creating the eOrganizer Layout

As you've learned in previous chapters, the key to a good application is getting started right. In this chapter, you'll learn how to create a good structure for the application, one that you'll be able to use throughout the rest of the book. This structure comes in two parts: visual and code. You'll be doing both in this chapter.

To refresh your memory, the eOrganizer application window looks like the one shown in Figure 23-1.

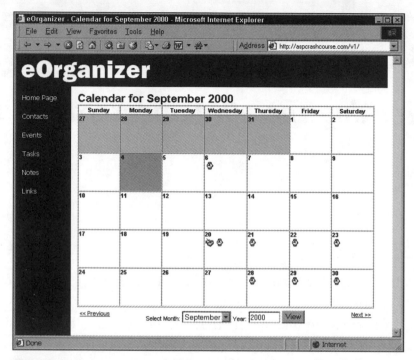

Figure 23-1
The eOrganizer application window

No matter what is going on in the right-hand side of the window, you always see the application logo on the top and the toolbar on the left. This provides a consistent look and enables the user to navigate to any part of the application from anywhere else.

The first thing you have to do is create the graphical layout for the application. In this case, a toolbar made sense. However, depending on the application you make, you might not want a toolbar. You might want to create a bar across the top or bottom, or create a separate floating window with the available commands. That's all up to you (and your client).

In our case, we're going to build a toolbar with an area on the top for the application logo. A couple things to note:

- The blue color being used is color #000099 in HTML format. The graphic at the top was created in Jasc Software's Paint Shop Pro 6.0. It is just a GIF file, but the blue in the graphic was marked as the transparent color, so the background color shows through properly.

- The blue toolbar is created using a background stripe that is a few pixels high and 1,600 pixels wide. The blue ends at around 100 pixels from the left, which results in a toolbar running from top to bottom. You can replicate this using background colors on a table, but I prefer the stripe method.

- We make extensive use of a spacing graphic, which is a 1 x 1 pixel graphic that is transparent. You can create this using any decent paint program that supports GIF transparency. We stretch this tiny graphic (as you'll see when you build the toolbar and the calendar page in Chapter 29) to force the Web page to enforce certain spacing on the page. This is one of the older tricks in the Web designers' book to coax HTML into the right format.

With the basic design principles out of the way, let's take a look at the include file that you'll be using throughout the application to make this work. One of the functions you'll use will bring in some of the HTML for the page, so we'll save the particular HTML code for a little bit later.

20 Min. To Go

Creating the include.asp File

The include.asp file will contain all the commonly used code throughout the application. This section shows you how to build it, function by function. A funny thing about include files — once you start using them, you'll end up using the same functions in lots of applications. It's a good idea to keep copies of your include files so that when you need a function, it's always available to you.

Constants and Other Declarations

At the top of the include.asp file, we have to declare our constants and reference several system libraries. The code to do this is as follows:

```
<!-- METADATA TYPE="typelib" FILE="c:\program files\common
files\system\ado\msado15.dll"-->
<!-- METADATA TYPE="typelib" FILE="c:\winnt\system32\scrrun.dll"--
>
<%
Option Explicit
Const DQ = """"
Const SQ = "'"
Const ACTION = "a"
```

```
Const ACTION_CREATE = "c"
Const ACTION_CREATE_SAVE = "cs"
Const ACTION_UPDATE = "u"
Const ACTION_UPDATE_SAVE = "us"
Const ACTION_DELETE = "d"
Const ACTION_DELETE_SAVE = "ds"
Const ACTION_RETRIEVE = "r"
```

The first two lines of the preceding code should be written on the same line of the file.

The first two lines of the file reference several system libraries so that we can use the built-in constants made available by them. The first reference is for the ADO constants we need, such as those used when you open a recordset. The second reference is for the Microsoft Scripting Runtime, which is used with the FileSystemObject. We'll be using the FileSystemObject to open and include several files in our HTML output. As long as you know that Windows was installed to the C: drive, the pathnames specified in the METADATA tag will be correct. These pathnames aren't "negotiable" and the files in question always get put in these directories when Windows is installed on the machine.

After that, we declare a number of constants that will be used throughout the other pages. We declare constants for the double and single quote characters, as well as constants for all the typical actions performed by each data entry page.

Adding the Database Functions

We have two database functions in the include.asp file: OpenDB and CloseDB. These functions are similar to those you learned about in previous chapters, so we'll just list them here:

```
' , , , , , , , , , , , , , , , , , , , , , , , , , , , , , , , , , , , , , , , , , , , , , , , , , , , , , , , , , , , , , ,
'
' Function OpenDB
'
```

```
' This routine opens up a database connection and returns
' a live database connection to the caller.
'
'''''''''''''''''''''''''''''''''''''''''''''''''''''''''''''''
Function OpenDB()
   Dim cnDB          ' As ADODB.Connection
   Set cnDB = Server.CreateObject("ADODB.Connection")
   cnDB.ConnectionString = _
      "Provider=SQLOLEDB;" _
        & "Data Source=ENTERPRISE;" _
        & "Initial Catalog=CrashCourse;" _
        & "User ID=crashcourse;" _
        & "Password=crashcourse;"
   cnDB.Open
   Set OpenDB = cnDB
End Function


'''''''''''''''''''''''''''''''''''''''''''''''''''''''''''''''
'
' Sub CloseDB
'
' This routine closes the database connection and clears
' the object reference.
'
'''''''''''''''''''''''''''''''''''''''''''''''''''''''''''''''
Sub CloseDB(cnDB)
   cnDB.Close
   Set cnDB = Nothing
End Sub
```

The connection string used in OpenDB needs to be changed for your particular system. Refer to Chapter 19 for more information about creating connection strings.

Part V—Sunday Morning
Session 23

Output Functions

We have two functions that you've learned about in earlier chapters: WriteLine and WriteComment. While we don't use WriteComment as part of the code you'll see, it's a handy debugging tool that I always include in my code. The code for these functions is shown here:

```
'''''''''''''''''''''''''''''''''''''''''''''''''''''''''''''
'
' Sub WriteLine
'
' This routine prints a line of HTML to the browser and
' includes a carriage return/line feed at the end of the
' line. That cleans up the HTML output for debugging
' purposes.
'
'''''''''''''''''''''''''''''''''''''''''''''''''''''''''''''
Sub WriteLine(strData)
    Response.Write strData & vbCrLF
End Sub


'''''''''''''''''''''''''''''''''''''''''''''''''''''''''''''
'
' Sub WriteComment
'
' This routine prints a comment into the HTML output.
'
'''''''''''''''''''''''''''''''''''''''''''''''''''''''''''''
Sub WriteComment(strData)
    WriteLine "<!-- " & strData & " -->"
End Sub
```

We also have another function that is used to read in a file and print it to the screen. This function is called IncludeFile and is shown here:

```
'''''''''''''''''''''''''''''''''''''''''''''''''''''''''''''
'
' Sub IncludeFile
```

```
'
' This routine reads a file and dumps it to the screen. It
' allows for variable names to be included instead of the
' hardcoded names required by the SSI directives.
'
''''''''''''''''''''''''''''''''''''''''''''''''''''''''''''''''
Sub IncludeFile(strFilename)
   If strFilename = "" Then Exit Sub

   On Error Resume Next
   Dim objFSO, objFile, strContents
   Set objFSO = CreateObject("Scripting.FileSystemObject")
   Set objFile = _
      objFSO.OpenTextFile(Server.MapPath(strFilename), _
      ForReading, False)
   strContents = objFile.ReadAll
   Response.Write strContents & vbCrLf
   objFile.Close
   Set objFile = Nothing
   Set objFSO = Nothing
End Sub
```

We first create a FileSystemObject, which gives us access to the server's file system. We then have to read in a particular file, whose path is given to the function as a virtual pathname. For instance, we will use the following function call:

```
IncludeFile "toolbar.html"
```

While we know that this file is located in the same directory as the ASP file, the system doesn't. We use the Server.MapPath routine to turn toolbar.html into a fully qualified pathname to the file. We can then open it, read it all into a string, and then print it out to the Web page.

Header and Footer Functions

These functions are the key functions to making the pages look similar. As mentioned earlier, we have an HTML layout that we need to apply to the page to make it look the same as others. To do this, we're going to print some of the HTML through ASP, and then we'll bring in the toolbar and the style sheet. This lets those common files stay external to the ASP code, which makes them easier to modify later. The following `PrintHeader` function is first:

```
'''''''''''''''''''''''''''''''''''''''''''''''''''''''''''''''''''''''
'
' Sub PrintHeader
'
' This routine prints the HTML at the top of each
' page in the system. It also includes the toolbar
' on the side of each file.
'
'''''''''''''''''''''''''''''''''''''''''''''''''''''''''''''''''''''''
Sub PrintHeader(strTitle)
    WriteLine "<html>"
    WriteLine "<head><title>eOrganizer - " & strTitle & "</title>"
    IncludeFile "styles.css"
    WriteLine "</head>"
    IncludeFile "toolbar.html"
    WriteLine "<span class=ph>" & strTitle & "</span>"

End Sub
```

Each page will have its own title, so we pass that as an argument to this function and then print it into the TITLE tag. Next, we open the styles.css file, which is our style sheet. That file is then dumped into the heading section of the page. The file is shown here:

```
<style type="text/css" title="eOrganizer Style Sheet">
<!--
.tb
{
   font-size : 10pt;
   font-family: Tahoma, Arial, Helvetica;
   font-weight: normal;
   color: #FFFFFF;
   text-decoration: none
}
.ph
{
   font-size : 16pt;
   font-family: Arial, Helvetica;
```

```
      font-weight: bold;
      color: #000099;
      text-decoration: none
   }
   .pt
   {
      font-size : 10pt;
      font-family: Arial, Helvetica;
      font-weight: normal;
      color: #000000;
      text-decoration: none
   }
   th
   {
      font-size : 9pt;
      font-family: Arial, Helvetica;
      font-weight: normal;
      color: #FFFFFF;
      background-color: #000099;
      text-decoration: none
   }
   td
   {
      font-size : 9pt;
      font-family: Arial, Helvetica;
      font-weight: normal;
      color: #000000;
      text-decoration: none
   }
   .calhead
   {
      font-size : 8pt;
      font-family: Arial, Helvetica;
      font-weight: bold;
      color: #000099;
      text-decoration: none;
      text-align : center;
   }
   .calcell
   {
```

```
     font-size : 8pt;
     font-family: Arial, Helvetica;
     font-weight: normal;
     color: #000000;
     text-decoration: none
 }


 -->
 </style>
```

You can find numerous books and Web sites that go into great depth about how to create style sheets, so they aren't covered in detail here. However, the format for a style sheet is as you see in the preceding code. The first line following the STYLE tag names the style you're creating. You have the option to create a new style or to redefine an existing tag with new style properties. New styles are prefixed with a period; and as you can see, we do both. First we create three styles: tb (toolbar text), ph (page heading text), and pt (page content text). We then provide style information for the TH and TD tags. This causes the style we've specified to be applied to all TH and TD tags throughout the application, saving us quite a bit of code. The last thing we do is define the styles that will be used with the calendar page, calhead and calcell.

The properties are somewhat self-explanatory here, but for a complete list, refer to another book that covers CSS and/or Dynamic HTML.

Once we've got the style sheet included, we include the toolbar file. This file sets up the HTML layout for the page:

```
<body
   leftmargin=0
   topmargin=0
   marginheight=0
   marginwidth=0
   background="/pics/stripe.gif">
<table width=700 border=0 cellspacing=0 cellpadding=0>

<tr>
<td colspan=3 width=640 bgcolor=#000099>
<img src="/pics/logo.gif"
   vspace=5
   width="260"
   height="50"
```

```
    alt=""
    border="0">
</td>
</tr>

<tr>
<td colspan=3>
<img src="/pics/spacer.gif" height=10 width=1>
</td>
</tr>

<tr>
<td width=90 valign=top>
<table width=100%>
<tr>
<td>
<span class="tb">
<p><a href="default.asp"><span class="tb">Home Page</span></a></p>
<p><a href="contacts.asp"><span class="tb">Contacts</span></a></p>
<p><a href="events.asp"><span class="tb">Events</span></a></p>
<p><a href="tasks.asp"><span class="tb">Tasks</span></a></p>
<p><a href="notes.asp"><span class="tb">Notes</span></a></p>
<p><a href="links.asp"><span class="tb">Links</span></a></p>
</span>
</td>
</tr></table>
</td>
<td width=10><img src="/pics/spacer.gif" height=10 width=20></td>
<td width=540 valign=top>
```

This page lays out a table that is 700 pixels wide, which easily fits in an 800 x 600 screen (width-wise, anyway). It then creates a row for the logo that spans three columns, followed by a spacer row that is ten pixels high. Finally, we set up the table into which the page content will go. The first column contains the toolbar items, which are links to each of the pages you'll create. There is a spacer column in between, and then we create a TD tag that is 540 pixels wide, and that's the end of the file. The reason for this abrupt end is that each page will put its own content following the call to PrintHeader, so all we have to do is set up the table; the page will take care of the rest.

The last function we have to create is the `PrintFooter` function, which closes out the table we created here:

```
' , , , , , , , , , , , , , , , , , , , , , , , , , , , , , , , , , , , , , , , , , , , , , , , , , , , ,
'
' Sub PrintFooter
'
' This routine prints the HTML at the bottom of each
' page in the system.
'
' , , , , , , , , , , , , , , , , , , , , , , , , , , , , , , , , , , , , , , , , , , , , , , , , , , , ,
Sub PrintFooter()
   WriteLine "</td></tr></table>"
   WriteLine "</body></html>"
End Sub
```

Done!

REVIEW

The file you created in this chapter is the foundation for everything else you'll build in this book. The functions you created here are used throughout the system. The advantages of this should be clear; if your database name or user ID changes, for instance, you only have to make one change. The same thing goes for the HTML toolbar or the style sheet — one change takes care of the entire application at once.

QUIZ YOURSELF

1. What tag goes at the start of a style sheet? The end of the style sheet? (See "Header and Footer Functions")

2. What object do we create to make a database connection? (See "Adding the Database Functions")

3. What HTML structure do we use to create the toolbar on the page? (See "Header and Footer Functions")

Building the Notes Manager

Session Checklist

✔ Building a page to show all the notes in the database

✔ Creating code to add new records

✔ Updating existing records

✔ Deleting records with ASP code

✔ Validating data before making database changes

**30 Min.
To Go**

Have you ever had information strewn all over your office(s) and when you need that one important piece of information, it's nowhere to be found? The Note Manager is designed to alleviate that problem. It allows for free-form text entry of anything you want — passwords, Web sites, birthdays, and so on. In this chapter, you'll learn how to build this portion of the eOrganizer application.

Introduction to the Notes Manager

The Notes portion of the eOrganizer is probably the simplest, which means you'll be able to get comfortable with the code arrangement before getting into the uglier tables, such as Contacts. The Notes system is designed to hold all those little bits of text that get scattered throughout your e-mail and your hard drive. For instance, you might use Notes to store your user IDs and passwords for various Web sites, your frequent flyer numbers, or just about anything else.

In this chapter, you'll be writing code to create, retrieve, update, and delete notes. You'll also be validating input data; so that notes aren't added without a name, for instance. The skills you develop in this chapter will be immediately applicable to the following chapters, as the basic structure of all these pages is identical.

Table structure

Just as a reminder, the table being used is the tblNotes table in the sample database, and the fields are shown in Table 24-1.

Table 24-1
tblNotes Fields

Field Name	Data Type	Description
pkNoteID	int	Primary key–identity value
Name	varchar(80)	Short description of the note
Description	text	Long text block for entering data

Note entry form

The form you'll be building for entering notes is shown in Figure 24-1.

As far as validation rules go, the title field on the note is required, but the user won't be required to put text into the text area of the form.

This is a simple form, but you'll exercise all your skills before getting to the more complex forms later in the book.

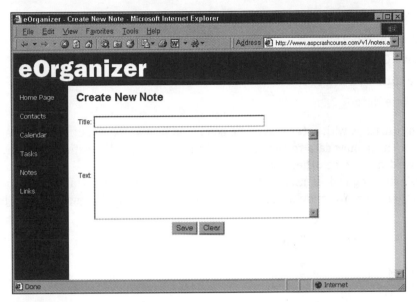

Figure 24-1
Notes entry form in the eOrganizer

Each part of the final notes.asp file is explained throughout this chapter, and you can find a completed copy of the file on the CD-ROM included with this book.

Setting up the File

The first thing you need to do is create a new ASP file called notes.asp. You don't have to name it notes.asp, but if you change the name, be sure to change the toolbar that you created in Chapter 23. You will encounter numerous comments as you proceed so that you can tell what is going on all along the way. Whether or not you put these comments in is up to you.

The basic methodology behind how this page works is to combine all the related functions into a single file. For this data type, you need to have all of the following functions:

- Retrieve All
- Retrieve Single Note (*)
- Create Note (*)

- Save New Note
- Update Note (*)
- Save Changes
- Confirm Deletion of Note
- Delete Note

The functions with asterisks can be combined into a single routine, because all three of them show data to the user in a form. This helps eliminate a lot of the work we'd have to do otherwise.

The following code is used at the beginning of the file and includes the page dispatcher code. You should note that it includes cases for all eight functions just listed.

```
<!--#include file="include.asp" -->
<%
Call Main
'''''''''''''''''''''''''''''''''''''''''''''''''''''''''''''
'
' Sub Main
'
' Processing for this page starts in this routine. It
' contains a dispatcher to call the appropriate routine,
' based on what function was needed.
'
'''''''''''''''''''''''''''''''''''''''''''''''''''''''''''''
Sub Main
    Dim cnDB          ' As ADODB.Connection
    Set cnDB = OpenDB()

    Select Case Request(ACTION)
       Case ACTION_CREATE, ACTION_RETRIEVE, ACTION_UPDATE
          BuildForm cnDB, ""
       Case ACTION_CREATE_SAVE
          CreateSave cnDB
       Case ACTION_UPDATE_SAVE
          UpdateSave cnDB
       Case ACTION_DELETE
          Delete cnDB
       Case ACTION_DELETE_SAVE
```

```
        DeleteSave cnDB
    Case Else
        Retrieve(cnDB)
    End Select

    CloseDB cnDB
End Sub
```

We start out with the SSI directive to include our utility file, include.asp, which you learned about in the last chapter. Because all our code will be in subroutines, we initially call the Main subroutine, and then we define it. The Main subroutine's job is to interpret which mode the page is in and send the control to the appropriate subroutine. Another job of the Main subroutine is to take care of opening and closing the database as necessary. This is done with the common OpenDB and CloseDB functions located in the include.asp file.

The first three functions that the Select Case statement handles are Create Note, Update Note, and Retrieve Single Note. You should notice that the BuildForm subroutine takes two arguments: the active database connection and an empty string. The empty string takes the place of a data validation error that you'll learn about later in the chapter. We'll turn these "logical" functions into actual subroutines as we work through the chapter.

The rest of the dispatcher handles the other five functions. The Case Else function will retrieve all the notes, which is the default action. If you bring up notes.asp by itself (as the toolbar does), you don't want to have an empty page, so you always create a default action by putting a value in Case Else.

The only other line of code that you don't see here is the ending ASP delimiter at the end of the file, so be sure you put that in or you will get a syntax error.

Creating the Note List Function

**20 Min.
To Go**

The next piece of code to add is the default action for the page, which is to retrieve the notes from the database and display a brief portion of the text. In the dialog box shown in Figure 24-2, you can see how notes are displayed in this view.

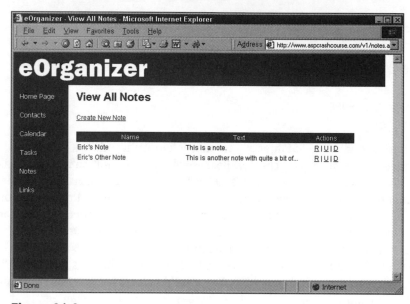

Figure 24-2

All notes in the system are shown on this page.

The first note has a short amount of text, all of which is shown in the second column. However, the second note has more text than can be shown, and an ellipsis is used after 40 characters. There's nothing magical about 40 characters, by the way. You can use any amount you wish, but I chose 40 because it enables the text to be shown without wrapping, based on the size of the table.

Besides the title and excerpt of the text, you also see three links at the end of the line. The R enables users to retrieve a note, U handles updates, and D is for delete. You should also note the Create New Note link at the top of the page. Each one of those URLs has the appropriate action code that the dispatcher is looking for.

Here's the Retrieve subroutine that does all this for you:

```
' , , , , , , , , , , , , , , , , , , , , , , , , , , , , , , , , , , , , , , , , , , , , , , , , , , , ,
'
' Sub Retrieve
'
' This routine lists all records of this data type. It
' also provides links to create, retrieve, update, and
' delete records.
'
' , , , , , , , , , , , , , , , , , , , , , , , , , , , , , , , , , , , , , , , , , , , , , , , , , , , ,
```

```
Sub Retrieve(cnDB)
   Dim rsData        ' As ADODB.Recordset
   Dim strURL        ' As String
   Dim strSQL        ' As String

   strSQL = "SELECT * FROM tblNotes ORDER BY Name"
   Set rsData = cnDB.Execute(strSQL)

   PrintHeader "View All Notes"

   WriteLine "<p><a href=" & DQ & Request("SCRIPT_NAME") _
      & "?" & ACTION & "=" & ACTION_CREATE _
      & DQ & ">Create New Note</a></p>"

   WriteLine "<table cellspacing=0 cellpadding=2>"
   WriteLine "<tr><th width=200>Name</th>"
   WriteLine "<th width=200>Text</th>"
   WriteLine "<th width=100>Actions</th></tr>"
   Do Until rsData.EOF
      WriteLine "<tr>"
      WriteLine "<td>" & rsData("Name") & "</td>"
      WriteLine "<td>"
      If Len(rsData("Text")) >= 40 Then
         WriteLine Left(rsData("Text"), 40) & "..."
      Else
         WriteLine rsData("Text")
      End If
      WriteLine "</td>"
      WriteLine "<td align=center>"
      strURL = "<a href=" & DQ & Request("SCRIPT_NAME") _
         & "?" & ACTION & "=" _
         & "###" & "&id=" _
         & rsData("pkNoteID") & DQ & ">"
      WriteLine _
         Replace(strURL, "###", ACTION_RETRIEVE) & "R</a> | "
      WriteLine _
         Replace(strURL, "###", ACTION_UPDATE) & "U</a> | "
      WriteLine _
         Replace(strURL, "###", ACTION_DELETE) & "D</a>"
      WriteLine "</td>"
```

```
        WriteLine "</tr>"
        rsData.MoveNext
    Loop
    rsData.Close
    PrintFooter
End Sub
```

As with the rest of the HTML you are writing within your ASP files, we are using WriteLine statements to generate the code. The WriteLine subroutine is in the common include.asp file you created before.

After declaring our variables, we create the SQL statement to run against the database. In this case, we're sending a SQL statement directly to the database. The more efficient method would be to create and use a stored procedure. A stored procedure is essentially a query that is saved as part of the database structure. You can refer to Chapter 30 for more information on stored procedures and their benefits. If you want to do this, you can use the following code in SQL Server to create a stored procedure called sp_RetrieveAllNotes:

```
CREATE PROCEDURE sp_RetrieveAllNotes
AS
SELECT *
FROM tblNotes
ORDER BY Name
```

If you use a stored procedure, change the statement

```
strSQL = "SELECT * FROM tblNotes ORDER BY Name"
```

to

```
strSQL = "sp_RetrieveAllNotes"
```

For this application, either method will work fine. We then execute the stored procedure and put the resulting data in the rsData recordset that we declared. After calling the PrintHeader routine, we build the link that enables the user to create a new note. Here's what the HTML will look like when we're done creating it:

```
<p><a href="/v1/notes.asp?a=c">Create New Note</a></p>
```

The /v1/notes.asp is coming from the ServerVariables SCRIPT_NAME value. On the aspcrashcourse.com site, where this application is running live, this version of the code is in the v1 directory, hence the URL. Depending on where you run your code, your URL will vary. The rest of the URL has the action parameter using the ACTION_CREATE code. To build this whole string, we also use the DQ constant to embed double quote characters in the output. It makes it somewhat easier to code, so you don't have three double quote characters next to one another all over the place.

Once that link is created, we build our table and its headings. We then start looping through the data, printing out the relevant fields along with the actions for each record. For the large text field, we check whether the data is more than 40 characters. If so, we use the first 40 characters and add an ellipsis. That indicates to the user that more text follows.

For the actions, we've used the `Replace` function to save ourselves some typing. Each of the URLs for the actions looks like the following:

```
<a href="/v1/notes.asp?a=r&id=11">R</a>
```

Instead of duplicating the code to generate this link three times, we create a generic link that has three pound (#) signs where the action code will go. When we want to print the Retrieve Record link (represented by the R), we simply replace the three pound signs with the retrieve record code. The same thing happens when we want to create the Update and Delete links.

After that, we wrap things up and print out the common footer to the page. Now that you've got the retrieval working, you can move on to the individual functions, starting with the BuildForm routine.

Creating the BuildForm Routine

The BuildForm routine is the most complex routine you'll build for this subsystem. Many people ask me why I write ASP code using all the subroutines, rather than embedding values in HTML. This particular routine shows what you can do when you don't think of ASP as just enhanced HTML. This routine dynamically fills boxes based on a number of different conditions. If you can understand this routine and replicate it yourself, you'll be well on your way to writing good ASP code that really hums.

Following is the BuildForm routine:

```
'''''''''''''''''''''''''''''''''''''''''''''''''''''''
'
' Sub BuildForm
'
' This routine displays a data entry and display
' form. It is used for the create, retrieve, and
```

```
' update modes.
'
'''''''''''''''''''''''''''''''''''''''''''''''''''''
Sub BuildForm(cnDB, strError)
   Dim lngNoteID   ' As Long
   Dim strName     ' As String
   Dim strText     ' As String
   Dim rsData      ' As ADODB.Recordset
   Dim strTitle    ' As String
   Dim strAction   ' As String

   If strError = "" Then
      Select Case Request(ACTION)
         Case ACTION_CREATE
            strAction = ACTION_CREATE_SAVE
            strTitle = "Create New Note"
            lngNoteID = -1
            strName = ""
            strText = ""
         Case ACTION_UPDATE, ACTION_RETRIEVE
            strAction = ACTION_UPDATE_SAVE
            If Request(ACTION) = ACTION_UPDATE Then
               strTitle = "Update Note"
            Else
               strTitle = "Retrieve Note"
            End If
            lngNoteID = Request("ID")
            Set rsData = cnDB.Execute("SELECT * FROM tblNotes " _
               & "WHERE pkNoteID = " & lngNoteID)
            strName = rsData("Name")
            strText = rsData("Text")

            rsData.Close
            Set rsData = Nothing
      End Select
   Else

      strAction = Request(ACTION)

      Select Case strAction
```

```
        Case ACTION_CREATE_SAVE
            strTitle = "Create New Note"
        Case ACTION_UPDATE_SAVE
            strTitle = "Update Note"
    End Select

    If Request("ID") = "" Then
        lngNoteID = -1
    Else
        lngNoteID = Request("ID")
    End If
    strName = Request("dbtName")
    strText = Request("dbtText")
End If
PrintHeader strTitle
If strError <> "" Then
    WriteLine strError
End If

WriteLine "<form action=" & DQ & Request("SCRIPT_NAME") _
    & DQ & " method=post>"
WriteLine "<input type=hidden name=" _
    & ACTION & " value=" & strAction & ">"
WriteLine "<input type=hidden name=ID " _
    & " value=" & lngNoteID & ">"
WriteLine "<table>"
WriteLine "<tr><td>Title:</td>"
WriteLine "<td><input type=text size=50 name=dbtName value=" _
    & DQ & strName & DQ & "></td></tr>"

WriteLine "<tr><td>Text:</td>"
WriteLine "<td><textarea rows=10 cols=50 name=dbtText>" _
    & strText & "</textarea></td></tr>"
If Request(ACTION) <> ACTION_RETRIEVE Then
    WriteLine "<tr><td colspan=2 align=center>" _
        & "<input type=submit name=cmdSubmit value=Save>" _
        & " " _
        & "<input type=reset name=cmdReset" _
        & " value=Clear></td></tr>"
Else
```

```
        WriteLine "<tr><td colspan=2><a href=" _
            & DQ & Request("SCRIPT_NAME") & DQ _
            & ">Return to List</a></td></tr>"
    End If
    WriteLine "</table>"
    PrintFooter
End Sub
```

The basic flow of this routine is as follows:

1. Determine whether the form is being shown with or without an error having occurred during validation.

2. If no error occurred, determine what the user asked to do (retrieve, update, or create new). For the retrieve and update cases, look up the selected record and put the data into temporary variables. For create, clear out those variables, just in case.

3. If an error occurred during a save, use the data that is in the Request object for each field and repopulate the form with what the user just typed.

4. Display any error that occurred to the user.

5. Build the form and populate each box with any values that were retrieved from either the database or the input data from the previous save attempt.

6. If you are just retrieving the record, don't show the Submit button. Instead, just show a link back to the list. Otherwise, show the buttons.

The error text we're talking about comes in via the strError parameter. We haven't covered the validation routine yet, but it will play a part in every page created here. When we call this subroutine from Sub Main, we supply an empty string that goes in the strError parameter. This indicates to the BuildForm routine that no error has been generated. We'll call BuildForm from the validation code later, in which case an actual error will be supplied in this parameter.

For the case in which there is no error, you can see that the code clears out the variables strName and strText, but it also sets the strTitle variable. The strTitle variable is used to supply a title for the page, both in the browser's title bar and on the page. This lets the user know what they are doing at all times. Based on the value of the action that was selected, we set the appropriate title, whether that is create, retrieve, or update. For retrieve and update, we use the Request("ID") parameter to look up the note that was selected. The reason we use variables, other than for efficiency, will be obvious shortly.

At this point, we've retrieved all the data necessary and we start building the data form. We show the title, and if there is an error, we display the error at the top of the page, between the page title and the form itself. We then start building the form. For the create case, no data is put into the VALUE parameters of each input box; however, retrieve and update both need to show data. That's why we used variables. At this point, regardless of the mode we're in, we simply dump out the value of the variable into the VALUE parameter of the input box. It doesn't matter whether there is a value or not; the input box will work fine either way.

Note a couple of things at the top of the form. The form tag is set up to be "self-referencing." The data entered in this form will be submitted to the same ASP page; however, because we're using the ACTION parameter to determine what to do, we have embedded the new ACTION parameter in the form as a hidden input field.

Regarding the creation of the input boxes, note that we did set the MAXLENGTH property of the first text box. This is because our database field has limited space for this field. This is a very easy check you can do (and we'll do it throughout) that will ensure that you don't get database errors for data being too long. We don't have to worry about a maximum length for the Text field, which is defined as a text data type in SQL Server.

We then have to determine whether or not to show the Save and Reset buttons at the bottom of the page. If we are just showing a record, we don't need to have the buttons, but we do need a link back to the list page. Based on the action, we either show the buttons or the link. That closes out the page's code.

Validating Input Data

The next subroutine that you'll build is the ValidateData subroutine. You'll be calling this routine from the create and update save routines that you'll write next. The point of the validation is to ensure that we get all the logically required fields into the database. In this case, it doesn't make sense to have a note without a title (Name field). While you could easily make a case to require that the text be populated, I'll leave that one up to you.

The validation you'll be doing here is considered server-side validation. The alternative to this is client-side validation, which is typically done with JavaScript. In the last chapter, you learned how you can move some of this validation to client-side code instead of having it all server-side code. However, there are logical arguments for both sides. Having all the validation on the server makes it easier to manage the code. You have one location for all the validation code, including the validation code that requires the server to operate properly. For instance, you wouldn't be able to do zip code to city/state validation on the client. There's too much data required. If you had some of the validation on the client, you'd still have validation to do on the server. However, having good client-side validation eliminates some of the trips to the server, if you're flagging one error at a time in the validation routine on the server.

One additional problem that many users forget is that client-side scripting can be disabled. This may be done for a variety of reasons, but the end result is that any client-side validation code you do will be ignored by browsers that don't support it. This can result in having bad data enter your system. Using server-side validation eliminates this problem entirely, since server-side validation can't be disabled by the users of the site.

We're going to take the middle road between these two approaches. The validation code will be located on the server, but we will find all the errors that we can before displaying an error message. If five fields are missing, the user will get a single message with all of the problems listed. I've used this particular method with real-world clients and it works nicely. It also gets around any issues involved with using client-side scripting. One particular client I worked with had determined that client-side scripting posed a security risk, and it was therefore not allowed. Server-side validation took care of the problem.

The ValidateData subroutine is shown here:

```
'''''''''''''''''''''''''''''''''''''''''''''''''''''
'
' Function ValidateData
'
' This routine validates the input data and
' causes the form to be shown if the data is
' not correct. A True result indicates that
' the data was OK, and a False indicates that
' the data was in error.
'
'''''''''''''''''''''''''''''''''''''''''''''''''''''
Function ValidateData(cnDB)
   Dim strError        ' As String
   strError = ""

   If Request("dbtName") = "" Then
      strError = strError _
         & "<li>The note's title must be entered."
   End If

   If strError <> "" Then
      strError = "<p><font color=#FF0000><b>" _
         & "The following data errors were detected:</b><br>" _
```

```
                    & "<ul>" & strError & "</ul></font></p>"
        BuildForm cnDB, strError
        ValidateData = False
    Else
        ValidateData = True
    End If

End Function
```

This is a fairly short routine, as only one field needs to be validated. However, the structure we use here is identical to the routines we'll use in all the other pages in the application.

We first start by creating an empty variable called strError. This variable will hold any errors that we detect in the routine along the way. If the variable is empty when we get done, we return a True to the caller and it saves the new or updated record. If we get error, we add some additional text to the error message and call the BuildForm routine. The BuildForm routine already knows how to handle a case in which an error has occurred, as you already learned.

The only validation check we do is to make sure that the title of the note is filled in. If that data is missing, we add some text to the error message. Figure 24-3 shows what happens when this error is triggered.

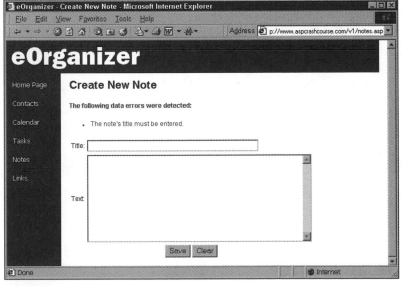

Figure 24-3
Validation errors are shown at the top of the form in red.

The error message needs to provide enough explanation to the user so that he/she knows what to fix. Just indicating that "errors occurred" isn't good enough. You need to be thorough when you create these error messages.

If we were validating more than one field, the UL tag would create a bulleted list of the errors that occurred. Feel free to change the formatting as you see fit. This particular method is my favorite, but I've used graphics and other widgets on occasion.

Saving a New Record

10 Min. To Go

The rest of the code is straightforward. This following code handles the creation of a new record:

```
'''''''''''''''''''''''''''''''''''''''''''''''''''''''''''
'
' Sub CreateSave
'
' This routine creates a new record in the database.
'
'''''''''''''''''''''''''''''''''''''''''''''''''''''''''''
Sub CreateSave(cnDB)

   Dim rsData        ' As ADODB.Recordset

   If Not ValidateData(cnDB) Then Exit Sub

   Set rsData = Server.CreateObject("ADODB.Recordset")
   rsData.Open "tblNotes", cnDB, adOpenDynamic, adLockOptimistic
   rsData.AddNew
   rsData("Name") = Request("dbtName")
   rsData("Text") = Request("dbtText")
   rsData.Update
   rsData.Close

   Response.Redirect Request.ServerVariables("SCRIPT_NAME")

End Sub
```

This is the most straightforward method of adding a record to a database table. After first making sure that the data is valid, we create and open a recordset of the tblNotes table. The parameters we use here make the recordset updateable. The AddNew method here lets us create a new record, and we supply each of the fields from the Request object. The Update method saves the new record, and then we close the recordset. Finally, we send the user back to the list window so that the new record is visible.

There are a number of other ways to do this:

- Create an INSERT statement in your code, as we did in previous chapters.
- Use a Command object with a stored procedure to pass parameters to the database.
- Use a COM+ object (which isn't covered in this book) to do the work for you.

Some of these methods are covered in the last chapter, along with the pros and cons of each. For the application you're writing, this particular method is the easiest to implement and understand.

Updating a Record

The next block of code, which looks almost identical to the creation routine, enables you to update an existing record with changes:

```
'''''''''''''''''''''''''''''''''''''''''''''''''''''
'
' Sub UpdateSave
'
' This routine performs an update on the table for this
' particular item.
'
'''''''''''''''''''''''''''''''''''''''''''''''''''''
Sub UpdateSave(cnDB)
    Dim rsData      ' As ADODB.Recordset

    If Not ValidateData(cnDB) Then Exit Sub

    Set rsData = Server.CreateObject("ADODB.Recordset")
    rsData.Open "SELECT * FROM tblNotes WHERE pkNoteID = " _
        & Request("ID"), cnDB, adOpenDynamic, adLockOptimistic
```

```
rsData("Name") = Request("dbtName")
rsData("Text") = Request("dbtText")
rsData.Update
rsData.Close
Response.Redirect Request.ServerVariables("SCRIPT_NAME")
```

```
End Sub
```

In this case, we follow virtually the same steps, except that instead of opening the table, we select one record in our recordset, based on the record ID passed in the ID parameter of the Request object. After that, the code is identical to the CreateSave routine you just created.

Like the CreateSave routine, there are a number of other ways you could write this code. Instead of opening the recordset, you could create a SQL UPDATE statement, like you've done before. However, the preceding method is the easiest to understand.

Handling Deletions

As discussed in previous chapters, it's not always a good idea to allow deletions of data. However, in this particular case, deleting a note isn't going to break referential integrity in any way, so we'll deal with it. The first thing we'll do is write the code that generates the message shown in Figure 24-4 when the user chooses to delete a record.

The code to do this is pretty easy to write:

```
'''''''''''''''''''''''''''''''''''''''''''''''''''''
'
' Sub Delete
'
' This routine confirms that the user wants to delete an
' item from the system.
'
'''''''''''''''''''''''''''''''''''''''''''''''''''''
Sub Delete(cnDB)
    Dim rsData         ' As ADODB.Recordset

    Set rsData = cnDB.Execute("SELECT Name FROM tblNotes " _
        & "WHERE pkNoteID = " & Request("ID"))
```

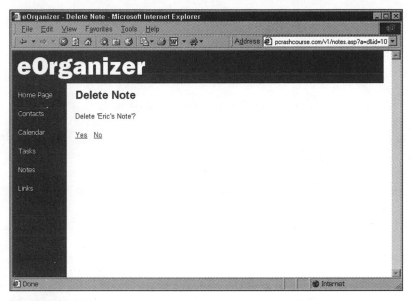

Figure 24-4
Deletion confirmation message

```
    PrintHeader "Delete Note"
    WriteLine "<span class=pt><p>Delete '" _
        & rsData("Name") & "'?</p>"
    WriteLine "<p><a href=" & DQ & Request("SCRIPT_NAME") & "?" _
        & ACTION & "=" & ACTION_DELETE_SAVE _
        & "&id=" & Request("ID") _
        & DQ & ">Yes</a>   " _
        & "<a href=" & DQ & Request("SCRIPT_NAME") & DQ _
        & ">No</a></p>"
    WriteLine "</span>"
    PrintFooter
    rsData.Close
End Sub
```

We first look up the data for the note so that we can generate the proper confirmation message. You can also use a stored procedure here if you want to. Once we've got the data, we create two links: a Yes link that goes to the next step and actually deletes the record, and a No link that goes back to the list.

The next part of this routine actually does the deletion and is quite short:

```
'''''''''''''''''''''''''''''''''''''''''''''''''''''''
'
' Sub DeleteSave
'
' This routine performs the deletion of a record.
'
'''''''''''''''''''''''''''''''''''''''''''''''''''''''
Sub DeleteSave(cnDB)

    cnDB.Execute "DELETE FROM tblNotes WHERE pkNoteID = " _
        & Request("ID")
    Response.Redirect Request("SCRIPT_NAME")

End Sub
```

Done!

This code deletes the record and then returns to the list window. That's it; no fuss, no muss. Like all the other database calls, this could be done using a stored procedure or a COM+ object as well.

REVIEW

As you can see, even a simple entity like the Notes table requires all the same structures and code as the more complex ones. Now that you've successfully built and used this part of the application, the rest of the pages are going to be nearly identical across the board.

You learned to display data to the user, as well as provide links to request other actions. You also learned about validating data, as well as how to perform the requested changes on the database. These applications are somewhat simplified versions of real-world applications that I've built for clients, but the basic structure is the same. It's not the only way to write this type of code, but it's one of the most efficient and easy to understand.

Quiz Yourself

1. What SQL clause do we use to sort data by a particular field? (See "Creating the Note List Function")

2. What SQL clause do we use to create a new record? (See "Saving a New Record")

3. What ADO object do we use to hold the results of a query? (See "Creating the Note List Function")

4. What happens if you leave off the WHERE clause on an UPDATE query? (See "Updating a Record")

Building the Link Manager

Session Checklist

✔ Building a page to show all the links in the database

✔ Creating code to add new records

✔ Updating existing records

✔ Deleting records with ASP code

✔ Validating data before making database changes

**30 Min.
To Go**

I n this chapter, you'll build the Link Manager component of the eOrganizer application. This portion of the application is designed to let you keep your Web site links in a common location if you've got more than one computer. You'll learn how to take the methodology you learned in the last chapter and apply it to a different type of data.

Introduction to the Link Manager

I created the Link Manager for myself a long time ago. Having several machines, I always had a problem keeping track of my bookmarks and favorites. I eventually built a static Web site with all my favorites on it. However, I didn't have a good way (other than manually updating the pages) to maintain the links. I eventually built a system similar to this one that I still use at `http://links.northcomp.com`.

You'll be building a simplified version of this application that doesn't include all the categories that mine has. However, Chapter 30 shows you how to add categories for your data so that you can add more data without having to download it all simultaneously.

Table structure

Just as a reminder, the table being used is the tblLinks table in the sample SQL Server database, and the fields are shown in Table 25-1.

Table 25-1
tblLinks Fields

Field Name	Data Type	Description
pkLinkID	int	Primary key–identity value
Name	varchar(80)	Short description of the link
URL	varchar(160)	Space for fairly long URLs
Description	text	Long description of the link

Link entry form

The form you'll be building for entering links is shown in Figure 25-1.

As far as validation rules go, the Name and URL field on the link are required, but the user won't be required to put a description of the link into the text area of the form.

Each part of the final links.asp file is explained throughout this chapter, and you can find a completed copy of the file on the CD-ROM included with this book.

Figure 25-1
Link entry form in the eOrganizer

**20 Min.
To Go**

Setting up the File

Because the structure for this page is nearly identical to the last one you created for the Note Manager, we're not going to go through it in great depth. The list of functions that the file supports is the same:

- Retrieve All
- Retrieve Single Link (*)
- Create Link (*)
- Save New Link
- Update Link (*)
- Save Changes
- Confirm Deletion of Link
- Delete Link

Once again, we'll be using a single BuildForm routine to handle the three blocks of code that are starred. The main difference between this page and the last one, besides the titles, is that this type of data will be displayed in a slightly different way. When we show the name of the link, we'll turn it into a clickable link using the URL field. For this reason, both the name and URL will be required fields when we write the ValidateData routine later in the chapter.

Following is the code that your file should start with:

```
<!--#include file="include.asp" -->
<%
Call Main
''''''''''''''''''''''''''''''''''''''''''''''''''''''''''''''''''''''
'
' Sub Main
'
' Processing for this page starts in this routine. It
' contains a dispatcher to call the appropriate routine,
' based on what function was needed.
'
''''''''''''''''''''''''''''''''''''''''''''''''''''''''''''''''''''''
Sub Main
    Dim cnDB       ' As ADODB.Connection
    Set cnDB = OpenDB()

    Select Case Request(ACTION)
        Case ACTION_CREATE, ACTION_RETRIEVE, ACTION_UPDATE
            BuildForm cnDB, ""
        Case ACTION_CREATE_SAVE
            CreateSave cnDB
        Case ACTION_UPDATE_SAVE
            UpdateSave cnDB
        Case ACTION_DELETE
            Delete cnDB
        Case ACTION_DELETE_SAVE
            DeleteSave cnDB
        Case Else
            Retrieve(cnDB)
    End Select

    CloseDB cnDB
End Sub
```

Creating the Link List Function

Building the list of links is very similar to the list of notes you created in the last chapter. The only difference is that when we show the name of the link, it should be shown as a clickable link. After all, what's the point of having links if you can't click on them?

Following is the code for the Retrieve routine:

```
''''''''''''''''''''''''''''''''''''''''''''''''''''''''''''''''''
'
' Sub Retrieve
'
' This routine lists all records of this data type. It
' also provides links to create, retrieve, update, and
' delete records.
'
''''''''''''''''''''''''''''''''''''''''''''''''''''''''''''''''''
Sub Retrieve(cnDB)
    Dim rsData        ' As ADODB.Recordset
    Dim strURL        ' As String
    Dim strSQL        ' As String
    strSQL = "SELECT * FROM tblLinks ORDER BY Name"
    Set rsData = cnDB.Execute(strSQL)
    PrintHeader "View All Links"

    WriteLine "<p><a href=" & DQ & Request("SCRIPT_NAME") _
        & "?" & ACTION & "=" & ACTION_CREATE _
        & DQ & ">Create New Link</a></p>"

    WriteLine "<table cellspacing=0 cellpadding=2>"
    WriteLine "<tr>"
    WriteLine "<th width=200>Name</th>"
    WriteLine "<th width=200>Description</th>"
    WriteLine "<th width=100>Actions</th></tr>"
    Do Until rsData.EOF
        WriteLine "<tr>"
        WriteLine "<td><a href=" & DQ & rsData("URL") & DQ & ">" _
            & rsData("Name") & "</a></td>"
        WriteLine "<td>"
        If Len(rsData("Description")) >= 40 Then
```

```
              WriteLine Left(rsData("Description"), 40) & "..."
          Else
              WriteLine rsData("Description")
          End If
          WriteLine "</td>"
          WriteLine "<td align=center>"
          strURL = "<a href=" & DQ & Request("SCRIPT_NAME") _
              & "?" & ACTION & "=" _
              & "####" & "&id=" _
              & rsData("pkLinkID") & DQ & ">"
          WriteLine Replace(strURL, "####", ACTION_RETRIEVE) _
              & "R</a> | "
          WriteLine Replace(strURL, "####", ACTION_UPDATE) _
              & "U</a> | "
          WriteLine Replace(strURL, "####", ACTION_DELETE) _
              & "D</a>"
          WriteLine "</td>"

          WriteLine "</tr>"
          rsData.MoveNext
      Loop
      rsData.Close
      PrintFooter
  End Sub
```

The difference here is that when we show the name of the link, instead of just printing out the name, we print the URL within the <A> tag, and wrap the end of the name with a </A> tag. This creates a link for the name that the user can click on.

We again use the Replace function to create the three action links at the end of the page. Other than the fields we're showing, the list looks basically the same as the notes viewer in Chapter 24. Figure 25-2 shows what the page looks like at runtime.

After that, we wrap things up and print out the common footer to the page. Now that you've got the retrieval working, you can move on to the individual functions, starting with the BuildForm routine.

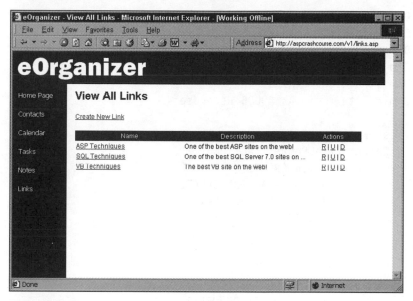

Figure 25-2
The Retrieve Links view of eOrganizer

Creating the BuildForm Subroutine

The BuildForm routine in this page is nearly identical to the one for the Note Manager, except that there are three fields instead of two. This means that you need three temporary variables for your data instead of two, and three fields on the form instead of two. Other than that, the code is basically the same. The code for the BuildForm subroutine is shown here:

```
'''''''''''''''''''''''''''''''''''''''''''''''''''''''''''''''''''''
'
' Sub BuildForm
'
' This routine displays a data entry and display form. It
' is used for the create, retrieve, and update modes.
'
'''''''''''''''''''''''''''''''''''''''''''''''''''''''''''''''''''''
Sub BuildForm(cnDB, strError)
   Dim lngLinkID  ' As Long
```

```
Dim strName     ' As String
Dim strURL      ' As String
Dim strDesc     ' As String
Dim strTitle    ' As String
Dim strAction   ' As String
Dim rsData      ' As ADODB.Recordset


If strError = "" Then
    Select Case Request(ACTION)
        Case ACTION_CREATE
            strAction = ACTION_CREATE_SAVE
            strTitle = "Create New Link"
            lngLinkID = -1
            strName = ""
            strURL = ""
            strDesc = ""
        Case ACTION_UPDATE, ACTION_RETRIEVE
            strAction = ACTION_UPDATE_SAVE
            If Request(ACTION) = ACTION_UPDATE Then
                strTitle = "Update Link"
            Else
                strTitle = "Retrieve Link"
            End If
            lngLinkID = Request("ID")
            Set rsData = cnDB.Execute("SELECT * FROM tblLinks " _
                & "WHERE pkLinkID = " & lngLinkID)
            strName = rsData("Name")
            strURL = rsData("URL")
            strDesc = rsData("Description")

            rsData.Close
            Set rsData = Nothing
    End Select
Else

    strAction = Request(ACTION)

    Select Case strAction
        Case ACTION_CREATE_SAVE
            strTitle = "Create New Link"
```

```
        Case ACTION_UPDATE_SAVE
            strTitle = "Update Link"
    End Select

    If Request("ID") = "" Then
        lngLinkID = -1
    Else
        lngLinkID = Request("ID")
    End If
    strName = Request("dbtName")
    strURL = Request("dbtURL")
    strDesc = Request("dbtDescription")
End If

PrintHeader strTitle
If strError <> "" Then
    WriteLine strError
End If

WriteLine "<form action=" & DQ & Request("SCRIPT_NAME") _
    & DQ & " method=post>"
WriteLine "<input type=hidden name=" _
    & ACTION & " value=" & strAction & ">"
WriteLine "<input type=hidden name=ID " _
    & " value=" & lngLinkID & ">"
WriteLine "<table>"
WriteLine "<tr><td>Name:</td>"
WriteLine "<td><input type=text size=40 maxlength=40 " _
    & "name=dbtName value=" _
    & DQ & strName & DQ & "></td></tr>"

WriteLine "<tr><td>URL:</td>"
WriteLine "<td><input type=text size=40 maxlength=120 " _
    & "name=dbtURL value=" _
    & DQ & strURL & DQ & "></td></tr>"

WriteLine "<tr><td>Description:</td>"
WriteLine "<td><textarea rows=10 cols=50 " _
    & "name=dbtDescription>" _
    & strDesc & "</textarea></td></tr>"
```

```
If Request(ACTION) <> ACTION_RETRIEVE Then
    WriteLine "<tr><td colspan=2 align=center>" _
        & "<input type=submit name=cmdSubmit value=Save>" _
        & " " _
        & "<input type=reset name=cmdReset " _
        & "value=Clear></td></tr>"
Else
    WriteLine "<tr><td colspan=2><a href=" _
        & DQ & Request("SCRIPT_NAME") & DQ _
        & ">Return to List</a></td></tr>"
End If
WriteLine "</table>"
PrintFooter
End Sub
```

Like the previous version, we have integrated our error handling into the Build-Form routine by printing the error before we display the form's table. Both the Name and URL fields have maximum lengths set in the HTML form, corresponding to the maximum length allowed by the database. Depending on the length of the URLs you're allowing people to store, you might want to increase the size of the URL field. However, 120 characters will handle all but the longest URLs.

Validating Input Data

**10 Min.
To Go**

As before, we want to make sure that data is properly entered into the form. We can start by making sure that the Name and URL fields are supplied. An additional validation makes sure that the user enters the http:// in front of every link. Note that this isn't required. If we wanted to, we could automatically add the prefix before creating the link on the list page. However, it's preferable to ensure that the data going into the system is valid, rather than working around bugs later. It also makes it easier to migrate the data to another system later if need be. Requiring that the data be valid before accepting it takes some of the burden off the software, but it doesn't really require the user to do more than they would have to elsewhere. This validation could also be done using client-side JavaScript, and there is information in Chapter 30 that explains more in detail how to do this.

The ValidateData subroutine is shown here:

```
'''''''''''''''''''''''''''''''''''''''''''''''''''''''''''
'
' Function ValidateData
```

```
'
' This routine validates the input data and
' causes the form to be shown if the data is
' not correct. A True result indicates that
' the data was OK, and a False indicates that
' the data was in error.
'
'''''''''''''''''''''''''''''''''''''''''''''''''''
Function ValidateData(cnDB)
    Dim strError        ' As String
    strError = ""

    If Request("dbtName") = "" Then
        strError = strError _
            & "<li>The link's name must be entered."
    End If

    If Request("dbtURL") = "" Then
        strError = strError _
            & "<li>The link's URL must be entered."
    Else
        If Left(LCase(Request("dbtURL")), 7) <> "http://" Then
            strError = strError _
                & "<li>Each link must be " _
                & "prefixed with <b>http://</b>."
        End If
    End If

    If strError <> "" Then
        strError = "<p><font color=#FF0000><b>" _
            & "The following data errors were detected:</b><br>" _
            & "<ul>" & strError & "</ul></font></p>"
        BuildForm cnDB, strError
        ValidateData = False
    Else
        ValidateData = True
    End If

End Function
```

A further validation you could perform ensures that the URL has at least one period in it, as most Web sites you visit are something .com or .net, for instance. However, if you're visiting intranet sites in your company, for instance, you won't necessarily have any periods in the URL. The following is also a valid URL, assuming a machine named goofy exists on your network:

```
http://goofy/
```

Saving a New Link

Creating a link in the database is similar to creating a note. Here's the code for the CreateSave routine:

```
'''''''''''''''''''''''''''''''''''''''''''''''''''
'
' Sub CreateSave
'
' This routine creates a new record in the database.
'
'''''''''''''''''''''''''''''''''''''''''''''''''''
Sub CreateSave(cnDB)

    Dim rsData      ' As ADODB.Recordset

    If Not ValidateData(cnDB) Then Exit Sub

    Set rsData = Server.CreateObject("ADODB.Recordset")
    rsData.Open "tblLinks", cnDB, adOpenDynamic, adLockOptimistic
    rsData.AddNew
    rsData("Name") = Request("dbtName")
    rsData("URL") = Request("dbtURL")
    rsData("Description") = Request("dbtDescription")
    rsData.Update
    rsData.Close

    Response.Redirect Request.ServerVariables("SCRIPT_NAME")

End Sub
```

If you wanted to, you could create a stored procedure that accepts the arguments for the link. Depending on the load on your system, this can improve performance in SQL Server because the stored procedure knows how to update any relevant indexes on the table.

Saving Changes to a Link

The next subroutine handles any updates you might need to make to existing links. The code for the UpdateSave routine is shown here:

```
'''''''''''''''''''''''''''''''''''''''''''''''''''''
'
' Sub UpdateSave
'
' This routine performs an update on the table for this
' particular item.
'
'''''''''''''''''''''''''''''''''''''''''''''''''''''
Sub UpdateSave(cnDB)
    Dim rsData      ' As ADODB.Recordset

    If Not ValidateData(cnDB) Then Exit Sub

    Set rsData = Server.CreateObject("ADODB.Recordset")
    rsData.Open "SELECT * FROM tblLinks WHERE pkLinkID = " _
        & Request("ID"), cnDB, adOpenDynamic, adLockOptimistic
    rsData("Name") = Request("dbtName")
    rsData("URL") = Request("dbtURL")
    rsData("Description") = Request("dbtDescription")
    rsData.Update
    rsData.Close
    Response.Redirect Request.ServerVariables("SCRIPT_NAME")

End Sub
```

In this code, we look for the link matching the ID specified in the ID parameter that we passed from the data input form. Once we have it, we update the record and save the changes. The user is then bounced back to the list of links.

Deleting Links

The last pieces of code you need take care of deletions. As before, we confirm the deletion before doing it. Following are the two routines that you need:

```
'''''''''''''''''''''''''''''''''''''''''''''''''''''''''''''''''
'
' Sub Delete
'
' This routine confirms that the user wants to delete an
' item from the system.
'
'''''''''''''''''''''''''''''''''''''''''''''''''''''''''''''''''
Sub Delete(cnDB)

    Dim rsData          ' As ADODB.Recordset

    Set rsData = cnDB.Execute("SELECT * FROM tblLinks " _
        & "WHERE pkLinkID = " _
        & Request("ID"))

    PrintHeader "Delete Link"
    WriteLine "<span class=pt><p>Delete '" _
        & rsData("Name") & "'?</p>"
    WriteLine "<p><a href=" & DQ & Request("SCRIPT_NAME") _
        & "?" _
        & ACTION & "=" & ACTION_DELETE_SAVE _
        & "&id=" & Request("ID") _
        & DQ & ">Yes</a>   " _
        & "<a href=" & DQ & Request("SCRIPT_NAME") & DQ _
        & ">No</a></p>"
    WriteLine "</span>"
    PrintFooter
End Sub


'''''''''''''''''''''''''''''''''''''''''''''''''''''''''''''''''
'
' Sub DeleteSave
'
```

```
' This routine performs the deletion of a record.
'
'''''''''''''''''''''''''''''''''''''''''''''''''''''''''''''''
Sub DeleteSave(cnDB)

    cnDB.Execute "DELETE FROM tblLinks WHERE pkLinkID = " _
        & Request("ID")
    Response.Redirect Request("SCRIPT_NAME")

End Sub
```

Feel free to used stored procedures as you see fit. The SQL code used here to select the record is exactly what you use when you retrieve or update a link. That's one benefit of stored procedures that you learned earlier — no duplicate code.

Done!

In this case, we confirm the deletion by showing the user the name of the link. You might also want to show the URL that the user is deleting. This could be done in a separate line or instead of the name. However, showing the name is probably the most useful piece of information you can provide the user.

REVIEW

This chapter shows that with a little bit of forethought, you can create a template and structure for your Web site that is easily replicable for other types of data. In the next chapter, you'll create a similar page for listing your current tasks, but with more fields. The basic code structure of the page remains the same, however.

QUIZ YOURSELF

1. Why should you validate input data? (See "Validating Input Data")
2. Explain how you would add an additional type of view to this page. (See "Creating the File")
3. What ASP structure allows us to share code between this and other files in the application? (See "Creating the File")

Building the Task Manager

Session Checklist

✔ Building a page to show all the tasks in the database

✔ Creating code to add new records

✔ Updating existing records

✔ Deleting records with ASP code

✔ Validating data before making database changes

**30 Min.
To Go**

Keeping track of everything I have to do is becoming a full-time job. Each project I'm working on has lots of tasks that need to be done, and they all seem to be due on the same date. To help me keep track of what's due when, I designed the Task Manager that you're going to build in this chapter. While we're not tracking a lot of information, the application can easily be expanded to accommodate whatever data you need.

Introduction to the Task Manager

If you're like most people, you have more things to do than you can remember. I've kept my task list in everything from a Casio PDA to a whiteboard to a spreadsheet; and right now, I have all three. In addition, my office manager has to keep track of my tasks so that bills get sent and I keep on schedule. As you've seen with the other features you've created for this application, however, the only way to keep everything straight is to have a single source for the information. The Task Manager you're going to build will enable you to do this.

Table structure

Just as a reminder, the table being used is the tblTasks table in the sample SQL Server database, and the fields are shown in Table 26-1.

Table 26-1
tblTasks Fields

Field Name	Data Type	Description
pkTaskID	int	Primary key — identity value
Name	varchar(80)	Short description of the task
Description	text	Long description of the task
Priority	tinyint	Priority level of the task — currently 1 through 3
StartDate	datetime	Start date for the task
DueDate	datetime	Date the task must be completed

Task entry form

The form you'll be building for entering tasks is shown in Figure 26-1.

The data here is more complex than before, so we'll have a few more validation rules. However, using the controls that we do helps eliminate a little bit of validation. The other key point that you should take away from this chapter is that you can validate data and be flexible at the same time. More about that later, though.

Each part of the final tasks.asp file is explained throughout this chapter, and you can find a completed copy of the file on the CD-ROM included with this book.

Figure 26-1
Task entry form in the eOrganizer

Setting up the File

Because the structure for this page is nearly identical to the one you created for the Note Manager, it is not covered in detail here. The list of functions that the file supports is the same:

- Retrieve All
- Retrieve Single Task (*)
- Create Task (*)
- Save New Task
- Update Task (*)
- Save Changes
- Confirm Deletion of Task
- Delete Task

Once again, we'll use a single BuildForm routine to handle the three blocks of code that are starred. One feature we'll be putting into this page is that when a task is overdue, its due date will be shown in red and boldface, to help it stand out.

Here's the code that your file should start with:

```
<!--#include file="include.asp" -->
<%
Call Main
',,,,,,,,,,,,,,,,,,,,,,,,,,,,,,,,,,,,,,,,,,,,,,,,,,,,,,,,,,,,,,,
'
' Sub Main
'
' Processing for this page starts in this routine. It
' contains a dispatcher to call the appropriate routine,
' based on what function was needed.
'
',,,,,,,,,,,,,,,,,,,,,,,,,,,,,,,,,,,,,,,,,,,,,,,,,,,,,,,,,,,,,,,
Sub Main
    Dim cnDB      ' As ADODB.Connection
    Set cnDB = OpenDB()

    Select Case Request(ACTION)
        Case ACTION_CREATE, ACTION_RETRIEVE, ACTION_UPDATE
            BuildForm cnDB, ""
        Case ACTION_CREATE_SAVE
            CreateSave cnDB
        Case ACTION_UPDATE_SAVE
            UpdateSave cnDB
        Case ACTION_DELETE
            Delete cnDB
        Case ACTION_DELETE_SAVE
            DeleteSave cnDB
        Case Else
            Retrieve(cnDB)
    End Select

    CloseDB cnDB
End Sub
```

Creating the Task List Function

Retrieving all the tasks in the system is a fairly straightforward operation. However, because we have to incorporate the concept of priority for a task, we want to think about how to order the data. The way we're going to sort the data is as follows:

1. **Priority.** High-priority tasks are listed first.
2. **Due Date.** The earlier a task is due, the earlier it should be listed.
3. **Name.** This sorts everything due on the same date and with the same priority alphabetically. Realistically, we probably won't have any items that have exactly the same priority and due date, but there's always a possibility of it.

The code to make this work is as follows:

```
''''''''''''''''''''''''''''''''''''''''''''''''''''''''''''''''''''
'
' Sub Retrieve
'
' This routine lists all records of this data type. It
' also provides actions to create, retrieve, update, and
' delete records.
'
''''''''''''''''''''''''''''''''''''''''''''''''''''''''''''''''''''
Sub Retrieve(cnDB)
    Dim rsData        ' As ADODB.Recordset
    Dim strURL        ' As String
    Dim strSQL        ' As String

    strSQL = "SELECT * FROM tblTasks " _
        & "ORDER BY Priority, DueDate, Name"
    Set rsData = cnDB.Execute(strSQL)
    PrintHeader "View All Tasks"

    WriteLine "<p><a href=" & DQ & Request("SCRIPT_NAME") _
        & "?" & ACTION & "=" & ACTION_CREATE _
        & DQ & ">Create New Task</a></p>"

    WriteLine "<table cellspacing=0 cellpadding=2>"
```

```
    WriteLine "<tr>"
    WriteLine "<th width=50>Priority</th>"
    WriteLine "<th width=250>Name</th>"
    WriteLine "<th width=150>Due Date</th>"
    WriteLine "<th width=100>Actions</th></tr>"
    Do Until rsData.EOF
        WriteLine "<tr>"
        WriteLine "<td align=center>" & rsData("Priority") & "</td>"
        WriteLine "<td>" & rsData("Name") & "</td>"
        WriteLine "<td align=center>"
        If DateDiff("s", rsData("DueDate"), Now) > 0 Then
            WriteLine "<b><font color=#FF0000>"
        End If
        WriteLine FormatDateTime(rsData("DueDate"), vbShortDate)
        If DateDiff("s", rsData("DueDate"), Now) > 0 Then
            WriteLine "</font></b>"
        End If
        WriteLine "</td>"
        WriteLine "<td align=center>"
        strURL = "<a href=" & DQ & Request("SCRIPT_NAME") _
            & "?" & ACTION & "=" _
            & "###" & "&id=" _
            & rsData("pkTaskID") & DQ & ">"
        WriteLine Replace(strURL, "###", ACTION_RETRIEVE) _
            & "R</a> | "
        WriteLine Replace(strURL, "###", ACTION_UPDATE) _
            & "U</a> | "
        WriteLine Replace(strURL, "###", ACTION_DELETE) _
            & "D</a>"
        WriteLine "</td>"

        WriteLine "</tr>"
        rsData.MoveNext
    Loop
    rsData.Close
    PrintFooter
End Sub
```

The main difference between this Retrieve subroutine and the others you've written so far is in how we display the due date for the task. If the task's due date is after the current date, it's still on time. Otherwise, it is marked in boldface and in red. The code that makes this work uses the DateDiff function, shown here:

```
If DateDiff("s", rsData("DueDate"), Now) > 0 Then
    WriteLine "<b><font color=#FF0000>"
End If
```

The first argument to DateDiff is the unit of time to use. Because a due date can include a date and time portion, we check to the second, represented by a lower-case S. We then list the two dates: the due date, and the current date and time provided by the Now function. The DateDiff function will return a positive result if the second date provided is later than the first date. As long as the task is on time, the result will be negative. Once the due date passes, the red font will be used. We have a similar block of code following the place where we print the date to close out the FONT and B tags.

**20 Min.
To Go**

Creating the BuildForm Routine

For adding a new task, the BuildForm routine is similar to the previous ones you've built. However, we've added a new twist by creating a drop-down list of the available priorities for tasks. This common feature is a bit more work to implement, but it provides some built-in validation. The user has no choice but to pick one of the priority values you've listed. In fact, we pre-select Medium priority for new records using this code.

Here's the BuildForm routine for this page:

```
'''''''''''''''''''''''''''''''''''''''''''''''''''''''''''''''''''''
'
' Sub BuildForm
'
' This routine displays a data entry and display form. It
' is used for the create, retrieve, and update modes.
'
'''''''''''''''''''''''''''''''''''''''''''''''''''''''''''''''''''''
Sub BuildForm(cnDB, strError)
    Dim lngTaskID   ' As Long
    Dim strName     ' As String
    Dim strDesc     ' As String
    Dim intPriority   ' As Integer
    Dim datStart    ' As Date
```

```
    Dim datDue      ' As Date
    Dim strTitle    ' As String
    Dim strAction   ' As String
    Dim rsData      ' As ADODB.Recordset

    If strError = "" Then
        Select Case Request(ACTION)
            Case ACTION_CREATE
                strAction = ACTION_CREATE_SAVE
                strTitle = "Create New Task"
                lngTaskID = -1
                strName = ""
                strDesc = ""
                intPriority = 2
                datStart = ""
                datDue = ""
            Case ACTION_UPDATE, ACTION_RETRIEVE
                strAction = ACTION_UPDATE_SAVE
                If Request(ACTION) = ACTION_UPDATE Then
                    strTitle = "Update Task"
                Else
                    strTitle = "Retrieve Task"
                End If
                lngTaskID = Request("ID")
                Set rsData = cnDB.Execute("SELECT * FROM tblTasks " _
                    & "WHERE pkTaskID = " & lngTaskID)

                strName = rsData("Name")
                strDesc = rsData("Description")
                intPriority = rsData("Priority")
                datStart = rsData("StartDate")
                datDue = rsData("DueDate")

                rsData.Close
                Set rsData = Nothing
        End Select
    Else
        strAction = Request(ACTION)

        Select Case strAction
            Case ACTION_CREATE_SAVE
```

```
            strTitle = "Create New Task"
        Case ACTION_UPDATE_SAVE
            strTitle = "Update Task"
    End Select

    If Request("ID") = "" Then
        lngTaskID = -1
    Else
        lngTaskID = Request("ID")
    End If
    strName = Request("dbtName")
    strDesc = Request("dbtDescription")
    intPriority = Request("dbnPriority")
    datStart = Request("dbtStartDate")
    datDue = Request("dbtDueDate")
End If

PrintHeader strTitle
If strError <> "" Then
    WriteLine strError
End If

WriteLine "<form action=" & DQ & Request("SCRIPT_NAME") _
    & DQ & " method=post>"
WriteLine "<input type=hidden name=" _
    & ACTION & " value=" & strAction & ">"
WriteLine "<input type=hidden name=ID " _
    & " value=" & lngTaskID & ">"
WriteLine "<table>"
WriteLine "<tr><td>Name:</td>"
WriteLine "<td><input type=text size=40 maxlength=40 " _
    & "name=dbtName value=" _
    & DQ & strName & DQ & "></td></tr>"

WriteLine "<tr><td>Priority:</td>"
WriteLine "<td>"
WriteLine "<select name-dbnPriority>"
Response.Write "<option value=1"
If intPriority = 1 Then Response.Write " SELECTED"
WriteLine ">High</option>"
```

```
    Response.Write "<option value=2"
    If intPriority = 2 Then Response.Write " SELECTED"
    WriteLine ">Medium</option>"

    Response.Write "<option value=3"
    If intPriority = 3 Then Response.Write " SELECTED"
    WriteLine ">Low</option>"
    WriteLine "</select>"
    WriteLine "</td></tr>"

    WriteLine "<tr><td>Start Date:</td>"
    WriteLine "<td><input type=text size=40 maxlength=40 " _
       & "name=dbtStartDate value=" _
       & DQ & datStart & DQ & "></td></tr>"

    WriteLine "<tr><td>Due Date:</td>"
    WriteLine "<td><input type=text size=40 maxlength=40 " _
       & "name=dbtDueDate value=" _
       & DQ & datDue & DQ & "></td></tr>"

    WriteLine "<tr><td>Description:</td>"
    WriteLine "<td><textarea rows=10 cols=50 " _
       & "name=dbtDescription>" _
       & strDesc & "</textarea></td></tr>"

    If Request(ACTION) <> ACTION_RETRIEVE Then
       WriteLine "<tr><td colspan=2 align=center>" _
          & "<input type=submit name=cmdSubmit " _
          & "value=Save>" _
          & " " _
          & "<input type=reset name=cmdReset " _
          & "value=Clear></td></tr>"
    Else
       WriteLine "<tr><td colspan=2><a href=" _
          & DQ & Request("SCRIPT_NAME") & DQ _
          & ">Return to List</a></td></tr>"
    End If
    WriteLine "</table>"
    PrintFooter
End Sub
```

Each time we add a few new fields, this routine gets a little bit longer. We're now managing five fields, which means we have to read data into five variables and create five input boxes. In Chapter 30, you'll learn some ways to create subroutines to do some of this work for you, once you're comfortable with how this particular method works.

Recall that one new feature we've added to this page is a drop-down list with three priorities. The resulting HTML for this list is as follows:

```
<select name=dbnPriority>
<option value=1>High</option>
<option value=2 SELECTED>Medium</option>
<option value=3>Low</option>
</select>
```

The trick here is to put the word SELECTED into the right option, based on which one should be selected. The intPriority variable holds this data, so we check it for each data value. If you stored the priorities in a database table, you could easily loop through the priorities checking for the value in question. However, we're not doing that here for reasons of simplicity — one less table to deal with.

Note that some places in the code use `Response.Write` and other places use `WriteLine`. This is because we want the OPTION tag to show up on one line. To do this, we have to Response.Write everything except for the last portion of it. This isn't required, but you might find it preferable.

Other than that, this routine is similar to the others you've created.

Validating Input Data

We have a number of new validation steps to perform in this routine, as we have date/time data to validate. However, using some of the built-in functions, this is easier to do than you might think. Here's the code for the ValidateData subroutine:

```
'''''''''''''''''''''''''''''''''''''''''''''''''''''
'
' Function ValidateData
'
' This routine validates the input data and
' causes the form to be shown if the data is
' not correct. A True result indicates that
' the data was OK, and a False indicates that
' the data was in error.
'
```

```
''''''''''''''''''''''''''''''''''''''''''''''''''''''
Function ValidateData(cnDB)
   Dim strError        ' As String
   strError = ""

   If Request("dbtName") = "" Then
      strError = strError _
         & "<li>The task's name must be entered."
   End If

   If Request("dbtStartDate") = "" Then
      strError = strError _
         & "<li>The start date must be entered."
   Else
      If Not IsDate(Request("dbtStartDate")) Then
         strError = strError _
            & "<li>The start date is not a valid date/time value."
      End If
   End If

   If Request("dbtDueDate") = "" Then
      strError = strError _
         & "<li>The due date must be entered."
   Else
      If Not IsDate(Request("dbtDueDate")) Then
         strError = strError _
            & "<li>The due date is not a valid date/time value."
      End If
   End If

   If strError <> "" Then
      strError = "<p><font color=#FF0000><b>" _
         & "The following data errors were detected:</b><br>" _
         & "<ul>" & strError & "</ul></font></p>"
      BuildForm cnDB, strError
      ValidateData = False
   Else
      ValidateData = True
   End If

End Function
```

Validating the name of the task is the same as what you've been doing all along. For the Priority field, the user must select one of the values. Because we pre-select a value, we don't have to worry about this field ever being empty. The start date and due date are handled in a similar fashion. We first make sure that the fields aren't empty. We then use the built-in IsDate function to check the contents to ensure that the data is a valid date/time value.

You might be wondering why we have two checks, as an empty date isn't valid and would be caught by the IsDate function. The reason is because we want to display a different message when the date is missing. Again, we want to be specific when we display an error message. Telling the user that an empty box is an invalid date might be understood, but the message we have here is a bit clearer.

The best part about IsDate is that it's incredibly flexible. Following are some valid dates that you could enter and have interpreted properly:

```
01 Dec 2000
December 1, 2000
01 Dec 2000 20:00
01 Dec 2000 8:00 PM
```

The IsDate function uses whatever rules are used in your country for formatting dates and times. If you use periods to separate date portions, that will be considered valid by the IsDate function.

As in the other chapters that have validation steps, you can use client-side JavaScript to do this work for you. Look at Chapter 30 for more tips on using this method of validation.

Saving a New Task

**10 Min.
To Go**

Saving a new task is exactly like saving other data. However, because we're using date/time data, we have to validate the input before attempting to save it. The database will reject invalid date/time values. Here's the code for CreateSave:

```
'.............................................
'
' Sub CreateSave
'
' This routine creates a new record in the database.
'
'.............................................
Sub CreateSave(cnDB)
```

```
Dim rsData        ' As ADODB.Recordset

If Not ValidateData(cnDB) Then Exit Sub

Set rsData = Server.CreateObject("ADODB.Recordset")
rsData.Open "tblTasks", cnDB, adOpenDynamic, adLockOptimistic
rsData.AddNew
rsData("Name") = Request("dbtName")
rsData("Description") = Request("dbtDescription")
rsData("Priority") = Request("dbnPriority")
rsData("StartDate") = Request("dbtStartDate")
rsData("DueDate") = Request("dbtDueDate")
rsData.Update
rsData.Close

Response.Redirect Request.ServerVariables("SCRIPT_NAME")

End Sub
```

Note that saving the date/time data, as well as the numeric value in the Priority drop-down list, works exactly the same as the text data we've been adding all along.

Saving Changes to a Task

Updating a task is similar to creating one. You still have to be careful with your date/time values because the database will perform some validation to prevent bad data from getting into the system. Here's the code for the UpdateSave routine:

```
'''''''''''''''''''''''''''''''''''''''''''''''''''
'
' Sub UpdateSave
'
' This routine performs an update on the table for this
' particular item.
'
'''''''''''''''''''''''''''''''''''''''''''''''''''
Sub UpdateSave(cnDB)
   Dim rsData        ' As ADODB.Recordset
```

```
If Not ValidateData(cnDB) Then Exit Sub

Set rsData = Server.CreateObject("ADODB.Recordset")
rsData.Open "SELECT * FROM tblTasks WHERE pkTaskID = " _
    & Request("ID"), cnDB, adOpenDynamic, adLockOptimistic
rsData("Name") = Request("dbtName")
rsData("Description") = Request("dbtDescription")
rsData("Priority") = Request("dbnPriority")
rsData("StartDate") = Request("dbtStartDate")
rsData("DueDate") = Request("dbtDueDate")
rsData.Update
rsData.Close
Response.Redirect Request.ServerVariables("SCRIPT_NAME")

End Sub
```

Deleting Tasks

Deleting tasks is the same as for previous pages, other than the table names in use. Here's the code for the Delete and DeleteSave routines:

```
''''''''''''''''''''''''''''''''''''''''''''''''''''''''''''''
'
' Sub Delete
'
' This routine confirms that the user wants to delete an
' item from the system.
'
''''''''''''''''''''''''''''''''''''''''''''''''''''''''''''''
Sub Delete(cnDB)

    Dim rsData          ' As ADODB.Recordset

    Set rsData = cnDB.Execute("SELECT * FROM tblTasks " _
        & "WHERE pkTaskID = " & Request("ID"))

    PrintHeader "Delete Task"
    WriteLine "<span class=pt><p>Delete '" _
        & rsData("Name") & "'?</p>"
```

```
    WriteLine "<p><a href=" & DQ & Request("SCRIPT_NAME") & "?" _
        & ACTION & "=" & ACTION_DELETE_SAVE _
        & "&id=" & Request("ID") _
        & DQ & ">Yes</a>   " _
        & "<a href=" & DQ & Request("SCRIPT_NAME") & DQ _
        & ">No</a></p>"
    WriteLine "</span>"
    PrintFooter
End Sub




'''''''''''''''''''''''''''''''''''''''''''''''''''''''''''''''''''
'
' Sub DeleteSave
'
' This routine performs the deletion of a record.
'
'''''''''''''''''''''''''''''''''''''''''''''''''''''''''''''''''''
Sub DeleteSave(cnDB)

    cnDB.Execute "DELETE FROM tblTasks WHERE pkTaskID = " _
        & Request("ID")
    Response.Redirect Request("SCRIPT_NAME")

End Sub
```

REVIEW

Once again, we've been able to create a new type of data for our system with only minor changes to the code we've built so far. In this chapter, you learned how to provide lists of information for the user to pick from, as well as how to handle date/time information. By using the built-in functions, you save yourself a lot of effort. Just think about how ugly the code would be to validate your date and time combinations otherwise. In addition, you learned how using drop-down lists eliminates a validation step, because the user is forced to choose from the available data values. This is a good way to ensure that essential fields are always filled in.

Quiz Yourself

1. Which function is used to determine if one date is before another? (See "Creating the Task List Function")

2. What code do you use to retrieve the name of the ASP file from within the same file? (See "Creating the Task List Function")

3. If you have two possible choices for a data value, what two HTML controls can be used to restrict input to just those two items? (See "Creating the BuildForm Routine")

PART

V

Sunday Morning Part Review

1. Write a ConnectionString property to connect to a SQL Server whose server name is COMPANY, database name is ORDERS, with a user ID of visitor and password of visitor5.

2. Write a server-side include directive to include the functions.asp file from the /includes virtual directory on the server.

3. Create a subroutine that automatically prints a piece of text followed by a <BR> tag and a carriage return/line feed character pair.

4. Which properties of the <TEXTAREA> tag control the size of the box?

Which style sheet attributes are responsible for each of the following formatting features:

5. Name of the font to use

6. Color of the text

7. Whether to underline hyperlinks or not

8. Are server-side include directives evaluated before or after the ASP code is executed?

9. What type of field is useful for creating database table primary keys in Access?

10. What type of field is useful for creating database table primary keys in SQL Server?

PART

VI

Sunday
Afternoon

Building the Contact Manager

Session Checklist

✔ Setting up the file

✔ Creating the contact list function

✔ Creating the BuildForm routine

✔ Validating the input data

✔ Saving new contacts

✔ Saving changes to contacts

**30 Min.
To Go**

Take a walk through any computer software store and you'll see how big a business contact management is. In fact, there are several multibillion-dollar companies whose primary business is writing software to manage customer contact information. Every time I go to a conference I get a new handful of business cards. This portion of the application lets you create records for each contact and view them using a Web-based interface.

Introduction to the Contact Manager

The biggest table in the application is your phone/address book, but the structure of the page is exactly the same as the other portions of the application you've built so far.

Table Structure

Just as a reminder, the table being used is the tblContacts table in the sample SQL Server database; the fields are shown in Table 27-1.

Table 27-1
tblContacts Fields

Field Name	Data Type	Description
pkContactID	int	Primary key — identity value
FirstName	varchar(40)	First name
LastName	varchar(40)	Last name
Title	varchar(80)	Person's title
CompanyName	varchar(120)	Company name
Address1	varchar(120)	Space for address
Address2	varchar(120)	Space for address
City	varchar(40)	City
State	varchar(2)	State
ZIP	varchar(10)	Zip code (with space for zip code + 4)
Phone	varchar(40)	Phone number
Fax	varchar(40)	Fax number
EMail	varchar(120)	E-mail address

As discussed when this database table was created, you may want to use a slightly different set of fields, based on the information you're storing for a person. For instance, you might want to include an additional address line if you have long addresses, as some outside the United States are. You may also want to change how you store city, state, and zip code if you're dealing with international addresses. Finally, you may want to add extra telephone and e-mail fields. If you change the fields that are in the database, the code covered through the rest of the chapter won't be exactly the code you need. If you add a new field, you'll need to add a new control to accept input and change the SQL statements to create, retrieve and update that record.

If this is a personal database, you might choose to include a birth date field, an anniversary date field, or a large notes field in which you can keep track of other information about the person. It's up to you.

Contact Entry Form

The form you'll be building for entering contacts is shown in Figure 27-1.

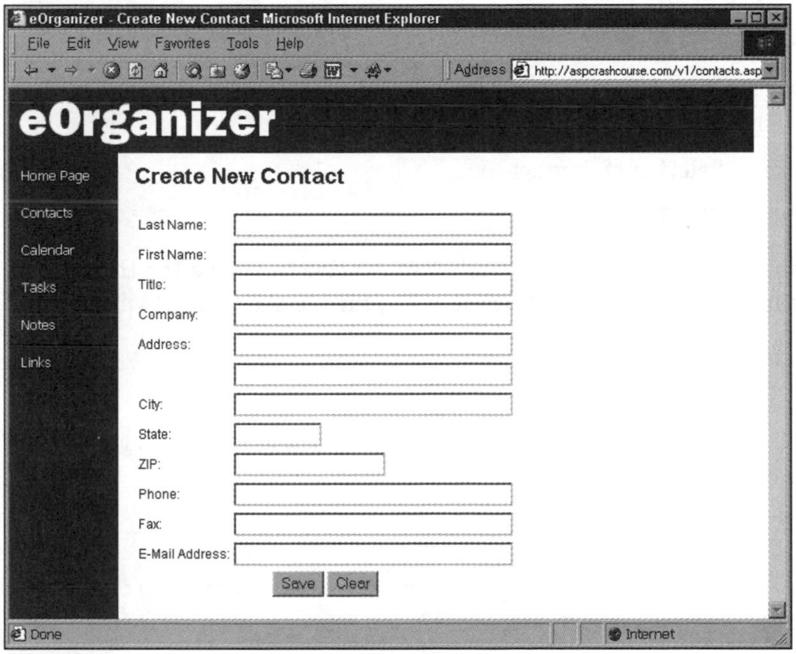

Figure 27-1
Contact entry form in the eOrganizer

The data here is lengthier than before, but we have to be more flexible about what data is entered. In fact, we'll be doing very little validation at all for this one. It's really up to the user what data is entered.

Each part of the final Contacts.asp file is explained throughout this chapter, and there is a complete listing at the end of the chapter.

Setting up the File

Because the structure for this page is nearly identical to the one you created for the Note Manager, it isn't covered in great depth here. The list of logical functions that the file supports is the same:

- Retrieve All
- Retrieve Single Contact (*)
- Create Contact (*)
- Save New Contact
- Update Contact (*)
- Save Changes
- Confirm Deletion of Contact
- Delete Contact

Again, we'll be using a single BuildForm routine to handle the three blocks of code that are starred. Here's the code that your file should start with:

```
<!--#include file="include.asp" -->
<%
Call Main
''''''''''''''''''''''''''''''''''''''''''''''''''''''''''''''''''
'
' Sub Main
'
' Processing for this page starts in this routine. It
' contains a dispatcher to call the appropriate routine,
' based on what function was needed.
'
''''''''''''''''''''''''''''''''''''''''''''''''''''''''''''''''''
Sub Main
    Dim cnDB      ' As ADODB.Connection
    Set cnDB = OpenDB()
```

```
    Select Case Request(ACTION)
        Case ACTION_CREATE, ACTION_RETRIEVE, ACTION_UPDATE
            BuildForm cnDB, ""
        Case ACTION_CREATE_SAVE
            CreateSave cnDB
        Case ACTION_UPDATE_SAVE
            UpdateSave cnDB
        Case ACTION_DELETE
            Delete cnDB
        Case ACTION_DELETE_SAVE
            DeleteSave cnDB
        Case Else
            Retrieve(cnDB)
    End Select

    CloseDB cnDB
End Sub
```

Creating the Contact List Function

As mentioned in the last section, the contact table is probably the most flexible of all the database tables. Because you may only need to store a company name and telephone number, or a name and telephone number, the list window has to take this into account when it's showing the data. Following are the rules we'll follow when showing the contact's name, in order of precedence:

1. If last name and first name are supplied, show them in the following format: Last Name, First Name.

2. If only a last name or first name is supplied, show the field without a comma.

3. If only a company name is supplied, show it instead of a first or last name.

The validation rules we'll create will require that the user enter information in at least one of these three fields. Here's the code for the Retrieve subroutine:

```
' , , , , , , , , , , , , , , , , , , , , , , , , , , , , , , , , , , , , , , , , , , , , , , , , , , , , , , , , , , , , , , , , ,
'
' Sub Retrieve
'
```

```
' This routine lists all records of this data type. It
' also provides actions to create, retrieve, update, and
' delete records.
'
'...............................................................

Sub Retrieve(cnDB)
    Dim rsData          ' As ADODB.Recordset
    Dim strSQL          ' As String
    Dim strURL          ' As String
    strSQL = "SELECT * FROM tblContacts " _
        & "ORDER BY LastName, FirstName, CompanyName"
    Set rsData = cnDB.Execute(strSQL)
    PrintHeader "View All Contacts"

    WriteLine "<p><a href=" & DQ & Request("SCRIPT_NAME") _
        & "?" & ACTION & "=" & ACTION_CREATE _
        & DQ & ">Create New Contact</a></p>"

    WriteLine "<table cellspacing=0 cellpadding=2>"
    WriteLine "<tr>"
    WriteLine "<th width=150>Name</th>"
    WriteLine "<th width=150>E-Mail</th>"
    WriteLine "<th width=100>Phone</th>"
    WriteLine "<th width=100>Fax</th>"
    WriteLine "<th width=100>Actions</th></tr>"
    Do Until rsData.EOF
        WriteLine "<tr>"
        WriteLine "<td>"
        If rsData("LastName") <> "" _
        And rsData("FirstName") <> "" Then
            WriteLine rsData("LastName") & ", " _
                & rsData("FirstName")

        ElseIf _
            (rsData("LastName") = "" _
            And rsData("FirstName") <> "") _
        Or _
            (rsData("LastName") <> "" _
            And rsData("FirstName") = "") Then
            WriteLine rsData("LastName") & rsData("FirstName")
```

```
            ElseIf rsData("CompanyName") <> "" Then
                WriteLine rsData("CompanyName")
            End If

            WriteLine "</td>"
            WriteLine "<td>"
            If rsData("EMail") <> "" Then
                WriteLine "<a href=" & DQ _
                & "mailto:" & rsData("EMail") & DQ & ">" _
                & rsData("EMail") & "</a>"
            End If
            WriteLine "</td>"
            WriteLine "<td>" & rsData("Phone") & "</td>"
            WriteLine "<td>" & rsData("Fax") & "</td>"
            WriteLine "<td align=center>"
            strURL = "<a href=" & DQ & Request("SCRIPT_NAME") _
                & "?" & ACTION & "=" _
                & "###" & "&id=" _
                & rsData("pkContactID") & DQ & ">"
            WriteLine Replace(strURL, "###", ACTION_RETRIEVE) _
                & "R</a> | "
            WriteLine Replace(strURL, "###", ACTION_UPDATE) _
                & "U</a> | "
            WriteLine Replace(strURL, "###", ACTION_DELETE) _
                & "D</a>"
            WriteLine "</td>"

            WriteLine "</tr>"
            rsData.MoveNext
        Loop
        rsData.Close
        PrintFooter
    End Sub
```

Besides the extra logic needed to display a name properly, we also create the e-mail address as a link. That makes it easy to send an e-mail to someone just by clicking the mailto link on the page. If a field is empty, no data is printed. If you want, you can print something like "No Value" when you have a field without data in it. However, I prefer to simply leave the empty fields blank in this view.

**20 Min.
To Go**

Creating the BuildForm Routine

Other than being quite a bit longer than before, this routine is identical to the
others you've created:

```
'..................................................................
'
' Sub BuildForm
'
' This routine displays a data entry and display form. It
' is used for the create, retrieve, and update modes.
'
'..................................................................
Sub BuildForm(cnDB, strError)
    Dim lngContactID     ' As Long
    Dim strLastName      ' As String
    Dim strFirstName     ' As String
    Dim strContactTitle  ' As String
    Dim strCompany       ' As String
    Dim strAddress1      ' As String
    Dim strAddress2      ' As String
    Dim strCity          ' As String
    Dim strState         ' As String
    Dim strZIP           ' As String
    Dim strPhone         ' As String
    Dim strFax           ' As String
    Dim strEMail         ' As String
    Dim strTitle         ' As String
    Dim strAction        ' As String
    Dim rsData           ' As ADODB.Recordset

    If strError = "" Then
        Select Case Request(ACTION)
            Case ACTION_CREATE
                strAction = ACTION_CREATE_SAVE
                strTitle = "Create New Contact"
                lngContactID = -1
                strLastName      = ""
                strFirstName     = ""
                strContactTitle  = ""
```

```
                strCompany        = ""
                strAddress1       = ""
                strAddress2       = ""
                strCity           = ""
                strState          = ""
                strZIP            = ""
                strPhone          = ""
                strFax            = ""
                strEMail          = ""
            Case ACTION_UPDATE, ACTION_RETRIEVE
                strAction = ACTION_UPDATE_SAVE
                If Request(ACTION) = ACTION_UPDATE Then
                    strTitle = "Modify Contact"
                Else
                    strTitle = "View Contact"
                End If
                lngContactID = Request("ID")
                Set rsData = _
                    cnDB.Execute("SELECT * FROM tblContacts " _
                    & "WHERE pkContactID = " & lngContactID)
                strLastName       = rsData("LastName")
                strFirstName      = rsData("FirstName")
                strContactTitle   = rsData("Title")
                strCompany        = rsData("CompanyName")
                strAddress1       = rsData("Address1")
                strAddress2       = rsData("Address2")
                strCity           = rsData("City")
                strState          = rsData("State")
                strZIP            = rsData("ZIP")
                strPhone          = rsData("Phone")
                strFax            = rsData("Fax")
                strEMail          = rsData("EMail")

                rsData.Close
                Set rsData = Nothing
        End Select
    Else
        strAction = Request(ACTION)

        Select Case strAction
```

```
        Case ACTION_CREATE_SAVE
            strTitle = "Create New Contact"
        Case ACTION_UPDATE_SAVE
            strTitle = "Update Contact"
    End Select

    If Request("ID") = "" Then
        lngContactID = -1
    Else
        lngContactID = Request("ID")
    End If
    strLastName      = Request("dbtLastName")
    strFirstName     = Request("dbtFirstName")
    strContactTitle  = Request("dbtTitle")
    strCompany       = Request("dbtCompanyName")
    strAddress1      = Request("dbtAddress1")
    strAddress2      = Request("dbtAddress2")
    strCity          = Request("dbtCity")
    strState         = Request("dbtState")
    strZIP           = Request("dbtZIP")
    strPhone         = Request("dbtPhone")
    strFax           = Request("dbtFax")
    strEMail         = Request("dbtEMail")
End If

PrintHeader strTitle
If strError <> "" Then
    WriteLine strError
End If
WriteLine "<form action=" & DQ _
    & Request("SCRIPT_NAME") & DQ & " method=post>"
WriteLine "<input type=hidden name=" _
    & ACTION & " value=" & strAction & ">"
WriteLine "<input type=hidden name=ID " _
    & " value=" & lngContactID & ">"
WriteLine "<table>"
WriteLine "<tr><td>Last Name:</td>"
WriteLine "<td><input type=text size=40 " _
    & "maxlength=40 name=dbtLastName value=" _
    & DQ & strLastName & DQ & "></td></tr>"
```

```
WriteLine "<tr><td>First Name:</td>"
WriteLine "<td><input type=text size=40 " _
    & "maxlength=40 name=dbtFirstName value=" _
    & DQ & strFirstName & DQ & "></td></tr>"

WriteLine "<tr><td>Title:</td>"
WriteLine "<td><input type=text size=40 " _
    & "maxlength=80 name=dbtTitle value=" _
    & DQ & strContactTitle & DQ & "></td></tr>"

WriteLine "<tr><td>Company:</td>"
WriteLine "<td><input type=text size=40 " _
    & "maxlength=80 name=dbtCompanyName value=" _
    & DQ & strCompany & DQ & "></td></tr>"

WriteLine "<tr><td>Address:</td>"
WriteLine "<td><input type=text size=40 " _
    & "maxlength=120 name=dbtAddress1 value=" _
    & DQ & strAddress1 & DQ & "></td></tr>"

WriteLine "<tr><td></td>"
WriteLine "<td><input type=text size=40 " _
    & "maxlength=120 name=dbtAddress2 value=" _
    & DQ & strAddress2 & DQ & "></td></tr>"

WriteLine "<tr><td>City:</td>"
WriteLine "<td><input type=text size=40 " _
    & "maxlength=40 name=dbtCity value=" _
    & DQ & strCity & DQ & "></td></tr>"

WriteLine "<tr><td>State:</td>"
WriteLine "<td><input type=text size=10 " _
    & "maxlength=2 name=dbtState value=" _
    & DQ & strState & DQ & "></td></tr>"

WriteLine "<tr><td>ZIP:</td>"
WriteLine "<td><input type=text size=20 " _
    & "maxlength=10 name=dbtZIP value=" _
    & DQ & strZIP & DQ & "></td></tr>"
WriteLine "<tr><td>Phone:</td>"
```

```
      WriteLine "<td><input type=text size=40 " _
         & "maxlength=40 name=dbtPhone value=" _
         & DQ & strPhone & DQ & "></td></tr>"

      WriteLine "<tr><td>Fax:</td>"
      WriteLine "<td><input type=text size=40 " _
         & "maxlength=40 name=dbtFax value=" _
         & DQ & strFax & DQ & "></td></tr>"

      WriteLine "<tr><td>E-Mail Address:</td>"
      WriteLine "<td><input type=text size=40 " _
         & "maxlength=120 name=dbtEMail value=" _
         & DQ & strEMail & DQ & "></td></tr>"

      If Request(ACTION) <> ACTION_RETRIEVE Then
         WriteLine "<tr><td colspan=2 align=center>" _
            & "<input type=submit name=cmdSubmit value=Save>" _
            & " " _
            & "<input type=reset name=cmdReset " _
            & "value=Clear></td></tr>"
      Else
         WriteLine "<tr><td colspan=2><a href=" _
            & DQ & Request("SCRIPT_NAME") & DQ _
            & ">Return to List</a></td></tr>"
      End If
      WriteLine "</table>"
      PrintFooter
   End Sub
```

It's a bit tedious to put in all the input boxes on this form, but imagine if you had to create and manage this code in three different pages. You have much less work to do this way, and you already know how to easily work with this code. You can also easily add new fields here without having to go to other files.

Validating Input Data

Validation of a contact is going to be very short. In order for the name to show up properly in the list window, we simply need to make sure that the user enters a last name, first name, or company name. That's all the validation we really need to do. If you want to, however, you can require that additional fields are supplied; and then you can validate them. For instance, you can verify that all the characters in the Zip Code field are either numeric or a dash character. You might do some basic checking of the e-mail address to ensure there are no spaces in it and that it has an at sign (@) and at least one period. However, I'll leave that to you to decide. Here's the ValidateData subroutine for this page:

```
',,,,,,,,,,,,,,,,,,,,,,,,,,,,,,,,,,,,,,,,,,,,,,,,,,,,,,
'
' Function ValidateData
'
' This routine validates the input data and
' causes the form to be shown if the data is
' not correct. A True result indicates that
' the data was OK, and a False indicates that
' the data was in error.
'
',,,,,,,,,,,,,,,,,,,,,,,,,,,,,,,,,,,,,,,,,,,,,,,,,,,,,,
Function ValidateData(cnDB)
   Dim strError        ' As String
   strError = ""

   If Request("dbtLastName") = "" _
      And Request("dbtFirstName") = "" _
      And Request("dbtCompanyName") = "" Then
      strError = strError _
         & "<li>Please enter a last name, " _
         & "first name, and/or company name."
   End If

   If strError <> "" Then
      strError = "<p><font color=#FF0000><b>" _
         & "The following data errors were detected:</b><br>" _
         & "<ul>" & strError & "</ul></font></p>"
      BuildForm cnDB, strError
      ValidateData = False
   Else
      ValidateData = True
   End If

End Function
```

Saving a New Contact

Again, other than having a longer list of fields to save, you save this data exactly as you did with every other data type so far. Here's the code for CreateSave:

```
'''''''''''''''''''''''''''''''''''''''''''''''''''
'
' Sub CreateSave
'
' This routine creates a new record in the database.
'
'''''''''''''''''''''''''''''''''''''''''''''''''''
Sub CreateSave(cnDB)

    Dim rsData      ' As ADODB.Recordset

    If Not ValidateData(cnDB) Then Exit Sub

    Set rsData = Server.CreateObject("ADODB.Recordset")
    rsData.Open "tblContacts", cnDB, _
        adOpenDynamic, adLockOptimistic
    rsData.AddNew
    rsData("LastName")       = Request("dbtLastName")
    rsData("FirstName")      = Request("dbtFirstName")
    rsData("Title")          = Request("dbtTitle")
    rsData("CompanyName")    = Request("dbtCompanyName")
    rsData("Address1")       = Request("dbtAddress1")
    rsData("Address2")       = Request("dbtAddress2")
    rsData("City")           = Request("dbtCity")
    rsData("State")          = Request("dbtState")
    rsData("ZIP")            = Request("dbtZIP")
    rsData("Phone")          = Request("dbtPhone")
    rsData("Fax")            = Request("dbtFax")
    rsData("EMail")          = Request("dbtEMail")
    rsData.Update
    rsData.Close

    Response.Redirect Request.ServerVariables("SCRIPT_NAME")

End Sub
```

**10 Min.
To Go**

Saving Changes to a Contact

Changing a contact is basically the same code as adding one:

```
'''''''''''''''''''''''''''''''''''''''''''''''''''
'
' Sub UpdateSave
'
' This routine performs an update on the table for this
' particular item.
'
'''''''''''''''''''''''''''''''''''''''''''''''''''
Sub UpdateSave(cnDB)
    Dim rsData     ' As ADODB.Recordset

    If Not ValidateData(cnDB) Then Exit Sub

    Set rsData = Server.CreateObject("ADODB.Recordset")
    rsData.Open "SELECT * FROM tblContacts WHERE pkContactID = " _
        & Request("ID"), cnDB, adOpenDynamic, adLockOptimistic
    rsData("LastName")      = Request("dbtLastName")
    rsData("FirstName")     = Request("dbtFirstName")
    rsData("Title")         = Request("dbtTitle")
    rsData("CompanyName")   = Request("dbtCompanyName")
    rsData("Address1")      = Request("dbtAddress1")
    rsData("Address2")      = Request("dbtAddress2")
    rsData("City")          = Request("dbtCity")
    rsData("State")         = Request("dbtState")
    rsData("ZIP")           = Request("dbtZIP")
    rsData("Phone")         = Request("dbtPhone")
    rsData("Fax")           = Request("dbtFax")
    rsData("EMail")         = Request("dbtEMail")
    rsData.Update
    rsData.Close
    Response.Redirect Request.ServerVariables("SCRIPT_NAME")

End Sub
```

Deleting Contacts

Deleting data from this table is basically the same as before, except in this case, we're not going to look up the contact first. We'll simply ask the generic question, Delete this contact? This gives the user a chance to back out, but because we're not forcing the user to enter much data, the resulting question might look a bit strange. If you like, you can use logic similar to what we used in the Retrieve routine to show the message. However, for a confirmation message, that might be overkill. Here's the code for the Delete and DeleteSave routines:

```
'''''''''''''''''''''''''''''''''''''''''''''''''''''''''''''''''''''
'
' Sub Delete
'
' This routine confirms that the user wants to delete an
' item from the system.
'
'''''''''''''''''''''''''''''''''''''''''''''''''''''''''''''''''''''
Sub Delete(cnDB)

    PrintHeader "Delete Contact"
    WriteLine "<span class=pt><p>Delete this contact?</p>"
    WriteLine "<p><a href=" & DQ & Request("SCRIPT_NAME") & "?" _
        & ACTION & "=" & ACTION_DELETE_SAVE _
        & "&id=" & Request("ID") _
        & DQ & ">Yes</a>   " _
        & "<a href=" & DQ & Request("SCRIPT_NAME") & DQ _
        & ">No</a></p>"
    WriteLine "</span>"
    PrintFooter
End Sub


'''''''''''''''''''''''''''''''''''''''''''''''''''''''''''''''''''''
'
' Sub DeleteSave
'
' This routine performs the deletion of a record.
'
'''''''''''''''''''''''''''''''''''''''''''''''''''''''''''''''''''''
```

```
Sub DeleteSave(cnDB)

    cnDB.Execute "DELETE FROM tblContacts WHERE pkContactID = " _
        & Request("ID")
    Response.Redirect Request("SCRIPT_NAME")

End Sub
```

Done!

REVIEW

In this chapter, you learned the pros and cons of offering flexible data entry. Because you might not have much contact information for a person or company, we can't be quite as rigid about requiring that fields be filled in. At the same time, the display and data entry routines have to be flexible in how they display and accept data. There's always a fine line between requiring and not requiring data. In the end, it always comes down to what your users want and need to do. Whatever rules you choose, make sure that the user of the application understands the rules for the data he/she is entering.

QUIZ YOURSELF

1. In the tblContacts table, which fields are required by the database? Which are optional? Which are automatically supplied by the database? (See "Introduction to the Contact Manager")

2. What type of recordset do we create to add or update a record? (See "Saving a New Contact")

3. What fields, at a minimum, does the user have to supply to save the record? (See "Validating Input Data")

Building the Event Manager

Session Checklist

✔ Building a page to show all the events in the database

✔ Creating code to add new records

✔ Updating existing records

✔ Deleting records with ASP code

✔ Validating data before making database changes

**30 Min.
To Go**

Acommon application in most organizer and PDA programs is an event calendar. This enables you to see your day's tasks and plan for the future. This chapter shows you how to build the data entry page to let users add events to their calendar, which you'll build in Chapter 29.

Introduction to the Event Manager

This chapter shows you how to create events to add to that calendar, which will integrate your events along with your tasks so that you see everything in a single, concise view. The events we're using are nearly identical to the tasks you created earlier, except that there is no priority and the DueDate field is now known as EndDate.

Table Structure

Just as a reminder, the table being used is the tblEvents table in the sample SQL Server database, and the fields are shown in Table 28-1.

Table 28-1
tblEvents Fields

Field Name	Data Type	Description
pkEventID	int	Primary key — identity value
Name	varchar(80)	Short description of the event
Description	text	Long description of the event
StartDate	datetime	Start date for the event
EndDate	datetime	Date the event is completed

Event Entry Form

The form you'll be building for entering events is shown in Figure 28-1.

The data here is more complex than before, so we'll have a few more validation rules. However, you'll see that the controls we use help to eliminate a little bit of validation. You can validate data but be flexible at the same time.

Each part of the final events.asp file is explained throughout this chapter, and you can find a complete listing at the end of the chapter.

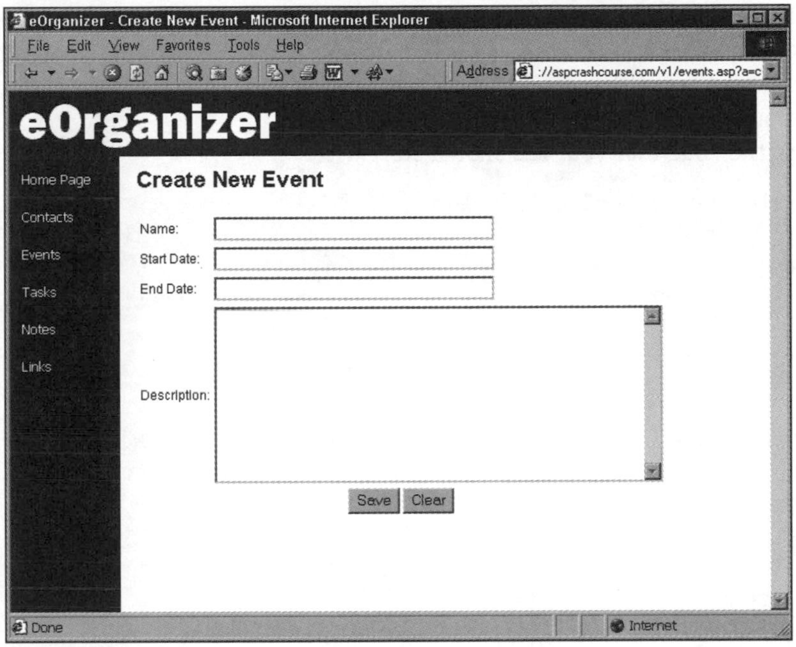

Figure 28-1
Event entry form in the eOrganizer

Setting up the File

The structure for this page is nearly identical to the one you created for the Note Manager, so we don't go through it in great depth here. The list of functions that the file supports is the same:

- Retrieve All
- Retrieve Single Event (*)
- Create Event (*)
- Save New Event
- Update Event (*)
- Save Changes
- Confirm Deletion of Event
- Delete Event

We'll again be using a single BuildForm routine to handle the three blocks of code that are starred. We'll also add a feature you might recall from Chapter 26; when an event is overdue, its due date will be shown in red and boldface, to help it stand out.

Here's the code that your file should start with:

```asp
<!--#include file="include.asp" -->
<%
Call Main
'''''''''''''''''''''''''''''''''''''''''''''''''''''''''''''''''
'
' Sub Main
'
' Processing for this page starts in this routine. It
' contains a dispatcher to call the appropriate routine,
' based on what function was needed.
'
'''''''''''''''''''''''''''''''''''''''''''''''''''''''''''''''''
Sub Main
    Dim cnDB        ' As ADODB.Connection
    Set cnDB = OpenDB()

    Select Case Request(ACTION)
        Case ACTION_CREATE, ACTION_RETRIEVE, ACTION_UPDATE
            BuildForm cnDB, ""
        Case ACTION_CREATE_SAVE
            CreateSave cnDB
        Case ACTION_UPDATE_SAVE
            UpdateSave cnDB
        Case ACTION_DELETE
            Delete cnDB
        Case ACTION_DELETE_SAVE
            DeleteSave cnDB
        Case Else
            Retrieve(cnDB)
    End Select

    CloseDB cnDB
End Sub
```

Creating the Event List Function

The Retrieve subroutine in this page is simpler than the one used in the task list, mainly because we don't have to indicate if a task is overdue. The code for this routine is shown here:

```
'''''''''''''''''''''''''''''''''''''''''''''''''''''''''''''
'
' Sub Retrieve
'
' This routine lists all records of this data type. It
' also provides actions to create, retrieve, update, and
' delete records.
'
'''''''''''''''''''''''''''''''''''''''''''''''''''''''''''''
Sub Retrieve(cnDB)
    Dim rsData         ' As ADODB.Recordset
    Dim strURL         ' As String
    Dim strSQL         ' As String

    strSQL = "SELECT * FROM tblEvents " _
        & "ORDER BY StartDate, Name"
    Set rsData = cnDB.Execute(strSQL)
    PrintHeader "View All Events"

    WriteLine "<p><a href=" & DQ & Request("SCRIPT_NAME") _
        & "?" & ACTION & "=" & ACTION_CREATE _
        & DQ & ">Create New Event</a></p>"

    WriteLine "<table cellspacing=0 cellpadding=2>"
    WriteLine "<tr>"
    WriteLine "<th width=200>Name</th>"
    WriteLine "<th width=150>Start Date</th>"
    WriteLine "<th width=150>End Date</th>"
    WriteLine "<th width=100>Actions</th></tr>"
    Do Until rsData.EOF
        WriteLine "<tr>"
        WriteLine "<td>" & rsData("Name") & "</td>"
        WriteLine "<td align=center>"
        WriteLine FormatDateTime(rsData("StartDate"), vbShortDate)
```

```
            WriteLine "</td>"
            WriteLine "<td align=center>"
            WriteLine FormatDateTime(rsData("EndDate"), vbShortDate)
            WriteLine "</td>"
            WriteLine "<td align=center>"
            strURL = "<a href=" & DQ & Request("SCRIPT_NAME") _
                & "?" & ACTION & "=" _
                & "###" & "&id=" _
                & rsData("pkEventID") & DQ & ">"
            WriteLine Replace(strURL, "###", ACTION_RETRIEVE) _
                & "R</a> | "
            WriteLine Replace(strURL, "###", ACTION_UPDATE) _
                & "U</a> | "
            WriteLine Replace(strURL, "###", ACTION_DELETE) _
                & "D</a>"
            WriteLine "</td>"

            WriteLine "</tr>"
            rsData.MoveNext
        Loop
        rsData.Close
        PrintFooter
    End Sub
```

The dates are sorted by their starting date, and then by name. Feel free to reverse this if you want, but I find that the events are easier to find when they are sorted in this manner. In addition, you might want to show the events in reverse order by StartDate. This would put all the old events at the bottom. However, you can easily switch the query as you see fit — try it out and see what works best for you.

20 Min. To Go

Creating the BuildForm Routine

Creating the event entry window is a bit shorter than before, because we don't have the drop-down list of priorities to deal with. The code for this routine is shown here:

```
' . . . . . . . . . . . . . . . . . . . . . . . . . . . . . . . . . . . . . . . . . . . . . .
'
' Sub BuildForm
'
```

```
' This routine displays a data entry and display form. It
' is used for the create, retrieve, and update modes.
'
,,,,,,,,,,,,,,,,,,,,,,,,,,,,,,,,,,,,,,,,,,,,,,,,,,,,,,,,,,,,
Sub BuildForm(cnDB, strError)
   Dim lngEventID  ' As Long
   Dim strName     ' As String
   Dim strDesc     ' As String
   Dim datStart    ' As Date
   Dim datEnd      ' As Date
   Dim strTitle    ' As String
   Dim strAction   ' As String
   Dim rsData      ' As ADODB.Recordset

   If strError = "" Then
      Select Case Request(ACTION)
         Case ACTION_CREATE
            strAction = ACTION_CREATE_SAVE
            strTitle = "Create New Event"
            lngEventID = -1
            strName = ""
            strDesc = ""
            datStart = ""
            datEnd = ""
         Case ACTION_UPDATE, ACTION_RETRIEVE
            strAction = ACTION_UPDATE_SAVE
            If Request(ACTION) = ACTION_UPDATE Then
               strTitle = "Update Event"
            Else
               strTitle = "Retrieve Event"
            End If
            lngEventID = Request("ID")
            Set rsData = cnDB.Execute("SELECT * FROM tblEvents " _
               & "WHERE pkEventID = " & lngEventID)

            strName = rsData("Name")
            strDesc = rsData("Description")
            datStart = rsData("StartDate")
            datEnd = rsData("EndDate")
```

```
                  rsData.Close
               Set rsData = Nothing
         End Select
      Else
         strAction = Request(ACTION)

         Select Case strAction
            Case ACTION_CREATE_SAVE
               strTitle = "Create New Event"
            Case ACTION_UPDATE_SAVE
               strTitle = "Update Event"
         End Select

         If Request("ID") = "" Then
            lngEventID = -1
         Else
            lngEventID = Request("ID")
         End If
         strName = Request("dbtName")
         strDesc = Request("dbtDescription")
         datStart = Request("dbtStartDate")
         datEnd = Request("dbtEndDate")
      End If

      PrintHeader strTitle
      If strError <> "" Then
         WriteLine strError
      End If

      WriteLine "<form action=" & DQ & Request("SCRIPT_NAME") _
         & DQ & " method=post>"
      WriteLine "<input type=hidden name=" _
         & ACTION & " value=" & strAction & ">"
      WriteLine "<input type=hidden name=ID " _
         & " value=" & lngEventID & ">"
      WriteLine "<table>"
      WriteLine "<tr><td>Name:</td>"
      WriteLine "<td><input type=text size=40 maxlength=40 " _
         & "name=dbtName value=" _
         & DQ & strName & DQ & "></td></tr>"
```

```
      WriteLine "<tr><td>Start Date:</td>"
      WriteLine "<td><input type=text size=40 maxlength=40 " _
         & "name=dbtStartDate value=" _
         & DQ & datStart & DQ & "></td></tr>"

      WriteLine "<tr><td>End Date:</td>"
      WriteLine "<td><input type=text size=40 maxlength=40 " _
         & "name=dbtEndDate value=" _
         & DQ & datEnd & DQ & "></td></tr>"

      WriteLine "<tr><td>Description:</td>"
      WriteLine "<td><textarea rows=10 cols=50 " _
         & "name=dbtDescription>" _
         & strDesc & "</textarea></td></tr>"

      If Request(ACTION) <> ACTION_RETRIEVE Then
         WriteLine "<tr><td colspan=2 align=center>" _
            & "<input type=submit name=cmdSubmit " _
            & "value=Save>" _
            & " " _
            & "<input type=reset name=cmdReset " _
            & "value=Clear></td></tr>"
      Else
         WriteLine "<tr><td colspan=2><a href=" _
            & DQ & Request("SCRIPT_NAME") & DQ _
            & ">Return to List</a></td></tr>"
      End If
      WriteLine "</table>"
      PrintFooter
   End Sub
```

Validating Input Data

Here we have rules similar to the task entry system; but in this page, we've added
an additional rule that you can feel free to add to your task entry page. Because the
graphical calendar we build later assumes that the start date is before the end date,
we need to validate this as being True before we save an event to the database. The
DateDiff function is used to make sure that the difference between the start date

and end date is greater than zero. Remember that the result of `DateDiff` is based on the ordering of the arguments to it. Make sure that the earliest date is first, followed by the later date. Here's the code for `ValidateData`:

```
'''''''''''''''''''''''''''''''''''''''''''''''''
'
' Function ValidateData
'
' This routine validates the input data and
' causes the form to be shown if the data is
' not correct. A True result indicates that
' the data was OK, and a False indicates that
' the data was in error.
'
'''''''''''''''''''''''''''''''''''''''''''''''''
Function ValidateData(cnDB)
   Dim strError        ' As String
   strError = ""

   If Request("dbtName") = "" Then
      strError = strError _
         & "<li>The event's name must be entered."
   End If

   If Request("dbtStartDate") = "" Then
      strError = strError _
         & "<li>The start date must be entered."
   Else
      If Not IsDate(Request("dbtStartDate")) Then
         strError = strError _
            & "<li>The start date is not a valid date/time value."
      End If
   End If

   If Request("dbtEndDate") = "" Then
      strError = strError _
         & "<li>The end date must be entered."
   Else
      If Not IsDate(Request("dbtEndDate")) Then
         strError = strError _
            & "<li>The end date is not a valid date/time value."
```

```
        End If
   End If

   If IsDate(Request("dbtStartDate")) _
      And IsDate(Request("dbtEndDate")) Then
      If DateDiff("s", Request("dbtStartDate"), _
         Request("dbtEndDate")) < 0 Then
         strError = strError _
            & "<li>The end date must come after the start date."
      End If
   End If

   If strError <> "" Then
      strError = "<p><font color=#FF0000><b>" _
         & "The following data errors were detected:</b><br>" _
         & "<ul>" & strError & "</ul></font></p>"
      BuildForm cnDB, strError
      ValidateData = False
   Else
      ValidateData = True
   End If

End Function
```

**10 Min.
To Go**

Saving a New Event

Saving a new event is like saving other data. One catch is that because you're using date/time data, you have to validate the input before attempting to save it. The database will reject invalid date/time values. Here's the code for CreateSave:

```
'''''''''''''''''''''''''''''''''''''''''''''''''''''''
'
' Sub CreateSave
'
' This routine creates a new record in the database.
'
'''''''''''''''''''''''''''''''''''''''''''''''''''''''
Sub CreateSave(cnDB)

   Dim rsData        ' As ADODB.Recordset
```

```
If Not ValidateData(cnDB) Then Exit Sub

Set rsData = Server.CreateObject("ADODB.Recordset")
rsData.Open "tblEvents", cnDB, adOpenDynamic, adLockOptimistic
rsData.AddNew
rsData("Name") = Request("dbtName")
rsData("Description") = Request("dbtDescription")
rsData("StartDate") = Request("dbtStartDate")
rsData("DueDate") = Request("dbtDueDate")
rsData.Update
rsData.Close

Response.Redirect Request.ServerVariables("SCRIPT_NAME")

End Sub
```

Note that saving the date/time data, as well as the numeric value in the Priority drop-down list, is handled the same as the text data we've been adding all along.

Saving Changes to a Event

Updating an event is similar to creating one. As we did when we added an event, we validate the changed data before saving to the database. Here's the code for the UpdateSave routine:

```
'''''''''''''''''''''''''''''''''''''''''''''''''''
'
' Sub UpdateSave
'
' This routine performs an update on the table for this
' particular item.
'
'''''''''''''''''''''''''''''''''''''''''''''''''''
Sub UpdateSave(cnDB)
    Dim rsData      ' As ADODB.Recordset

    If Not ValidateData(cnDB) Then Exit Sub

    Set rsData = Server.CreateObject("ADODB.Recordset")
```

```
        rsData.Open "SELECT * FROM tblEvents WHERE pkEventID = " _
            & Request("ID"), cnDB, adOpenDynamic, adLockOptimistic
        rsData("Name") = Request("dbtName")
        rsData("Description") = Request("dbtDescription")
        rsData("StartDate") = Request("dbtStartDate")
        rsData("DueDate") = Request("dbtDueDate")
        rsData.Update
        rsData.Close
        Response.Redirect Request.ServerVariables("SCRIPT_NAME")

    End Sub
```

Deleting Events

Other than the table names used, deleting events is the same as in previous pages. Here's the code for the Delete and DeleteSave routines:

```
    '.............................................................
    '
    ' Sub Delete
    '
    ' This routine confirms that the user wants to delete an
    ' item from the system.
    '
    '.............................................................
    Sub Delete(cnDB)

        Dim rsData        ' As ADODB.Recordset

        Set rsData = cnDB.Execute("SELECT * FROM tblEvents " _
            & "WHERE pkEventID = " & Request("ID"))

        PrintHeader "Delete Event"
        WriteLine "<span class=pt><p>Delete '" _
            & rsData("Name") & "'?</p>"
        WriteLine "<p><a href=" & DQ & Request("SCRIPT_NAME") & "?" _
            & ACTION & "=" & ACTION_DELETE_SAVE _
            & "&id=" & Request("ID") _
            & DQ & ">Yes</a>   " _
            & "<a href=" & DQ & Request("SCRIPT_NAME") & DQ _
```

```
            & ">No</a></p>"
        WriteLine "</span>"
        PrintFooter
    End Sub


    ''''''''''''''''''''''''''''''''''''''''''''''''''''''''''''''''
    '
    ' Sub DeleteSave
    '
    ' This routine performs the deletion of a record.
    '
    ''''''''''''''''''''''''''''''''''''''''''''''''''''''''''''''''
    Sub DeleteSave(cnDB)

        cnDB.Execute "DELETE FROM tblEvents WHERE pkEventID = " _
            & Request("ID")
        Response.Redirect Request("SCRIPT_NAME")

    End Sub
```

Done!

REVIEW

While a list of events might be helpful, this page is primarily used for data entry only. In the next chapter, you'll be using the calendar events that you created here, adding them to a graphical calendar that you'll learn to build.

QUIZ YOURSELF

1. What data type in SQL Server holds date/time information? (See "Introduction to the Event Manager")

2. What method do we use after we save data to send the user back to the View All Events screen? (See "Saving a New Event")

3. What fields does the database require? What fields does our validation routine require? (See "Validating Input Data")

Creating the eOrganizer Home Page

Session Checklist

✔ Creating a graphical calendar for the eOrganizer's home page

✔ Showing both calendar events and tasks on the calendar

✔ Showing the most recently added links on the page

**30 Min.
To Go**

With so many Web sites out there, it's hard to keep track of information that you've got spread across all these sites. An early idea that took off was the idea of a portal site. A portal site, like Yahoo or Excite, provided all your selected information in a single, integrated "home page." From that page, you can get to everything else you need. We're going to build the same thing for the eOrganizer application. From this home page, you'll be able to get to all the types of data, plus you'll see a calendar with all your events and tasks on it.

Creating the Home Page

So far, we've been working on the data entry and viewing pages for all the different types of data in the eOrganizer application. We don't have a home page for the site yet. That's what we're going to build in this chapter. The purpose of the home page is to provide the most important information at a glance. Users can always get to all the other information through the links on the left-hand toolbar. The point here is to minimize the time that users spend in the application. That may sound strange, but if the software is effective, it does what the user needs it to and doesn't get in the way too much.

We won't need to create any new tables for this page, as we'll be pulling data from the tables we've already created. Figure 29-1 shows what the home page will look like when we're done building it.

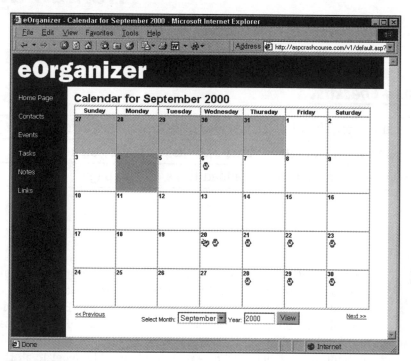

Figure 29-1
The monthly view of the calendar, with events and tasks shown as icons

Instead of trying to cram all the text into a tiny calendar cell, we've created icons for our events and tasks that are due. Using the alternate text assigned to the image (in the ALT attribute), you can see all the details on the task or event when you hover over the graphic with the mouse. Figure 29-2 shows what this looks like at runtime.

You could, of course, build other views for this calendar that show more information per cell, but we'll build the monthly view this way. It also saves users from having to click on each event to get more information. The information is already available; users just have to hover over the graphic to get it. Clicking on the graphic takes users to the edit window for the task or event, depending on what is clicked.

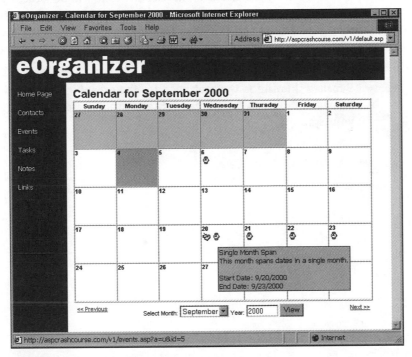

Figure 29-2
Details about an event or task are available when you hover over the icon for it.

At the bottom of the calendar, note the two links and a small form. The links on either side of the calendar take you the previous and next month's calendar. This makes it easy to browse your calendar. In addition, you have a small form that enables you to pick a month and year to jump directly to that month's calendar. Because this calendar could theoretically go forever, you need a way to jump months or years ahead without having to click through each month.

To colorize the calendar, we use gray to mark the cells that are part of either the previous month (in the first week) or part of the next month (in the last week). We don't show data in those cells, but the calendar would look strange without those days visible. We also mark the current day with a different color to help it stand out better. Most of the formatting is done by way of style sheets, except for the coloring of the previous/next month cells and the current day. Refer to Chapter 23 for more information about the style sheet we're using.

The first thing you need to do is set up the basic page structure. As before, we'll have a Sub Main subroutine that calls the appropriate routine. Because this page is only responsible for showing the calendar, most of the code will be located in the ShowCalendar routine. However, we still want to use this structure, because at some point, we may want to add extra views of the calendar. We'll be able to use a lot of the same code with a weekly or daily calendar that we use with a monthly calendar, so setting up the structure properly is important.

 Because this file is the root page for the organizer, it should be named default.asp (or whatever file is used as a default page on your system).

The code we start with is shown here:

```
<!--#include file="include.asp" -->
<%
Const ICON_TASK = 1
Const ICON_EVENT = 2

Call Main
'''''''''''''''''''''''''''''''''''''''''''''''''''''''''''''''
'
' Sub Main
'
' Processing for this page starts in this routine. It
' contains a dispatcher to call the appropriate routine,
' based on what function was needed.
'
'''''''''''''''''''''''''''''''''''''''''''''''''''''''''''''''
Sub Main
   Dim cnDB       ' As ADODB.Connection
   Set cnDB = OpenDB()

   If Request("month") = "" Or Request("year") = "" Then
      ShowCalendar cnDB, Month(Date), Year(Date)
   Else
      ShowCalendar cnDB, _
         CInt(Request("month")), CInt(Request("year"))
   End If
```

```
    CloseDB cnDB
End Sub
```

By default, we want to show the current month's calendar. If the page is loaded without any parameters (at startup, for instance), this code will call the ShowCalendar routine with the current month and year, as well as the database connection. If the user clicks a previous month or next month link, or uses the form at the bottom of the page, the calendar will be shown using those values. You'll learn how those links are created in the next section. We also take care of closing the database from this routine when the page is complete.

**20 Min.
To Go**

Displaying the Calendar

Creating the calendar involves quite a bit of date math, as you'll soon see. To help you understand all the parts of the ShowCalendar routine, you'll be seeing parts of it at a time.

Doing the Math

The first thing we have to do is to figure out how many days are in the current month. To do that, we don't have a built-in function, but we can do some basic date math to figure it out. If we are trying to figure out how many days there are in March, for instance, we know that the first day of the next month is one day later than the last day in March. While that may sound obvious, that's how we calculate the number of days in March. We add a month to the March date, and then subtract one day. When we use the Day function on the result, we get the number of days in March. We could hard-code the number of days for each month, but then we're responsible for dealing with leap years. It's easier, in my opinion, to do this little bit of math to get the result. Following is the beginning of the ShowCalendar routine:

```
, , , , , , , , , , , , , , , , , , , , , , , , , , , , , , , , , , , , , , , , , , , , , , , , , , , , , , , , , , , , ,
'
' Sub ShowCalendar
'
' This routine generates the calendar grid and puts all the
' events into it.
'
, , , , , , , , , , , , , , , , , , , , , , , , , , , , , , , , , , , , , , , , , , , , , , , , , , , , , , , , , , , , ,
Sub ShowCalendar(cnDB, intMonth, intYear)
```

```
Dim rsEvents        ' As ADODB.Recordset
Dim rsTasks         ' As ADODB.Recordset
Dim strSQL          ' As String

Dim datCurrent      ' As Date
Dim intWeekday      ' As Integer
Dim intPreviousMonthDays    ' As Integer
Dim intCurrentMonthDays     ' As Integer
Dim i               ' As Integer
Dim intMonthLink    ' As Integer
Dim intYearLink     ' As Integer
Dim strColor        ' As String

datCurrent = CDate(intMonth & "/1/" & intYear)
intCurrentMonthDays = _
    Day(DateAdd("d", -1, DateAdd("m", 1, datCurrent)))
intWeekday = Weekday(datCurrent)
```

In addition, we have to figure out what the current weekday's number is
(Sunday = 1, Monday = 2, and so on). That will help tell us how many cells need
to be on the first row for the previous month. We put all this information into
variables for later use.

Querying the Database

The next step is to retrieve the events and tasks from the database. We are looking
for any events that begin or end in the current month and year. If you think through
this, you'll see that this code won't be able to handle events that span three or more
months, for instance. If you have an event that goes from January to March, the
start date will show up in January, the end date will show up in March, but you
won't see the event in February because neither the beginning nor the end is in
February. I did this purposely because every event I put on my calendar begins and
ends within a two-month time frame. Occasionally I get an event that starts in one
month and ends the next, but I don't have any that start in March and aren't completed until May, for instance. As far as tasks go, we are going to show just the due
dates for the tasks, so we can retrieve all the tasks for which the due date month
and year are the same as the one we're showing. The code to do this is as follows:

```
Set rsEvents = Server.CreateObject("ADODB.Recordset")
strSQL = "SELECT * FROM tblEvents " _
    & " WHERE ((Month(StartDate) = " & intMonth _
```

```
    & " AND Year(StartDate) = " & intYear & "))" _
    & " OR ((Month(EndDate) = " & intMonth _
    & " AND Year(EndDate) = " & intYear & "))"
rsEvents.Open strSQL, cnDB, adOpenStatic

Set rsTasks = Server.CreateObject("ADODB.Recordset")
strSQL = "SELECT * FROM tblTasks " _
    & " WHERE Month(DueDate) = " & intMonth _
    & " AND Year(DueDate) = " & intYear
rsTasks.Open strSQL, cnDB, adOpenStatic
```

Note that the recordsets are being opened as static, read-only recordsets. We'll be looping through these recordsets for each cell in the table, so we don't want to re-create them each time. In addition, we need the capability to go to the first record with MoveFirst, which isn't allowed using the forward-only recordset created by the Connection's Execute method.

Setting up the Calendar Table

The next step is to print the page header and set up the calendar table. We also want to print the days of the week at the top of the table, which we can do using the WeekdayName function. Here's the next block of code:

```
'
' Print calendar header information and
' setup table.
'
PrintHeader "Calendar for " _
    & MonthName(intMonth) & " " & intYear

WriteLine "<table width=560 border=1 " _
    & "cellspacing=0 cellpadding=0>"

'
' Add weekday names to column headings
'
WriteLine "<tr>"
For i = 1 To 7
    WriteLine "<td width=80 align=center>"
    WriteLine "<span class=calhead>" _
        & WeekdayName(i) & "</span>"
```

```
   WriteLine "</td>"
Next ' i
WriteLine "</tr>"
```

We're making the table 560 pixels wide, which means that each cell will be 80 pixels wide. If you have a bigger page, feel free to use a larger size than this. This size, however, enables us to fit the calendar within our target browser, which is 800x600 for the page.

We're also using the calhead style here for the calendar headings, which are the days of the week. The calhead style is defined in styles.css and can be changed as you see fit. We've also explicitly set the width of these cells to be 80 pixels wide. This width will carry through the rest of the page, but we'll put it in each cell, just to be on the safe side.

Adding the CreateCell Routine

Before we continue, we need to add the CreateCell routine to the page. This routine is responsible for showing the date as well as any content for the cell. Following is the code for this subroutine:

```
' , , , , , , , , , , , , , , , , , , , , , , , , , , , , , , , , , , , , , , , , , , , , , , , , , , , , , ,
'
' Sub CreateCell
'
' This function puts content into a cell, including
' all the necessary HTML and formatting tags.
'
' , , , , , , , , , , , , , , , , , , , , , , , , , , , , , , , , , , , , , , , , , , , , , , , , , , , , , ,
Sub CreateCell(strNumber, strColor, strText)
   WriteLine "<td width=80 valign=top bgcolor=" & strColor & ">"
   WriteLine "<table cellpadding=0 cellspacing=0>"
   WriteLine "<tr><td width=1 valign=top>" _
      & "<img src=/pics/spacer.gif width=1 height=70></td>"
   WriteLine "<td width=79 valign=top><span class=calcell><b>" _
      & strNumber & "</b><br>"
   WriteLine strText
   WriteLine "</td></tr>"
   WriteLine "</table></td>"
End Sub
```

This routine saves us some typing later by putting all the HTML to create a table cell in one place. We start out with the initial TD tag. After that, we set up another table within the cell. This table has two columns. The first uses an invisible pixel to force the cell to be 70 pixels high. This gives us an approximately square cell; and because we're using the graphic, the browser won't collapse the table cell if there is no content in it. The other column of the table holds any HTML content we want to put in it. We start with the day number in the corner, followed by any other text we supplied the subroutine. We then close up all the tags.

Adding Previous Month Days

We now have to add the last few days of the previous month, if necessary, to the table. We show these in a gray color so that they're not confused with the current month. All we need to do here is print the day number and move on. Here's the code:

```
'
' The first row of calendar cells will contain gray
' boxes for all the days in the previous month.
'
WriteLine "<tr>"
If intWeekday <> 1 then
    intPreviousMonthDays = Day(DateAdd("d", -1, datCurrent))
    For i = intWeekday -1 to 1 Step - 1
        CreateCell intPreviousMonthDays - i + 1, "#CCCCCC", ""
    Next ' i
End If
```

We only need to run this code if the month doesn't begin on Sunday (weekday 1). If we run it, we first have to determine how many days are in the previous month. We do that by subtracting one from the value in datCurrent, which is the first day of the month being shown. That gives us the number of days when we use the Day function on the result. We then work backward for the number of weekdays before the first of the month. If the first of the month falls on a Thursday, we have to show blocks for Sunday through Wednesday. To show the HTML, we call the CreateCell routine with the number to show, the background color for the cell, and the text to show.

Building the Current Month's Calendar

The next step is to build the current month's calendar entries. The table may already have a few cells in it from the weekdays in the first week of the month, so we don't immediately start with a TR tag. Instead, we keep track of what weekday it is, and when we hit Saturday, we print the cell and then start a new row. Here's the code to do this:

```
'

' Start main loop through days of the month. When we hit
' 7 days in a row, the loop starts a new table row.
'


For i = 1 to intCurrentMonthDays
   '
   ' Mark the current date's box in a
   ' different color.
   '
   If Date = CDate(intMonth & "/" & i & "/" & intYear) Then
      strColor = "#66CCFF"
   Else
      strColor = "#FFFFFF"
   End If
   CreateCell i, strColor, _
      GetDayItems(rsEvents, rsTasks, intMonth, i, intYear)
   '
   ' Start a new row if we have 7 days in the grid
   '
   If intWeekday = 7 Then
      intWeekday = 1
      WriteLine "</tr>"
      WriteLine "<tr>"
   Else
      intWeekday = intWeekday + 1
   End If
Next  ' i
```

We add a bit of code to show the current cell in a color other than the default white color. We then call the CreateCell routine with the day number, the color to use, and the results of the new GetDayItems function that will be covered at the end of this section. This routine returns the HTML that lists all the events happening on the current day. We then check to see if the day is Saturday; if it is, we create a new table row.

Adding the Next Month's Days

To end the calendar building code, we have to show the first days of the next month if the current month didn't end on a Saturday. This code is similar to the code you used for the beginning of the code:

```
'
' Add days of next month to grid in last row.
'
If intWeekday <= 7 and intWeekday > 1 Then
    For i = intWeekday To 7
        CreateCell i - intWeekday + 1, "#CCCCCC", ""
    Next ' i
End If
WriteLine "</tr></table>"
rsTasks.Close
rsEvents.Close
```

We print empty cells for the beginning of the next month, and then close up the table row and table. We also close up the recordsets that we've been using, as we're all done with them at this point.

Adding the Previous Month Link

We now have to create a link to send the user to the previous month's calendar. The trick with this code is that we have to determine whether the previous month is in the current year or the previous year. Here's the code that does the work for you:

```
'
' Add navigation buttons (previous, next) to bottom of calendar
'
WriteLine "<table width=560 border=0 " _
    & "cellspacing=5 cellpadding=0><tr>"
intMonthLink = intMonth - 1
intYearLink = intYear
If intMonth = 1 Then
    intMonthLink = 12
    intYearLink = intYearLink - 1
End If
WriteLine "<td width=80 valign=top><span class=calcell>"
WriteLine "<a href=" & DQ & Request("SCRIPT_NAME") _
```

```
& "?month=" & intMonthLink _
& "&year=" & intYearLink & DQ _
& ">&lt;&lt; Previous</a></span></td>"
```

We first set up a new table at the bottom of the page. We use a new table because we don't want a border on it. We then determine what year and month to link to. If the current month is January, we use a month of 12 and subtract one from the year. We then format a link and include both the month and year parameters. If you remember, the Sub Main routine reads these and passes them into the ShowCalendar subroutine.

Adding the Navigation Form

We now have to add the small navigation form to the middle of the bottom of the calendar. This is fairly straightforward, as shown here:

```
'
' Add navigation to middle of bottom row of calendar. This
' allow the user to pick any month/year to view.
'
WriteLine "<td width=400 align=center>"
WriteLine "<form action=" _
    & DQ & Request.ServerVariables("SCRIPT_NAME") & DQ _
    & " method=post>"

WriteLine "<span class=calcell>Select Month: "
WriteLine "<select name=Month size=1>"
For i = 1 To 12
    Response.Write "<option value=" & DQ & i & DQ
    If i = Month(datCurrent) Then
        Response.Write " SELECTED"
    End If
    WriteLine ">" & MonthName(i) & "</option>"
Next  ' i
WriteLine "</select>"
WriteLine "Year: "
WriteLine "<input type=Text name=Year " _
    & "size=6 maxlength=4 value=" _
    & DQ & intYear & DQ & ">"
WriteLine "<input type=submit name=cmdSubmit value=View>"
```

```
WriteLine "</form>"
WriteLine "</td>"
```

We create a small form that has a list of the months, with the current month being displayed selected in the list. We also pre-populate the Year box with the current year value. This enables users to just pick a month and select the View button to continue.

Adding the Next Month Link

The last part of this routine creates a link to the next month's calendar. This code is similar to the code used to create the Previous Month link except that we have to determine if the current month is December. If so, we use a month of 1 and increment the year by one. Here's the code:

```
intMonthLink = intMonth + 1
intYearLink = intYear
If intMonth = 12 Then
    intMonthLink = 1
    intYearLink = intYearLink + 1
End If

WriteLine "<td width=80 valign=top align=right>" _
    & "<span class=calcell>"
WriteLine "<a href=" & DQ & Request("SCRIPT_NAME") _
    & "?month=" & intMonthLink _
    & "&year=" & intYearLink & DQ _
    & ">Next &gt;&gt;</a></span></td>"
WriteLine "</tr></table>"


PrintFooter
```

**10 Min.
To Go**

Creating the GetDayItems Function

The heart of the system isn't the grid builder. Instead, it's the GetDayItems function. This routine determines whether an event is active for each day in the calendar. It also is responsible for adding any tasks that come due on a particular day. However, this routine makes use of another function that you'll build in order to show an icon in the grid for an event or task. This helps reduce the amount of code in this one routine.

The code for the GetDayItems function is shown here:

```
'''''''''''''''''''''''''''''''''''''''''''''''''''''''''''''''
'
' Function GetDayItems
'
' This routine displays the events in each calendar cell.
' The events are returned to the caller as a string so that
' they can be printed into the calendar cell.
'
'''''''''''''''''''''''''''''''''''''''''''''''''''''''''''''''
Function GetDayItems(rsEvents, rsTasks, intCurMonth, _
    intCurDay, intCurYear)

    Dim blnShowEvent     ' As Boolean
    Dim i                ' As Integer
    Dim strResult        ' As String

    Dim intStartMonth
    Dim intStartDay
    Dim intStartYear

    Dim intEndMonth
    Dim intEndDay
    Dim intEndYear


    If rsTasks.RecordCount > 0 Then rsTasks.MoveFirst

    Do Until rsTasks.EOF

        If Day(rsTasks("DueDate")) = intCurDay Then
            strResult = strResult & CreateIcon(ICON_TASK, rsTasks)
        End If
        rsTasks.MoveNext
    Loop

    If rsEvents.RecordCount > 0 Then rsEvents.MoveFirst
    Do Until rsEvents.EOF
```

```
            blnShowEvent = False
            intStartMonth = Month(rsEvents("StartDate"))
            intStartDay = Day(rsEvents("StartDate"))
            intStartYear = Year(rsEvents("StartDate"))

            intEndMonth = Month(rsEvents("EndDate"))
            intEndDay = Day(rsEvents("EndDate"))
            intEndYear = Year(rsEvents("EndDate"))

            '
            ' Non-wrapping case - start and end month/year are the same.
            '
            If intStartMonth = intCurMonth _
               And intEndMonth = intCurMonth _
               And intStartYear = intCurYear _
               And intEndYear = intCurYear Then
                  blnShowEvent = (intStartDay <= intCurDay) _
                      And intEndDay >= intCurDay
            Else
               '
               ' Wrapping case - if event started in
               ' previous month, only check day.
               '
               If intStartMonth < intCurMonth Then
               ' event started before current month
                  blnShowEvent = (intCurDay <= intEndDay)
               ElseIf intEndMonth > intCurMonth Then
               ' event ended after current month
                  blnShowEvent = (intCurDay >= intStartDay)
               End If
            End If

            If blnShowEvent Then
               strResult = strResult & CreateIcon(ICON_EVENT, rsEvents)
            End If
            rsEvents.MoveNext
         Loop

         GetDayItems = strResult
      End Function
```

In the calendar, we show any tasks that are due first, followed by any appointments or events for the day. As mentioned in the last section, we maintain the recordsets of events and tasks for the life of the page and search them for each cell. We start by moving to the first record in the tasks recordset, but only if there are tasks in the recordset. If we called MoveFirst on a recordset with no data, we could get an error.

We then loop through all the tasks, looking for any that have a due date that is the same as the current day being shown. Because we only retrieved the tasks that end in the current month and year, we don't have to check them each time. If we find a task that is due on the current day, we add an icon for it using the CreateIcon routine. We pass in the code for task (ICON_TASK) that is a constant defined at the top of the page. We also pass in the tasks recordset, as it is already positioned at the correct record for this task. The CreateIcon routine generates some HTML and returns it. We add that HTML to our temporary strResult variable and go to the next task in the recordset.

The next step is to find the events that are active for the current day. This is trickier, because we have several different cases to consider:

- One-day events, which start and stop on the same day
- Multi-day events in same month, which start and stop on days in the current month
- Month-spanning events, which start in one month and end in another

The last type of event is further broken down as to whether the event begins or ends in the current month.

We start by "rewinding" the events recordset to the first record, and then we begin looping through them. Remember that this recordset contains all the events that either started or ended in the current month or year. For simplicity, we pull out all the individual month, day, and year values from the start and end dates for an event. This saves us some typing later.

We then take care of the first case: the one-day event. If the month, day, and year are all the same as the current month, day, and year, we set the blnShowEvent flag to True. You may be wondering why we're checking the entire date when we know that the event wouldn't have shown up if it didn't begin or end in the current month. The problem is that we don't know whether the event started or ended in the current month, so we have to check all three values. This code also takes care of the second case, in which the event starts and ends in the same month of the year. As long as the current day is surrounded by the starting day and ending day of the event, we can show the event.

The last case, month-spanning events, is the trickiest. If we have an event that began in the previous month and ended in the current month, we know that the valid days for the event extend from the first of the month until the day portion of the ending date. If we have an event that starts in the current month and ends in the next month, we know that the event extends from the day portion of the starting date until the last day of the month. This creates the last condition. The easiest way to understand this is to look at the calendar and determine what the data values will be for both the start and end dates. Luckily, the logic has already been done for you — you just have to put the code to work.

At the very end of this routine, we create the icon for this event if the preceding conditional code has determined that we should show the event.

Writing the CreateIcon Subroutine

The last block of code for this page is the CreateIcon subroutine. This routine is responsible for putting the pictures into the calendar cells. These icons' ALT text contains all the information about the task or event. The trick is that this routine has to know which fields to look at in each table. Storing the variable data into variables at the start of this routine avoids the use of several If/Then's later when we start writing the HTML out.

Here's the CreateIcon subroutine:

```
'''''''''''''''''''''''''''''''''''''''''''''''''''''''''''
'
' Function CreateIcon
'
' This function generates an icon for an item to
' be added to the calendar. This routine knows
' what fields to pull, based on the type of icon
' to be shown.
'
'''''''''''''''''''''''''''''''''''''''''''''''''''''''''''
Function CreateIcon(intCode, rsData)
    Dim strResult     ' As String
    Dim lngID         ' As Long
    Dim datStart      ' As Date
```

```
    Dim datEnd         ' As Date
    Dim strGraphic     ' As String
    Dim strPage        ' As String
    If intCode = ICON_TASK Then
        strGraphic = "/pics/task.gif"
        strPage = "tasks.asp"
        lngID = rsData("pkTaskID")
        datStart = rsData("StartDate")
        datEnd = rsData("DueDate")
    ElseIf intCode = ICON_EVENT Then
        strGraphic = "/pics/event.gif"
        strPage = "events.asp"
        lngID = rsData("pkEventID")
        datStart = rsData("StartDate")
        datEnd = rsData("EndDate")
    End If

    strResult = "<a href=" & DQ & strPage _
        & "?" & ACTION & "=" & ACTION_UPDATE _
        & "&id=" & lngID & DQ & ">" _
        & "<img src=" & DQ & strGraphic & DQ _
        & " height=16 width=16 border=0 alt=" & DQ _
        & rsData("Name")
    If rsData("Description") <> "" Then
        strResult = strResult & vbCrLf & rsData("Description")
    End If
    strResult = strResult & vbCrLf & vbCrLf _
        & "Start Date: " & FormatDateTime(datStart) & vbCrLf _
        & "End Date: " & FormatDateTime(datEnd) _
        & DQ & "></a> "
    CreateIcon = strResult
End Function
```

Clicking on an icon takes you to the edit page for that type of data. Because our pages are all designed the same, the only difference between the task's link and the event's link is the name of the page, so we store that in a variable. We also have two 16x16 icons for the event and task items, each of which is stored based on the code passed in. Finally, we need to retrieve specific fields from each record-set. An event will have a pkEventID, StartDate, and EndDate field, whereas a task will have a pkTaskID, StartDate, and DueDate field. However, the end result is that both tables have the same number of fields, which means that the data can be formatted in the same way.

We format a link that points to the edit page for the data type, and then we print the graphic. The trick is that the ALT tag will contain all the details of the event. One feature of the ALT tag is that it can span multiple lines, just like any data within double quotes in an HTML tag. We simply print out the name, description, and start and end dates, using vbCrLf characters to embed newline characters where necessary. This produces a nicely formatted entry that will pop up when the user hovers over a calendar entry.

When we're all done formatting the link, we return the HTML to the caller. Creating the routine like this makes it easier to add new types of data that you might want to show on the calendar. For instance, if you wanted to read the birthday fields from your own Contacts table, you could modify this routine to show a little birthday cake icon. In that case, the start and end dates for the "event" would be the person's birth date. You could either leave the output format as is, or slightly modify how a birthday icon is displayed. However, the structure is in place for expanding this for all types of data.

Done!

REVIEW

This is the most complex piece of code you wrote in the entire book. However, because we used modular programming techniques (subroutines and functions) and were able to tie into existing pages for editing tasks and events, we didn't have to do that much new work. We simply used the data created by the other pages in a slightly different way. That's the whole point of creating a system like this — to use the data you're collecting in as many useful ways as possible. Showing due dates on users' calendars helps remind them to get the job done. If you just offer a list of the tasks, you're not actively helping users with their job. The same thing goes for the events you schedule. If you just offer a list, users have to read the list to determine what is going on for a particular day.

QUIZ YOURSELF

1. What function do you use to determine the difference between two dates? (See "Displaying the Calendar")

2. Which attribute of an HTML image allows us to supply text that shows up when you hover over the graphic? (See "Creating the GetDayItems Function")

3. What function returns the current day's name? The month's name? (See "Building the Current Month's Calendar")

Where to Go Next

Session Checklist

✔ How to expand the eOrganizer application

✔ Using stored procedures to improve database performance

✔ Creating additional personalizations for the home page

✔ Supporting multiple users

*30 Min.
To Go*

If you're like me, you like learning by doing. However, it's hard to build software when you don't have an idea of what to build. This chapter offers you ideas that you can use to expand the eOrganizer application. You can see some of these new features online at the ASP Crash Course Web site (aspcrashcourse.com), but we're not going to build them into the application here. The point is to give you some ideas of what else you can do with this application.

What to Do Next?

The ideas presented in this chapter fall into three main categories:

- Improvements to existing code for performance, reliability, and reusability
- Minor features to improve eOrganizer's interface
- Major features to add, such as new types of data or changes to existing data types.

Some new routines are included, but version 1.0 of the eOrganizer application (included on the CD-ROM) doesn't include them.

Using Stored Procedures

The first thing that you can do to improve your application's performance is to create stored procedures for your SQL statements. Quite a few SQL statements are peppered throughout the ASP files you've created, and each one can benefit from being turned into a stored procedure. Stored procedures are SQL statements that have been saved as part of the database. When you save the stored procedure, the database determines the best way to run the query and saves that plan along with the stored procedure. This makes it faster to run later.

Some of the stored procedures are simple and don't require any input. Other stored procedures require parameters to be passed and take a bit more work to implement. However, they all make your code run better, because SQL Server is able to predetermine how best to run the query. For a small-scale system, you won't necessarily see any improvement; but for a heavily loaded system, stored procedures greatly increase the performance of your database code.

For example, take a look at the code used in the links.asp page to retrieve all the links. This code also sorts the links in order by the Name field. Here's the ASP code right now:

```
strSQL = "SELECT * FROM tblLinks ORDER BY Name"
Set rsData = cnDB.Execute(strSQL)
```

Your stored procedure might look like this:

```
CREATE PROCEDURE sp_RetrieveLinks
AS
SELECT *
FROM tblLinks
ORDER BY Name
```

You would then change the ASP code to the following:

```
Set rsData = cnDB.Execute("sp_RetrieveLinks")
```

At this point, anywhere you retrieved links, you could use this stored procedure. Access enables you to create queries and save them in the database. While they don't work quite the same way as stored procedures, they do offer some performance improvements. You create the query in a different way, but you can still call it using the Execute method of the Connection object.

You can also use a stored procedure as a data source when you call the Open method of a recordset, as shown here:

```
Set rsData = Server.CreateObject("ADODB.Recordset")
rsData.Open "sp_RetrieveLinks", cnDB, adOpenStatic
```

I generally make all my database calls stored procedures when I'm building my own ASP applications. Another benefit is that when you save your query, SQL Server will evaluate it and make sure that it is syntactically correct. This saves some debugging time if you missed a quote or a keyword, for instance.

Using SQL Statements Instead of Recordsets

**20 Min.
To Go**

In the code you wrote, you opened a recordset to modify or add a new record. Unfortunately, this is not the fastest way to add and modify records. The quickest way, other than a stored procedure, is to create a SQL statement. However, creating a SQL statement that way can be pretty tedious, especially for a table like the Contacts table.

To help alleviate the labor involved in creating a SQL statement like that, I came up with an automatic SQL builder that will look at your form's fields and generate the SQL statement needed to update or add a new record to the table.

When you were building your forms, you may have noticed that all the fields on the form are prefixed with either dbt or dbn. This isn't an accident. This automatic system uses the prefix dbt when for a text field, and dbn for a numeric field. That way, the SQL builder knows whether or not to use single quotes around the data.

The problem here is that if the data you are entering has single quotes, that can break the SQL statement. When you were entering data directly into the recordset, it wasn't an issue. However, we now have to "clean" the string, replacing all the single quotes with two single quotes. For instance, if you wanted to run a query that looks up a company named *O'Brien and Sons*, you have to replace the single quote in *O'Brien* with two single quotes, or the single quote is misinterpreted by the database as a delimiter character.

Following are three functions that you can add to your common file to make this work:

```
''''''''''''''''''''''''''''''''''''''''''''''''''''''''''''
'
' Function CreateStatement
'
' This routine builds the name and field lists used in the
' SQL CREATE statement.
'
''''''''''''''''''''''''''''''''''''''''''''''''''''''''''''
Function CreateStatement
    Dim strFields
    Dim strValues
    Dim varItem

    For Each varItem in Request.Form()
        If Left(varItem, 2) = "db" Then
            If strFields <> "" Then
                strFields = strFields & ", "
                strValues = strValues & ", "
            End If

            strFields = strFields & Mid(varItem, 4)
            If Left(varItem, 3) = "dbt" Then
                strValues = strValues _
                    & SQ & Clean(Request(varItem)) & SQ
            ElseIf Left(varItem, 3) = "dbn" Then
                strValues = strValues & Request(varItem)
            End If

        End If
    Next ' i
    CreateStatement = "(" & strFields & ") VALUES (" _
        & strValues & ")"

End Function
''''''''''''''''''''''''''''''''''''''''''''''''''''''''''''
'
' Function UpdateStatement
'
```

```
' This routine builds the name/value pairs used in the
' SQL UPDATE statement.
'
',,,,,,,,,,,,,,,,,,,,,,,,,,,,,,,,,,,,,,,,,,,,,,,,,,,,,,,,,,
Function UpdateStatement
   Dim strPairs
   Dim varItem

   strPairs = ""
   For Each varItem in Request.Form()
      If Left(varItem, 2) = "db" Then
         If strPairs <> "" Then
            strPairs = strPairs & ", "
         End If

         strPairs = strPairs & Mid(varItem, 4) & " = "
         If Left(varItem, 3) = "dbt" Then
            strPairs = strPairs _
               & SQ & Clean(Request(varItem)) & SQ
         ElseIf Left(varItem, 3) = "dbn" Then
            strPairs = strPairs & Request(varItem)
         End If
      End If
   Next ' i

   UpdateStatement = strPairs
End Function

',,,,,,,,,,,,,,,,,,,,,,,,,,,,,,,,,,,,,,,,,,,,,,,,,,,,,,,,,,
'
' Function Clean
'
' This routine changes all the single quotes in a value
' into two single quotes. This eliminates possible errors
' when building the SQL statement.
'
',,,,,,,,,,,,,,,,,,,,,,,,,,,,,,,,,,,,,,,,,,,,,,,,,,,,,,,,,,
Function Clean(strValue)
   Clean = Replace(strValue, SQ, SQ & SQ)
End Function
```

The first function creates most of an INSERT statement. It creates the list of fields into which data is being entered, and produces the list of values that follows. It does this by looping through the contents of the Request.Form collection, looking for any fields that are prefixed with db. If it finds a dbt, it lists the field name and the corresponding value (after it is cleared of single quotes) in single quotes in the strValues variable. If it finds a dbn, it lists the field and its value without quotes.

Calling the Clean function in a save routine reduces the amount of code you have to type. Here's a CreateSave routine that could be used in any of your pages:

```
'''''''''''''''''''''''''''''''''''''''''''''''''''''''''''''''''''''
'
' Sub CreateSave
'
' This routine creates a new record in the database.
'
'''''''''''''''''''''''''''''''''''''''''''''''''''''''''''''''''''''
Sub CreateSave(cnDB)
   Dim strSQL

   strSQL = "INSERT INTO tblContacts " & CreateStatement()
   cnDB.Execute strSQL
   Response.Redirect Request.ServerVariables("SCRIPT_NAME")

End Sub
```

The UpdateStatement function works in a similar way, but it creates name/value pairs that are used in an UPDATE statement. The same rules apply: dbt gets single quotes, dbn doesn't. Calling this function is performed as follows:

```
'''''''''''''''''''''''''''''''''''''''''''''''''''''''''''''''''''''
'
' Sub UpdateSave
'
' This routine performs an update on the table for this
' particular item.
'
'''''''''''''''''''''''''''''''''''''''''''''''''''''''''''''''''''''
Sub UpdateSave(cnDB)
   Dim strSQL
```

```
strSQL = "UPDATE tblContacts SET "
    & UpdateStatement() _
    & " WHERE pkContactID = " & Request("ID")
cnDB.Execute strSQL
Response.Redirect Request.ServerVariables("SCRIPT_NAME")

End Sub
```

As long as the name of each field corresponds to a database field, this code works quite well. It isn't a cure-all for every application, but it does take some of the tedium out of the basic ones such as you created here, where you don't have several different types of fields.

**10 Min.
To Go**

New Features

Now that you've learned a little bit about performance improvements you can add, take a look at some new features that might keep you busy working on this application. Some of these features will be added to the application running at www.aspcrashcourse.com, but they're all listed here as ideas you can borrow for your own use.

Adding Multi-User Capability

One feature I debated about putting into the book version of this software was the capability to handle multiple users. I ended up not putting it in, but it's easy to do. There are a few things you have to do to make it work, however.

First, all the data tables have to be changed to include a user ID field. This user ID field (fkUserID) would correspond to a tblUsers table that you would also have to create. From that point on, all data entered would have to be tied to a particular user.

You also have to create a way to sign up new users. You could go the easy way and enter the names, user IDs, and passwords directly into the database; or you could revamp one of the pages you've already built to enable the entry of user information.

Finally, once you have user IDs and passwords, you'll have to create a login page that looks up a user's unique ID and stores that — either in a cookie, a session variable, or as part of each page in a hidden input field. I'd opt for one of the first two methods. In fact, depending on how sensitive the data were, you could allow the user to sign up for the system and then store a permanent cookie on his/her machine with the user ID value assigned to him/her. The user wouldn't have to log back in after that.

Note and Link Categories

If you use this system the way it was intended, you're going to quickly amass a large list of links and notes. Another feature I debated putting in was the capability to categorize your notes and links. This would involve two more category tables: one for notes and one for links. If you were clever, you could create a single category table and tag each entry with a flag indicating whether it was a link or note category. I prefer the first method, but either one is an option.

When you showed notes, you would first list the categories in which the notes belonged. You might use a folder/document analogy, similar to the one I use at my ASPTechniques.com site, shown in Figure 30-1.

Figure 30-1
All notes can be contained within folders.

Once you click on a folder, you see the notes in that category. If you explore the ASP Techniques site, you'll notice that the categories are hierarchical; that is, there are multiple levels of categories. This involves creating a foreign key relationship within the category table, pointing back to the category table itself. Again, if you create these categories, you'll need a page that enables you to edit them. When you start adding these categories, you'll also need to change your note and link entry forms to accept a category entry as part of the data entry step. Hierarchical categories are even trickier, but it can be done.

Search Capabilities

Whenever you have a large amount of data, you'll inevitably forget where you put something and need to search for it. Because you have data in several different tables, searching becomes a bit tricky. However, SQL Server can help you out with its full-text search capabilities. This is covered in most SQL Server texts, but any of the large text fields we created can be set up for full-text search. Using a LIKE clause in your SQL statement, you can search each table.

In addition, you could create a search page that returns a combined set of results of your search keywords against all the different tables in the system. You could separate the results according to which section they came from, or list the name of the section as part of the result value. The idea is that you need to search every field in every table to be completely thorough.

Done!

REVIEW

This chapter was more of a suggestion list than a tutorial. Again, the best way to learn is to do, so have fun with the application you've created. Check my Web site for new features that you can add to your own application. At the same time, you'll be learning new ways of working with Active Server Pages on your own.

QUIZ YOURSELF

1. What SQL statement do you use to create a new record? (See "Using SQL Statements")
2. What SQL statement do you use to update an existing record? (See "Using SQL Statements")
3. What is a stored procedure? (See "Using SQL Statements")
4. What keyword can you use in a SQL statement to perform partial keyword searches? (See "Search Capabilities")

PART

VI

Sunday Afternoon
Part Review

1. Write code that creates a drop-down list of the days of the week.

2. Write the SQL statement to add a new note to the tblNotes table. Remember to include the text from the `Request.Form` collection that represents each field value.

3. Write a SQL statement to sort the events in order by ending date and then by name.

4. Write a VBScript function to do basic validation on a United States Zip Code. Each character is either a digit from 0–9 or a dash. For extra credit, make sure that the length of the string is either five or ten characters.

5. Write a SQL statement to empty the tblEvents table.

Answers to Part Reviews

Friday Evening Review Answers

1. IIS: Internet Information Server. This is the Web server provided with Windows NT.

2. ASP: Active Server Pages. This is the technology that enables you to build dynamically generated Web pages.

3. ADO: Active Data Objects. This is the data-access technology used within ASP.

4. ODBC: Open Database Connectivity. This technology allows an application to talk to any database without the application knowing exactly how each of the databases works.

5. MMC: Microsoft Management Console. This is the application that enables you to administer various Windows NT and Windows 2000 applications. Each specific application uses a "snap-in" that loads into the MMC.

6. To create a new Web site, right-click the name of the machine and select New ➪ Web Site from the popup menu. The dialog will walk you through all the properties that you have to set.

7. To change the home directory for a Web site, bring up the Properties dialog for the Web site and then change to the Home Directory tab.

8. To change the logging options for the Web site, bring up the Properties dialog for the Web site. On the Web Site tab, click the Properties button next to the type of log you want to create.

Saturday Morning Review Answers

1. The <HEAD> tag specifies the heading of the page, which typically includes the page title, style sheets, JavaScript code, and so on.

2. The <TD> tag stands for table data and is used to mark a table cell's contents.

3. The <B> tag causes text to be shown in boldface.

4. The <TH> tag stands for table heading and causes text to be centered and boldfaced within a table cell. Typically, the table heading is put at the top of the page.

5. The <FONT> tag enables you to control the color, size, and typeface of text on your Web pages.

6. The <UL> tag creates a bulleted list of items. <LI> tags are used to mark each item in the list.

7. Use this code to create the Roman numeral list:

   ```
   <OL TYPE="I">
   ```

8. Use this code to create a bulleted list using circles as the bullet:

   ```
   <UL TYPE="CIRCLE">
   ```

9. The Request.QueryString collection contains data included as parameters on the URL.

10. This is a trick question: the Request.Cookies collection only enables you to view cookies. The Response object creates cookies.

11. The Request.ServerVariables collection holds this and other information; the SCRIPT_NAME variable holds the name of the script.

12. The QueryString collection is read first, and the ServerVariables collection is read last. The complete order is as follows: QueryString, Form, Cookies, ClientCertificate, ServerVariables.

13. You create a temporary cookie with code like this:

    ```
    Response.Cookies("MyLoginID") = "543"
    ```

    Creating a permanent cookie involves adding an expiration date, like this:

    ```
    Response.Cookies("MyLoginID").Expires = "#1/1/2002#"
    ```

14. Response.Write does not add any formatting to the text you output. If you want line breaks or HTML tags, you have to add them yourself.

15. This error is typically generated if you've tried to change the header of the page after data have been sent. It is typically generated if you try to `Redirect` or change cookie values after you've already written other HTML data. If you need to do this, be sure to turn on buffering.

16. The `Response.End` statement will stop processing of a page immediately.

Saturday Afternoon Review Answers

1. Any numeric data type can hold the value.

2. This value would best be stored in a Long, but could also be stored in any of the floating-point data types (Single, Double, Decimal).

3. This value needs to be stored in one of the floating-point data types (Single, Double, Decimal).

4. This needs to be stored in a Date variable.

5. This value would best be stored in an Integer. An Integer can hold both positive and negative values.

6. All arrays in VBScript start with index 0.

7. `LBound` returns the lower bound, and `UBound` returns the upper bound.

8. An array can have up to 60 dimensions. A three-dimensional array might be declared like this:

   ```
   Dim a_intValues(5, 4, 3)
   ```

   This array would have indices 0 to 5, 0 to 4, and 0 to 3.

9. `LTrim` removes spaces from the left-hand side of a string, `RTrim` removes spaces from the right-hand side, and `Trim` removes spaces from both sides.

10. The `Space` function can generate a string with a given number of spaces in it.

11. Any function that has an optional case argument is case-sensitive by default. You can use the vbTextCompare constant on many of these functions to indicate case insensitivity.

12. You should use the `Randomize` statement in conjunction with the `Rnd` function to generate a random sequence of values.

13. The `Now` function returns both the date and the time, while the `Time` function only returns the time.

14. To determine the day I was born, I would use this code:

    ```
    Response.Write WeekdayName(Weekday(#6/19/1970#))
    ```

    This returns `Friday` as the result.

15. To add three months to the current date, you can do the following:

    ```
    Response.Write DateAdd("m", 3, Date)
    ```

16. A For/Next loop is the best type of loop to use when you have a fixed beginning and end point. You can use a Do loop if you like, but the For/Next loop is easier to set up.

17. This loop is not guaranteed to run any times. Having the condition at the top of the loop can prevent the loop from running at all, based on the value of x.

18. $x >= 5$

19. $x <= 5 \; Or \; x > 10$

20. $x <= 10 \; Or \; x = 15$

Saturday Evening Review Answers

1. A subroutine does not return a value, but a function does.

2. Unlike in Visual Basic, there is not a subroutine that will run automatically when the page is loaded. If you want to call a subroutine, you simply use either the subroutine's name by itself or the `Call` keyword.

3. Parameters in a subroutine/function declaration are separated by commas.

4. The `#include` directive can use either the file argument or the virtual argument. The file argument indicates that the included file is in the current directory or a subdirectory. The virtual argument allows the page to include a file from any part of the current Web site.

5. You create a temporary cookie with code like this:

    ```
    Response.Cookies("MyLoginID") = "543"
    ```

    Creating a permanent cookie involves adding an expiration date, like this:

    ```
    Response.Cookies("MyLoginID").Expires = "#1/1/2002#"
    ```

6. Remove a cookie by setting its value to an empty string, like so:

    ```
    Response.Cookies("MyLoginID") = ""
    ```

7. Cookie text cannot be automatically encrypted. To encrypt cookie text you need your own code or a third-party component.

8. A table represents a single type of record in the database. Each record contains a series of fields, each of which represents an attribute of the record.

9. A field is a part of a table that holds a particular attribute of the record.

10. The primary key is the field or series of fields that uniquely identify each record.

11. A foreign key is a copy of a primary key within another table. It enables you to relate two tables to each other.

12. An index allows the database to more quickly locate data in a table.

13. SELECT * FROM Customers

14. SELECT * FROM Customers ORDER BY Phone

15. SELECT * FROM Customers WHERE Phone LIKE '%703%'

16. Query:
```
INSERT INTO Customers
(ContactName, CompanyName,
Phone, Fax)
VALUES
('Joe Shmo', 'Joe Shmo Enterprises',
'(212) 555-1212', '(212) 555-1213')
```

17. Query:
```
INSERT INTO Customers
(ContactName, CompanyName,
Phone, Fax)
VALUES
('Brian O''Leary', 'O''Leary''s Foods',
'(202) 555-1212', '(202) 555-1213')
```

Sunday Morning Review Answers

1. Here's the ConnectionString you should create:
```
cnDB.ConnectionString = "Provider=SQLOLEDB;" _
    & "Data Source=COMPANY;Initial Catalog=ORDERS;" _
    & "User ID=visitor;Password=visitor5;"
```

2. Here's the directive you should use:

```
<!--#include virtual=/includes/functions.asp" -->
```

3. The subroutine can be created as follows:

```
Sub PrintText(strText)
    Response.Write strText & "<br>" & vbCrLf
End Sub
```

4. The ROWS and COLS attributes of the TEXTAREA tag control the size, to a point. The browser is ultimately responsible for drawing the box. This means that the same TEXTAREA tag may look different from browser to browser.

5. font-face

6. color

7. text-decoration

8. Server-side include directives are executed before any ASP code runs.

9. Access has an AutoNumber type that automatically supplies a unique number for each new record you create in a table. This helps guarantee that each primary key value is unique.

10. SQL Server has an IDENTITY feature that automatically supplies a unique number for each new record you create in a table. This helps guarantee that each primary key value is unique.

Sunday Afternoon Review Answers

1. Here's the code you might have written:

```
Dim i
Response.Write "<select name=""mylist"">"
For i = 1 To 7
    Response.Write "<option value=" & i & ">" _
        & WeekdayName(i) & "</option>"
Next  ' i
Response.Write "</select>"
```

2. Here's the code you might have used:

```
strSQL = "INSERT INTO tblNotes (Name, Text) VALUES ('" _
    & Request.Form("dbtName") & "', '" _
    & Request.Form("dbtText") & "')"
```

Note that this code does not replace any single quotes in the data values with two single quotes. This can be done using the Clean function talked about in Chapter 30.

3. Here's a SQL statement that will solve this problem:

```
SELECT * FROM tblEvents
ORDER BY EndDate, Name
```

4. Here's a sample of the function you might have written:

```
Function ValidateZipCode(strInput)
   Const VALIDCHARS = "0123456789-"
   Dim blnResult
   Dim intPos
   blnResult = True
   For intPos = 1 To Len(strInput)
      blnResult = blnResult And _
      (InStr(VALIDCHARS, Mid(strInput, intPos, 1) > 0)
   Next  ' intPos
   '
   ' For extra credit, check length
   '
   blnResult = blnResult And _
      (Len(strInput) = 5 Or Len(strInput) = 10)
   ValidateZipCode = blnResult
End Function
```

5. Here's a statement you might have written:

```
DELETE FROM tblEvents
```

This is a dangerous statement since it will wipe out the table without any recourse. Restrict this sort of code to administrators, only.

What's on the CD-ROM?

This appendix provides you with information on the contents of the CD-ROM that accompanies this book.

The following programs are included on this CD:

- ASPEMail from Persits Software
- HomeSite 4.5 from Allaire Corporation
- TextPad 4.31 from Helios Software
- ASPUpload from Persits Software
- ASPnGo from LiveWizards.com
- BrowserHawk 4.0 from cyScape, Inc.
- VSEMail from Vsoft Technologies
- SiteGalaxy ASPUpload Component
- Pie Chart Server from Dundas Software.
- DynuEncrypt from Dynu Systems, Inc.
- NewsSucker from 4net Software, Inc.
- Dundas Mailer from Dundas Software

Also included are source code examples from the book.

System Requirements

Make sure that your computer meets the minimum system requirements listed in this section. If your computer doesn't match up to most of these requirements, you may have a problem using the contents of the CD.

For Microsoft Windows 9*x* or Windows 2000:

- PC with a Pentium processor running at 120 Mhz or faster
- At least 32 MB of RAM
- Ethernet network interface card (NIC) or modem with a speed of at least 28,800 bps
- A CD-ROM drive — double-speed (2x) or faster

The components and software included on this CD-ROM may have higher requirements than these, so refer to each product's documentation for more information.

Using the CD with Microsoft Windows

To install the items from the CD to your hard drive, follow these steps:

1. Insert the CD into your computer's CD-ROM drive.
2. Start Windows (or Windows NT) Explorer and select your CD-ROM drive.
3. Double-click the folder you wish to view and the files in the directory will be shown in your window.

What's on the CD

The CD-ROM contains source code examples and applications. Following is a summary of the contents of the CD-ROM arranged by category.

Source code

Every complete listing in the book is on the CD in the folder named /bookcode. Only the complete listings that are numbered in the book are included — code snippets are not included because they are not complete files.

Applications

The following applications are on the CD-ROM:

Components

The following third-party components are included on the CD-ROM. These are some of the most commonly used components for ASP developers, based on independent reviews on several different web sites.

- **ASPEMail** — E-mail component from Persits Software, Inc. This component has more features and better performance than the built-in NewMail component. This component is a trial version.

  For more information: www.aspemail.com

- **HomeSite 4.5** — HTML/ASP editor from Allaire Corporation. This editor helps you write code but doesn't write it for you. This copy is a 30 day trial version.

  For more information: www.allaire.com

- **TextPad 4.31** — Text editor from Helios Software. This editor helps you write code but doesn't write it for you. This software is shareware with a "nag" message that disappears when you register it.

  For more information: www.textpad.com

- **ASPUpload** — Component that accepts uploaded files from users' web browsers. This component is a trial version from Persits Software.

  For more information: www.aspupload.com

- **ASPnGo** — Tool that helps you build interfaces to databases. This software is freeware from LiveWizards.com.

  For more information: www.livewizards.com

- **BrowserHawk 4.0** — This component detects the features available in the user's browser, including enabled/disabled cookies, scripting, and more. This component is an evaluation version of the software from cyScape, Inc.

  For more information: www.cyscape.com

- **VSEMail** — Easy-to-use, full-featured e-mail component. Freeware from Vsoft Technologies.

  For more information: www.vsoft-tech.com.au

- **SiteGalaxy ASPUpload** — Freeware component to allow uploads of files to your web server.

  For more information: www.geocities.com/sitegalaxy/

- **Pie Chart Server** — This component allows you to dynamically build graphs for your web site visitors. This is a commercial version of the the product produced by Dundas Software.

  For more information: www.dundas.com

- **DynuEncrypt** — This component lets you encrypt and decrypt data in your web pages, which is perfect for sensitive information like user IDs, credit card numbers, and more. This 30 day trial software is from Dynu Systems, Inc.

  For more information: www.dynu.com

- **NewsSucker** — This component knows how to read news from over 250 categories and make it available on your web site. This is a trial version from 4net Software, Inc.

  For more information: www.4netsoftware.com

- **Dundas Mailer** — This mail component includes features to let you post e-mail to NNTP newsgroups, send fully formatted HTML e-mail, and more. According to the web site, this is a free commercial control.

  For more information: www.dundas.com

Troubleshooting

If you have difficulty installing or using the CD-ROM programs, try the following solutions:

- **Turn off any anti-virus software that you may have running.** Installers sometimes mimic virus activity and can make your computer incorrectly believe that it is being infected by a virus. (Be sure to turn the anti-virus software back on later.)

- **Close all running programs.** The more programs you're running, the less memory is available to other programs. Installers also typically update files and programs; if you keep other programs running, installation may not work properly.

If you still have trouble with the CD, please call the IDG Books Worldwide Customer Service phone number: (800) 762-2974. Outside the United States, call (317) 572-3993. IDG Books will provide technical support only for installation and other general quality control items; for technical support on the applications themselves, consult the program's vendor or author.

Index

Continued

Continued

the Software is an update or has been updated, any transfer must include the most recent update and all prior versions.

4. **Restrictions on Use of Individual Programs.** You must follow the individual requirements and restrictions detailed for each individual program in Appendix B "What's on the CD-ROM" of this Book. These limitations are also contained in the individual license agreements recorded on the Software Media. These limitations may include a requirement that after using the program for a specified period of time, the user must pay a registration fee or discontinue use. By opening the Software packet(s), you will be agreeing to abide by the licenses and restrictions for these individual programs that are detailed in Appendix B and on the Software Media. None of the material on this Software Media or listed in this Book may ever be redistributed, in original or modified form, for commercial purposes.

5. **Limited Warranty.**

   (a) IDGB warrants that the Software and Software Media are free from defects in materials and workmanship under normal use for a period of sixty (60) days from the date of purchase of this Book. If IDGB receives notification within the warranty period of defects in materials or workmanship, IDGB will replace the defective Software Media.

   (b) **IDGB AND THE AUTHOR OF THE BOOK DISCLAIM ALL OTHER WARRANTIES, EXPRESS OR IMPLIED, INCLUDING WITHOUT LIMITATION IMPLIED WARRANTIES OF MERCHANTABILITY AND FITNESS FOR A PARTICULAR PURPOSE, WITH RESPECT TO THE SOFTWARE, THE PROGRAMS, THE SOURCE CODE CONTAINED THEREIN, AND/OR THE TECHNIQUES DESCRIBED IN THIS BOOK. IDGB DOES NOT WARRANT THAT THE FUNCTIONS CONTAINED IN THE SOFTWARE WILL MEET YOUR REQUIREMENTS OR THAT THE OPERATION OF THE SOFTWARE WILL BE ERROR FREE.**

   (c) This limited warranty gives you specific legal rights, and you may have other rights that vary from jurisdiction to jurisdiction.

6. **Remedies.**

   (a) IDGB's entire liability and your exclusive remedy for defects in materials and workmanship shall be limited to replacement of the Software Media, which may be returned to IDGB with a copy of your receipt at the following address: Software Media Fulfillment Department, Attn.: *Active Server Pages 3 Weekend Crash Course*, IDG Books Worldwide, Inc., 10475 Crosspoint Blvd., Indianapolis, IN 46256, or call 1-800-762-2974. Please allow three to four weeks for delivery. This Limited Warranty is void if failure of the Software Media has resulted from accident, abuse, or misapplication. Any replacement Software Media will be warranted for the remainder of the original warranty period or thirty (30) days, whichever is longer.

(b) In no event shall IDGB or the author be liable for any damages whatsoever (including without limitation damages for loss of business profits, business interruption, loss of business information, or any other pecuniary loss) arising from the use of or inability to use the Book or the Software, even if IDGB has been advised of the possibility of such damages.

(c) Because some jurisdictions do not allow the exclusion or limitation of liability for consequential or incidental damages, the above limitation or exclusion may not apply to you.

7. **U.S. Government Restricted Rights.** Use, duplication, or disclosure of the Software by the U.S. Government is subject to restrictions stated in paragraph (c)(1)(ii) of the Rights in Technical Data and Computer Software clause of DFARS 252.227-7013, and in subparagraphs (a) through (d) of the Commercial Computer — Restricted Rights clause at FAR 52.227-19, and in similar clauses in the NASA FAR supplement, when applicable.

8. **General.** This Agreement constitutes the entire understanding of the parties and revokes and supersedes all prior agreements, oral or written, between them and may not be modified or amended except in a writing signed by both parties hereto that specifically refers to this Agreement. This Agreement shall take precedence over any other documents that may be in conflict herewith. If any one or more provisions contained in this Agreement are held by any court or tribunal to be invalid, illegal, or otherwise unenforceable, each and every other provision shall remain in full force and effect.

my2cents.idgbooks.com

Register This Book — And Win!

Visit **http://my2cents.idgbooks.com** to register this book and we'll automatically enter you in our fantastic monthly prize giveaway. It's also your opportunity to give us feedback: let us know what you thought of this book and how you would like to see other topics covered.

Discover IDG Books Online!

The IDG Books Online Web site is your online resource for tackling technology — at home and at the office. Frequently updated, the IDG Books Online Web site features exclusive software, insider information, online books, and live events!

10 Productive & Career-Enhancing Things You Can Do at www.idgbooks.com

- Nab source code for your own programming projects.
- Download software.
- Read Web exclusives: special articles and book excerpts by IDG Books Worldwide authors.
- Take advantage of resources to help you advance your career as a Novell or Microsoft professional.
- Buy IDG Books Worldwide titles or find a convenient bookstore that carries them.
- Register your book and win a prize.
- Chat live online with authors.
- Sign up for regular e-mail updates about our latest books.
- Suggest a book you'd like to read or write.
- Give us your 2¢ about our books and about our Web site.

You say you're not on the Web yet? It's easy to get started with IDG Books' *Discover the Internet,* available at local retailers everywhere.

CD Installation Instructions

The CD-ROM that accompanies this book contains useful applications, third-party components, and source code from the lessons.

To install the items from the CD to your hard drive, follow these steps:

1. Insert the CD into your computer's CD-ROM drive.
2. Start Windows Explorer and select your CD-ROM drive.
3. Double-click the folder you wish to view and the files in the directory will be shown in your window.

For more information about the components of this CD, turn to Appendix B "What's on the CD-ROM?"